Drupal 7

TOM GELLER

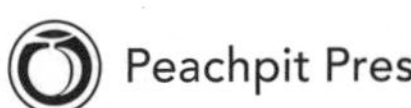

Peachpit Press

Visual QuickStart Guide
Drupal 7
Tom Geller

Peachpit Press
1249 Eighth Street
Berkeley, CA 94710
510/524-2178
510/524-2221 (fax)

Find us on the Web at: www.peachpit.com
To report errors, please send a note to: errata@peachpit.com
Peachpit Press is a division of Pearson Education.

Project Editor: Nancy Peterson
Development Editor: Robyn G. Thomas
Copyeditors: Darren Meiss and Scout Festa
Technical Editor: Emma Jane Hogbin
Production Coordinator: Myrna Vladic
Compositor: David Van Ness
Indexer: Joy Dean Lee
Cover Design: Peachpit Press
Interior Design: Peachpit Press

Notice of Rights

Notice of Liability

Trademarks

ISBN 13: 978-0-321-61921-1
ISBN 10: 0-321-61921-8

9 8 7 6 5 4 3 2 1

Printed and bound in the United States of America

Table of Contents

Introduction

With version 7, the web-publishing system Drupal stands at that frightening moment when it either enters the mainstream or falls into the abyss of niche enthusiasts. Until now its complexity has kept it mostly in the province of technology professionals, but I believe Drupal 7 will succeed for two reasons: The public is ready for it, and it's ready for the public.

First, the average web site builder understands—and demands—features that plain old HTML can't offer without extensive programming, such as user management and form processing. Drupal provides those features. Its architecture is elegant, its features broad and varied, and its community base unparalleled in the open-source software world (except by Linux, whose lead Drupal trails in terms of contributors).

But it's not the only contender, and in fact several others are easier to use. Drupal's boosters (*Drupalistas*) point out that their software does well against Joomla and other full-featured CMSes (content management systems), but I think they're missing the point: The real competition is anything that gives people the features they want. So for simple personal sites, it's Facebook and MySpace; for businesses, Yahoo Merchant Solutions, eBay, and Amazon; for publications, WordPress.com and Blogger.com; and for the rest, a hosted solution like Google Sites. Drupalistas would argue that none of these are technically CMSes. It doesn't matter—they have enough CMS-like features for the masses.

But time spent learning Drupal rewards its student handsomely. None of those other solutions compares to it in terms of flexibility, security, or support. Learning to exploit Drupal's advantages just takes time and attention.

I wrote this book because I wanted to help non-technical people discover the joy I found when I started building sites in Drupal in late 2007. Freshly downloaded, Drupal gave me the ability to run a blog (like WordPress) and host polls (like MySpace) in addition to everything I could do before with plain HTML. Dipping into the vast wealth of Drupal extensions (*modules*) gave me plug-and-play access to features

I hadn't even considered before. My first Drupal site (**`savemyhomebook.com`**) looked and functioned far better than anything I'd built since learning HTML in the mid-'90s; later sites included shopping carts, user interaction, and complex data display.

Which brings us to the second reason Drupal 7 is right for non-technical site builders: Its developers have focused on making it the easiest version of Drupal. In early 2009, project founder *Dries Buytaert* made it clear that he wanted "radical improvements in usability" to this version, even funding design improvements through his company, Acquia. Eye-tracking studies at the University of Baltimore pinpointed items of greatest confusion among first-time Drupal administrators, and outreach programs encouraged the participation of graphic designers and user-interface experts.

The results have fallen short of some of the more ambitious goals, but are impressive nonetheless. The Drupal community (as the saying goes) shot for the sky and missed—but landed among the stars.

Is This Book for You?

Drupal 7: Visual QuickStart Guide was written for anybody who wants to create a dynamic, easy-to-update web site that looks good and performs well. Unlike most current books about Drupal, it's written for anybody with even the most basic computer skills. That means you should be already able to:

- Use a computer to access the Internet through a web browser
- Download files
- Install software on your computer

Depending on how you intend to host your Drupal web site, you might also need to:

- Access a remote computer through programs other than a web browser
- Navigate by typing on a non-graphical, command-line interface such as is found in *nix operating systems
- Change file permission settings
- Understand written instructions from your web hosting provider

What This Book Will Teach You

By the time you've finished this book, you'll have all the skills you need to create an attractive and complete Drupal web site. Specifically, you'll learn how to:

- Install Drupal on your home computer (to prototype your site)
- Install Drupal on a remote server (to make your site available to the world at large)
- Give your site its basic identity
- Add, change, and delete text and images
- Modify your site's visual design
- Modify your site's functional interface, for example changing where information appears on the page and what links show up in menus
- Monitor and maintain your site to prevent malicious activity
- Make a backup for safety, and restore your site from that backup
- Allow site visitors to become members with their own user names and passwords
- Control member access
- Run interactive features, such as blogs, polls, and forums

- Find and add any of hundreds of modules that extend Drupal with new and interesting functions
- Find help from experienced Drupal administrators when you get stuck
- Further your Drupal career by understanding and participating in the project's vibrant user community

What This Book Won't Teach You

Alas, there are some Drupal-related subjects too big or tangential to include here, such as:

- Finding and signing up with a web host to make your site available to the world. (There is a list of companies that provide Drupal-ready hosting services at **`drupal.org/hosting`**.)
- Accessing files on, transferring files to, or navigating around your remote host's file system. In Chapter 1, "Getting Drupal Up and Running," I briefly show how to navigate one of the most common host interfaces—the command-line interface of *nix. But there's an enormous variation in how web hosts operate and what they allow their customers to do. If the instructions in this book don't fit, ask the support desk of your web host for help.
- Registering a domain name or making it refer to your Drupal site. Again, your web host's help desk is the best place to go.
- Suggesting anything about the *kind* of content to put on your site. That's your job!
- Programming or advanced theming.

How This Book Is Organized

Drupal 7: Visual QuickStart Guide is intended to take you from a standing start to running a web site that's both functional and useful. Because the definition of "useful" varies from person to person, this book makes only basic assumptions about what you're going to do with Drupal. The book is divided into four sections based on those assumptions:

I Setting Up (Chapters 1 and 2)

II Managing Content (Chapters 3–6)

III Managing Drupal (Chapters 7–9)

IV Appendix and Glossary

As you can see, the biggest section is devoted to creating and managing content: That's probably why you're learning a *content management* system! But this book also assumes that you'll want to:

- Open your site to a wider community, and therefore need to understand Drupal's user-management features (Chapter 7)
- Change your site's appearance (Chapter 8)
- Take advantage of Drupal's huge library of modules to extend what it can do (Chapter 9)
- Go beyond this book to interact with Drupal's user community, one of the most active in the open-source software world (Appendix)

In making these assumptions—and to best use limited space—I've left out some of Drupal's finer points. Typically these were features that will matter to you only after you've been administering Drupal sites for a while. For example, I decided not to discuss performance or security enhancements, because Drupal's built-in features are sufficient for all but the busiest web sites. The appendix, "Getting (and Giving) Help," gives you pointers about where to find such information should you need it.

At times, I use a very simple, fictional Drupal site to demonstrate various points. If you'd like inspiration from people who have taken Drupal much further, see **`drupalsites.net`**.

Standards Used In This Book

I use some conventions to provide guidance. This book:

- Uses **`this font`** whenever showing something that you should actually type (also known as *code*).
- Shows the code font in italics to indicate that you should replace the text with the equivalent for your situation, for example, **`http://`*`domain-name`*`/user/`*`user-id`***.
- Italicizes the first occurrence of words that are defined in the glossary.
- Refers to locations on your own Drupal site in the form **`http://`*`domain-name`***.
- Refers to other web sites in the form **`example.com`** (without the **`http://`**).
- Refers to directory paths on your web server in the form **`/path/to/location`** (with a leading slash, which indicates the top directory of your Drupal installation).
- Assumes that you're always logged in as the *superuser* (**`user/1`**)—that is, the user that you created when you first installed Drupal. (For details, see Chapter 1.) This user has full access to every administrative feature in a Drupal site. If you get the message "Access Denied" when you try to do something in this book, try logging out (by going to **`http://`*`domain-name`*`/logout`**) and then logging in again (**`http://`*`domain-name`*`/user`**).
- Gives instructions for Mac first, followed by Windows and *nix in those instances where differences among them arise. (Since you manage Drupal mostly through web browsers that work pretty much the same on all platforms, these distinctions are rare.)
- Provides screen shots of the **`drupal.org`** web site as it appeared immediately after its October 2010 renovation. In an example of bad timing, the site was undergoing profound reorganization as we were putting this book to bed. Some screen shots you see here are of the prerelease beta site, and might be different from what you see when you visit **`drupal.org`**.

What is Drupal, Anyway?

Drupal is in the content management system (CMS) category of web site tools. CMSes excel in letting you create *dynamic* sites, which show different information depending on a number of factors, such as the input of previous visitors, or whether the current visitor is logged in. Sites that don't have such features are called *static* and are typically created using a page-description language such as HTML. (You can also use Drupal to create sites that don't take advantage of its dynamic features.)

Drupal has many features common to CMSes, including:

- Administration through a web browser. You manage your Drupal site mostly by visiting it in a web browser such as Firefox or Safari, logging in as an administrator, and going to pages that let you change site settings.

- A user-management system that lets you identify, track, and control visitors' access.
- Fine-grained permissions that allow you to grant specific rights to specific groups of users.
- Streamlined methods for changing content. In Drupal, you edit basic pages (or other types of content) by clicking a tab labeled Edit and filling out a form. To do the same thing on a traditional HTML site, you'd need to download a file, figure out what parts to change, make the changes, and then upload the file again.
- Flexible methods of displaying content. One example is Drupal's Summary feature, which shows a shortened version of content where appropriate.
- Consistent appearance throughout the site. Certain features (such as menus and graphic design) remain the same regardless of what part of the site you visit.
- Changeable overall appearance. In Drupal, you change the look of the site as a whole by switching to a new *theme*, hundreds of which are available from **drupal.org** or through private designers. The content remains the same regardless of what theme you select.
- Extensibility so you can add features by writing (or downloading) a bit of programming code, typically in the PHP language. Drupal is usually extended through the use of modules, which you can read about in Chapter 9, "Extending Drupal with Modules."

How Drupal Works

The best way to understand how Drupal works is to compare it with other systems, specifically static HTML and hosted sites.

- Static HTML sites comprise text files that end in **.htm** or **.html**; image files (**.jpg**, **.gif**, **.png**); other media and downloadable files such as Adobe Portable Document Format files (**.pdf**) or QuickTime movies (**.mov**); and any custom programming files. These reside on a remote computer (the *host*) that's always on and connected to the Internet and that runs a program called a web server.

  When someone types the domain name of a static HTML site into a web browser, the web server finds a file called **index.html** (or **index.htm**) on the host. That file typically contains all the text on the site's home page, along with references to other files such as images and formatting information. The web server gathers all these pieces together and sends them back over the Internet to the web browser, which reassembles them into a web page **A**.

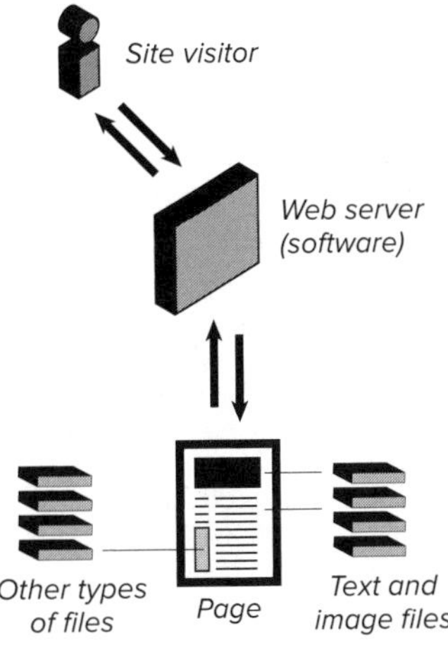

A How static HTML sites produce pages

To change a static HTML site, you either modify files directly on the server or on your personal computer and then transfer them to the server through a program such as FileZilla (**filezilla-project.org**), Secure Copy (SCP), or a web browser–based interface. Likewise, to copy your HTML site to another computer, you only need to copy its files.

- Hosted sites such as Yahoo Merchant Solutions and Google Sites vary widely in how they're set up, but they share some common traits. For one thing, you almost always build and modify your site through a simplified, web browser-based interface that hides the underlying HTML and programming code from you. As a result, such solutions tend to be easy to create but hard or impossible to customize beyond pre-defined limits. You neither need to know nor are able to know exactly *how* the site runs beyond what you can see through the web browser **B**. It's sometimes impossible to copy a hosted site to another computer in a useful form—you're stuck with the host for life.

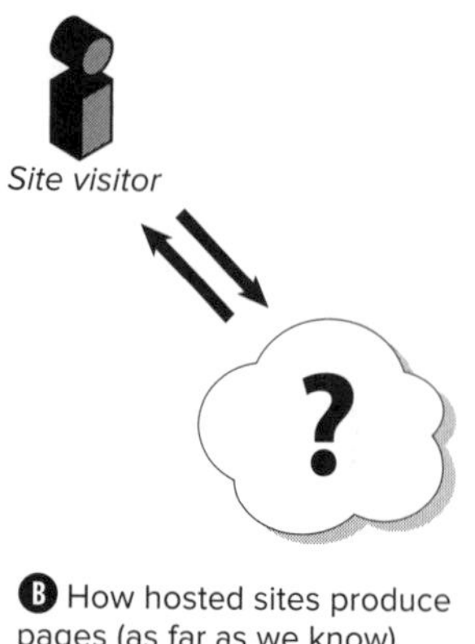

B How hosted sites produce pages (as far as we know)

- Drupal sites essentially comprise three parts: the Drupal software itself, which is written mostly in the PHP programming language; a database that contains your site's content and settings; and images and other files.

  When someone visits a Drupal site, the web server first finds the **index.php** file. Whereas a static HTML site's **index.html** file simply describes what the page should look like, Drupal's **index.php** file is a program that causes the host to look into dozens of files and the content database to determine what information should be sent to the visitor. When the process is finished, the web server responds with files from the host and content from the database, formatted (mostly) as simple HTML. The web server sends that HTML over the Internet to the web browser, which interprets and displays it just as if it had come from a static HTML site **C**.

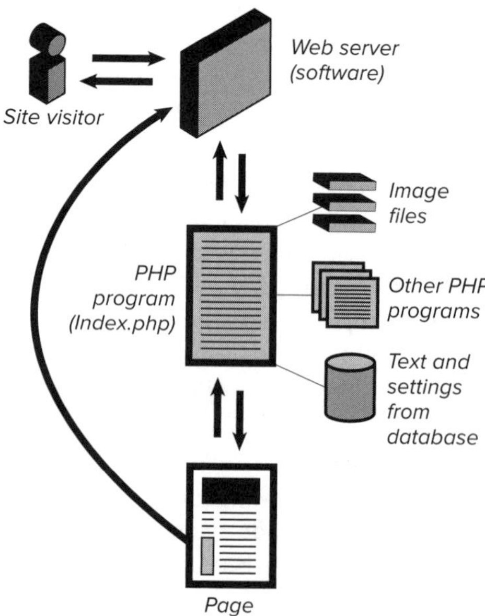

C How Drupal produces pages

Although this process seems impossibly complex to the human eye, the host interprets this chain of PHP and database instructions quickly and easily. Along the way, Drupal has opportunities to modify the output based on its own programming, modules you've installed, and any other circumstances.

You make most changes to a Drupal site by manipulating content in the database through a web browser–based interface. Except for Chapter 1, this book is almost entirely about how to use that web browser–based interface.

To copy a Drupal site to another location, you need to transfer both its files and its database. You'll learn how to do that in Chapter 2, "Establishing Your Drupal Site."

Drupal, CSS, PHP, JavaScript, and SQL

I mentioned that Drupal is mostly written in PHP, which was designed specifically for web development. Technically, PHP is a *scripting* language, which (among other things) means that programs written in it are stored in a form that you can easily read; an *interpreter* turns them into machine language at the time they're run. (By contrast, programs written in *compiled* languages such as C++ are converted into machine language before they're run, and then the computer uses the converted version from then on.) As a result, anyone who knows PHP can look at the Drupal program and understand how it works.

PHP is a *server-side* language, meaning that all of this interpretation happens on the host—typically, on the same remote computer that stores the files and sends the final HTML code out over the Internet.

But PHP isn't the only language involved in a Drupal site. Others are:

- SQL (Structured Query Language), a server-side database language that Drupal uses to add, change, and remove information. When someone posts a page to your site, for example, Drupal sends a command in SQL to the database that says, "insert this information into the **node** table" (actually, Drupal sends several SQL commands). When somebody reads that page, Drupal says, "retrieve that information from the **node** table." Here's an example.

```
INSERT INTO `node` (`nid`, `vid`,
→`type`, `language`, `title`, `uid`,
→`status`, `created`, `changed`,
→`comment`, `promote`, `moderate`,
→`sticky`, `tnid`, `translate`)
→VALUES (1, 1, 'page', '', 'Title
→goes here.', 1, 1, 1257477418,
→1257477418, 0, 0, 0, 0, 0, 0);
```

- CSS (Cascading Style Sheets), a descriptive language that defines typography, layout, and other display properties. One of the fastest ways to give your Drupal site the appearance you want is to download a free theme that has the basic layout you like, and then change its CSS files to indicate your preferred fonts, colors, and images. (You'll learn how to do this in Chapter 8, "Customizing Drupal's Look and Feel.")

  Unlike SQL and PHP, CSS is a client-side language that's sent over the Internet and then interpreted by site visitors' web browsers. Here's an example.

```
h1, h2, h3, h4, h5, h6 {
  margin: 0;
  padding: 0;
  font-weight: normal;
  font-family: Helvetica, Arial,
sans-serif;
}
```

- JavaScript, a language that mostly adds interface "spice" to your site. If an image changes when you move your mouse over it, that's JavaScript at work. Drupal itself includes several user-interface portions of the jQuery library, a JavaScript extension that allows developers to easily include lots of "eye candy," such as animations, resizable dialog boxes, and drag-and-drop effects.

  Like CSS, JavaScript interpretation happens in site visitors' web browsers, not on the server. A very small number of site visitors turn off JavaScript on their browsers and won't be able to see these effects. Fortunately, Drupal always tries to present them the same information without the effects. Here's some sample JavaScript.

  ```
  Drupal.progressBar.prototype.
  → startMonitoring = function
  → (uri, delay) {
    this.delay = delay;
    this.uri = uri;
    this.sendPing();
  };
  ```

You don't need to learn any of these languages to use Drupal! But doing so lets you create unique features for your sites and improve your overall computer knowledge. Besides, Drupal provides both motivation and opportunity to learn them: Why not take advantage of it? I personally had a hard time wrapping my head around CSS—until I started modifying Drupal themes. Likewise, my real first forays into PHP were to display information that couldn't be extracted in any other way.

Having said that, contributed modules sometimes take the place of these languages. For example, the Views module (which you can download for free from **drupal.org/project/views**) makes most custom SQL programming unnecessary.

The Long Road to Drupal 7

Drupal has come a long, long way since Belgian student Dries Buytaert started creating it in 2000 to stay in touch with his friends at the University of Antwerp. It received a big publicity boost in 2003 when supporters of U.S. presidential candidate Howard Dean organized campaign activities using Drupal 4, and since then it has grown by leaps and bounds.

By the time version 5 arrived in early 2007, Drupal ran such notable web sites as **theonion.com** and **mtv.co.uk**. Drupal 6 came a little over a year later, including features that eased installation, maintenance, content translation, and general administration.

Mr. Buytaert listed 11 key improvements he wanted when Drupal 7 development started in earnest in February 2008 (see **buytaert.net/starting-to-work-on-drupal-7**). As I mentioned, the one that got the most attention—and that's most visible to anyone who's tried earlier versions—is *usability*. That focus has frankly required a change within the community's social structure, as the text-minded developers who make up its inner circle needed to see the value of good visual design and user interaction. But with Drupal 7, they're beginning to see the light. They belatedly follow in the footsteps of Mr. Buytaert's own conversion, which he described in a January 2006 post:

"For long I focused, completely and utterly, on the aesthetics of Drupal's code, neglecting eye candy and ease of use... The aesthetics of Drupal's clean code has attracted many developers, but has also given Drupal the reputation of being developer-centric and hard to use... I have since learned that elegant design and ease of use are equally [as] important as clean source code."

A secondary goal of Drupal 7 was, put bluntly, to not repeat certain mistakes of the Drupal 6 launch. Three practices have given the Drupal 7 release plan a level of professionalism that any organization would envy:

- Drupal development tools are better. Testing, communication, and project tracking have all benefited from advances of the past two years.
- Drupal 7's release schedule was defined better. A series of "code freezes" set deadlines that both revved motivation and imposed discipline. While those finish lines moved a few times (introducing the giggle-worthy phrase "code slush"), and there were occasions of blatant disregard for some of those deadlines, there's no denying the clarity they attempted to give Drupal 7's development process.
- Support by Drupal module developers is better. One of the biggest complaints surrounding Drupal 6's release was that most modules—including those that nearly every Drupal site administrator needed—lagged the release by months or even years. This time around, Moshe Weitzman lobbied for developers to pledge release of their Drupal 7–compatible modules for the same time that Drupal 7 itself is released. That effort has garnered over 100 pledges. Of the 20 most popular modules, only six have neither taken the pledge nor been incorporated into Drupal 7 itself. Even without the pledge, Drupal 7 versions of every one of those six are in active development. (For details, see "Modules: The Drupal 7 Challenge" in Chapter 9.)

Drupal 6 vs. Drupal 7

So what finally came out of the Drupal 7 sausage grinder? Dozens of changes, described in minuscule detail in the periodic release notes linked from the Drupal project page at **`drupal.org/project/drupal`**. Although you could rightly argue about which are the most important, here's my take (summarized from my article on the Peachpit Press web site at **`peachpit.com/articles/article.aspx?p=1433049`**):

- New themes. Drupal 7 adds a new default theme (Bartik) as well as a separate theme, appropriately called Seven, that makes administration easier.
- Lighter workflow. For version 7, links to Drupal's administrative functions have been radically reorganized into what its developers hope is a more user-friendly configuration, although it might leave Drupal 6 administrators scratching their heads for a while. Drupal 7 also puts commonly used commands in easy reach, in the Toolbar and customizable Shortcut bar. Finally—and most visibly—there's now an administrative overlay that floats controls in front of the screen they affect, reducing the feeling that you're navigating through a maze of screens.

- Improved installation and update procedures. What probably most often tripped up users of Drupal 6 was installation and updating, both of which have been fundamentally improved in Drupal 7. First, the installer has some nice touches that make it more foolproof. Second, help texts during installation are a lot more, well, helpful. Once you have Drupal installed, you can now install and update themes and modules through Drupal's web-based interface instead of needing access to the server (via its sometimes obscure commands).
- Smarter defaults. User studies and administrator experience have made Drupal more ready for use immediately upon installation. You can still override such behaviors, but on the whole, Drupal administrators will do a lot less initial work to make their Drupal 7 sites work the way they want.
- Easier, more flexible content management. For a content management system, the procedure for entering content in Drupal has historically been more difficult than it needed to be. But Drupal 7 makes up for lost time with three standout features. First, a neat visual trick called "vertical tabs" makes the content-entry form cleaner and easier to navigate. Second, you no longer need to download additional modules to put images in content. Finally, you can define highly customized types of content, for example catalog pages that include *fields* for price, color, and size. Before Drupal 7, you needed a module called Content Construction Kit (CCK) for this functionality. (See Chapter 4, "Customizing Content," for details.)
- Fields in core. Drupal 7 has many improvements that are hidden from view—unless you're an experienced administrator or Drupal developer. "Fields in core" is one of those changes, but it has far-reaching benefits for everyone who uses Drupal. It essentially lets you break information into separate parts (*fields*) for truly original results. Fields in core actually goes beyond content, extending *profiles,* comments, and how you categorize content.
- Easier programming. As long as I'm talking about less-visible improvements, I should mention a huge raft of changes that have made programming for Drupal easier. The list is far too long to include here, but you can see it at **http://drupal.org/node/224333** and **http://drupal.org/node/394070**.
- Clean-up of unneeded bits. Some things removed from Drupal 7 include the little-used Throttle, Ping, and Blog API modules; the "related terms" feature for taxonomy (which never did anything, anyway); and the ability to block posts that don't have a minimum number of words. Of course, every bit of obsolete technology has its fans, so such removals are always controversial. If you find yourself needing those old Drupal 6 features, most (if not all) will still be available through downloadable modules.
- Better organization of user permissions. Drupal has long offered extremely fine-grained permission controls. For example, you could allow users to edit (but not delete) their own blog entries. With that flexibility comes confusion, though, and the dozens of check boxes on Drupal 6's default permissions screen often threw new administrators for a loop. Those permissions have

been reworked for clarity, and there's a new "administrator" *role*.

- Contextual edit links. When you're logged in as the administrator, a Drupal 7 site now presents options as you hover your pointer over certain items you can control. For example: To edit a block in Drupal 6, you had to go to the Blocks configuration page, guess the name of the block you wanted to change, and click "configure"; in Drupal 7, you just point at the block and click. Much better!

Acknowledgments

"No man is an island," wrote Renaissance poet John Donne, whose separate Elegy XIX ("To His Mistress Going to Bed") is a gleeful celebration of erotic anticipation. So mix the profound and the profane, as they do in everyday life. These acknowledgments, too, mix thanks to both central and incidental influences. Some made the book what it is; some made me what *I* am. Which is which is left as an exercise for the reader.

First, the obvious. Robyn Thomas has been an attentive and friendly development editor: She kept me (comparatively) honest. Project editor Nancy Peterson gave difficult decisions about timing and content the attention they deserved, ensuring this book's relevance and longevity. Technical editor Emma Jane Hogbin (**`emmajane.net`**) has been the *real* Drupal expert here, insisting on (among other things) the correct spelling, usage, and politics of "*nix" until I got it right. [Emma: I *did* finally get it right, didn't I?] Greg Knaddison (**`growingventuresolutions.com`**) took time away from his busy schedule to step in when we needed some emergency fact-checking.

Darren Meiss and Scout Festa polished the copy swiftly and silently, like literary Rumpelstiltskins. When it was all finished, product marketing manager Glenn Bisignani ensured that the resulting volume would find its way into your hot little hands.

Thanks also go to the two people who got this project off the ground: my agent, Neil Salkind of the Salkind Literary Agency (**`salkindagency.com`**), and Peachpit's senior acquisitions editor Wendy Sharp. By the same token, I'd like to thank the mob of computer book professionals who have guided me to this point over the years, particularly those met through various technical communities and the Studio B discussion list.

This list doesn't include the many, many people involved in the book's production and distribution, some of whom toil with names unknown to me. That they're not explicitly included shouldn't suggest a diminishment of their services or of my gratitude.

Thanks for other reasons go to Joanne Brodie, Laura Sherwood, Lisa Carlotta, and Ali Leal, along with others who recognize a pattern and believe they should be in that list. It's cliché to say "You keep me sane," so here's a greater truth: You keep me happy.

It's shocking that this is my third book, yet I haven't thanked the *ultimate* originators of this project: my parents, Mimi and Conrad Geller. What kind of son would do such a thing? And comb your hair, it looks like a rat's nest.

I'd like to also thank the good people of Oberlin, Ohio, where I decided to make my home a few weeks before starting this book. It was written almost entirely at the facilities of Oberlin College and the Oberlin Public Library, with occasional stints in several of the town's restaurants, bars, cafes, and lobbies, and in the Wi-Fi–enabled town square. I couldn't have chosen a better place.

Lastly, one more shot at the obvious: This book would have no purpose, and the web would be a poorer place, if not for the tens of thousands of people who program, test, use, document, critique, and otherwise enjoy Drupal. Its success has put high-quality, 21st-century web publishing within the reach of millions of people who'd otherwise be stuck with harder and less-capable options. It's my sincere hope that this book continues the community's work in some small way and strengthens the project's goals.

Getting Drupal Up and Running

In this chapter, you'll perform all the steps to install Drupal, the database behind it, and all the necessary support software.

If you've never installed server-based software before, you might find the procedure somewhat more complicated than you're used to, but don't worry: Although there are many steps, each one is fairly simple. The procedure includes:

- Preparing your computer by installing Apache, MySQL, and PHP (an "AMP stack") if needed
- Downloading and unpacking the Drupal package
- Setting up a Drupal database
- Running the Drupal installer through a web browser

This section takes you through all four steps, both on a development (*staging*) computer and on the production (*site*) server. When you're finished, you'll be ready to start adding content, design, and functionality to your Drupal site.

In This Chapter

Fulfilling Drupal's Requirements

Drupal can run on any Internet-connected computer on which you have sufficient access *permissions* to add, delete, and change files and directories. You'll also benefit greatly by installing the following software, if it's not already there:

- A program to transfer files between your Drupal installation and other places. An FTP program such as FileZilla (**`filezilla-project.org`**) is a common solution, although other utilities (such as Secure Copy [SCP]) also work fine.
- A text editor to modify programming, design, and configuration files. The free programs that come with Mac (TextEdit) and Windows (Notepad) are adequate, although other editors have advanced features that can be useful in Drupal development.

You can meet virtually all the other Drupal software requirements by installing a software package called an *AMP stack*, whose name comes from the first letter of the three programs it contains: the Apache web server, MySQL database program, and PHP programming language.

The downloadable package containing an AMP stack for Mac is called MAMP, and is available at **`mamp.info`**. The Windows version (WAMP) is at **`wampserver.com/en/`**. (There are several WAMP packages available: WampServer is the most common, and we'll refer to it simply as WAMP throughout this chapter. For a list of others, see **`http://en.wikipedia.org/wiki/Comparison_of_WAMPs`**.) Many *nix servers—that is, those running Unix,

Linux, or another Unix-like operating system—come with Apache, MySQL, and PHP configured and running; procedures for installing an AMP stack on those *nix servers that don't have one vary greatly. So we won't discuss installation of these programs in such environments in any detail, beyond the sidebar later in this chapter, "What about *nix Operating Systems?"

TIP I strongly recommend that you develop your Drupal site on a *local* computer—that is, a laptop or desktop machine. Then, when you're ready to launch, move your site to a server. (We'll show you how to do that in Chapter 2, "Establishing Your Drupal Site," in the section "To move your Drupal site to another computer.") Working on a local computer is generally faster, because you're not affected by Internet slowdowns. It's also easier, because you can manage files through your computer's familiar desktop interface.

TIP It's possible to run Drupal using other web servers and database servers, but the Apache/MySQL combination is by far the most popular: We'll assume you're using that pairing throughout this book.

TIP PHP is always required, as Drupal is technically a collection of PHP scripts.

But I Want to Do This the Easy Way!

The next few pages tell you how to download and install both an AMP stack and Drupal itself, for either Mac or Windows. But there's actually a single package that includes both: The *Acquia Drupal* stack installer, DAMP, available from `acquia.com/downloads`. DAMP also includes several additional Drupal modules and themes, as the sidebar "Understanding Acquia Drupal" describes.

So why bother installing the pieces separately? First, so you gain experience in customizing and troubleshooting your installation; and second, to help you install Drupal in places where DAMP won't work, such as on most *nix operating systems or on a pre-10.5 version of Mac OS X. But if you don't have such needs and are comfortable using Acquia Drupal, the Acquia Drupal stack installer is the faster option.

To install MAMP on a Mac:

1. Visit **`mamp.info`** in a web browser.
2. Click "Download now."

   MAMP is the free version; the **`mamp.info`** site also offers a commercial version (MAMP Pro) with additional features that aren't necessary for running Drupal.
3. Click the latest version of MAMP to download the file **A**. The file is quite large, so downloading may take several minutes.
4. Find the downloaded file: It's probably either on the Desktop or in **`/Users/`***`your-username`***`/Downloads`**, and has a name ending in .dmg.zip.
5. Double-click the file to uncompress it. The result is a file ending in .dmg **B**. You may now discard the .dmg.zip file.
6. Double-click the .dmg file. Read through the license agreement that appears **C** and click Agree to accept it.

A The link to download MAMP

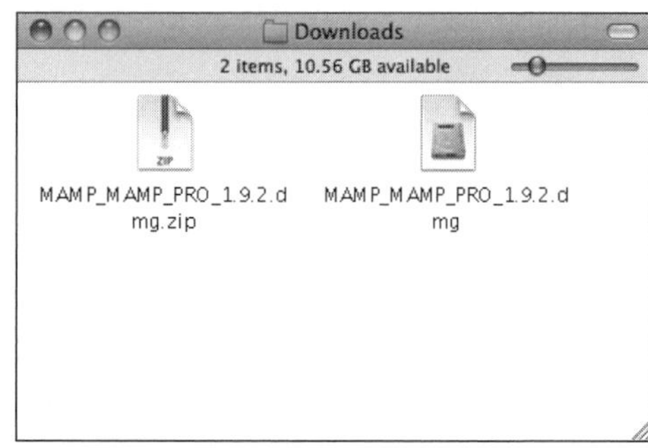

B The compressed .dmg.zip file and the uncompressed .dmg file

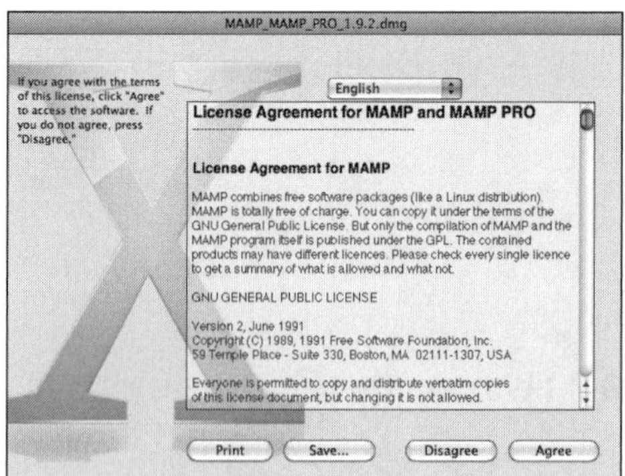

C The license agreement you must accept to install MAMP

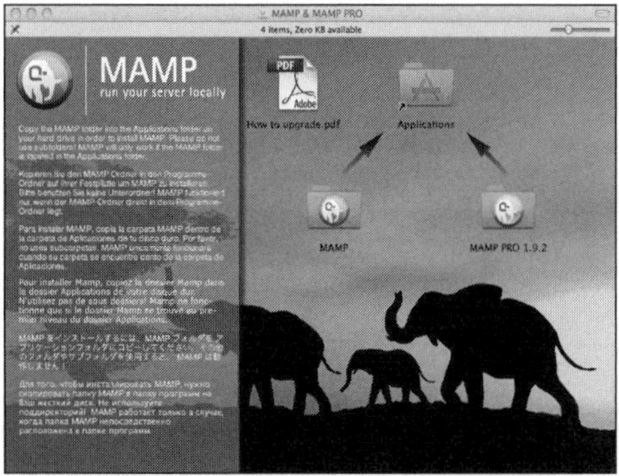

D The window that opens after you agree to MAMP's licensing terms

7. A disk appears on your Desktop, and a window opens with instructions on how to complete the installation **D**.
8. Drag the MAMP folder into the Applications folder alias as the instructions direct.
9. MAMP is now installed. To start it, go to `/Applications/MAMP` and double-click the MAMP icon.

TIP A default setting in MAMP often causes problems when you later try to install Drupal. To fix it, open the file at `/Applications/MAMP/conf/php5/php.ini` with a text editor. Search for the line that reads `memory_limit = 32M` and change the value to at least 64M (that is, so it reads `memory_limit = 64M`), then restart MAMP.

TIP When you first start MAMP, it will make some assumptions about how you want to run the web and MySQL servers—specifically, what ports to use, and where files will be located. We'll show you how to change those settings to work with your Drupal installation in the section "To Configure MAMP for Drupal on a Mac."

TIP As in *nix systems, MySQL installs an initial user named `root` that has *superuser* powers to do pretty much everything to MySQL databases. When you install MAMP, the default password for that superuser is also `root`. If you intend to use your Mac as a public-facing server, or simply want to make the MAMP installation more secure, change the password by opening the Terminal program found at `/Applications/Utilities/Terminal` and typing `/Applications/MAMP/Library/bin/mysqladmin -u root -p password` *`newpassword`*. Then enter the former password to confirm the change.

To install WAMP on a Windows computer:

1. Visit **wampserver.com/en/** in a web browser.
2. Click the link "Download the latest release of Wampserver 2" **E**.
3. On the resulting page, click the Download link. This page also specifies which versions of PHP and MySQL are part of the package **F**.

   A web page on **sourceforge.net** displays, and the file automatically starts downloading to your browser's default download location (usually the Desktop). The file is large, so downloading may take a few minutes.
4. Once downloaded, double-click the file **G**. You might see a dialog that gives special instructions for upgrading from a previous version. Assuming that you're not upgrading, click Yes to continue the installation.
5. The WAMP Setup Wizard appears **H**. Complete the necessary steps, accepting the license agreement and selecting preferred options as you go. By default, WAMP installs on the primary drive, as c:\wamp.

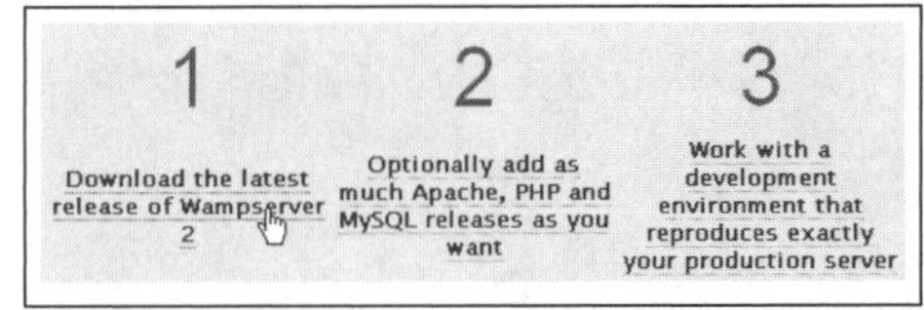

E The link on **wampserver.com** that leads to the page containing the downloadable file

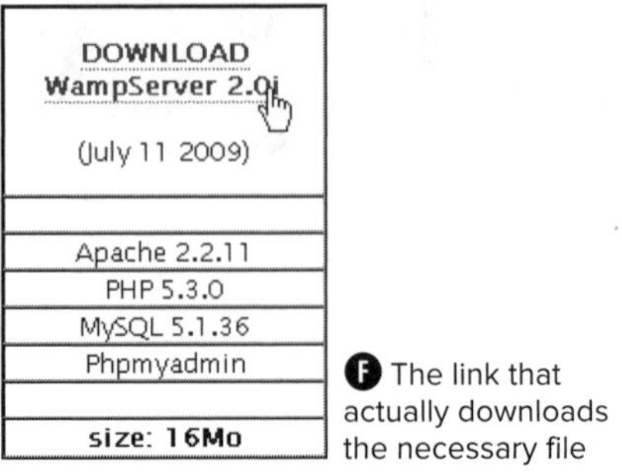

F The link that actually downloads the necessary file

G Icon to install WAMP

H WAMP Setup Wizard

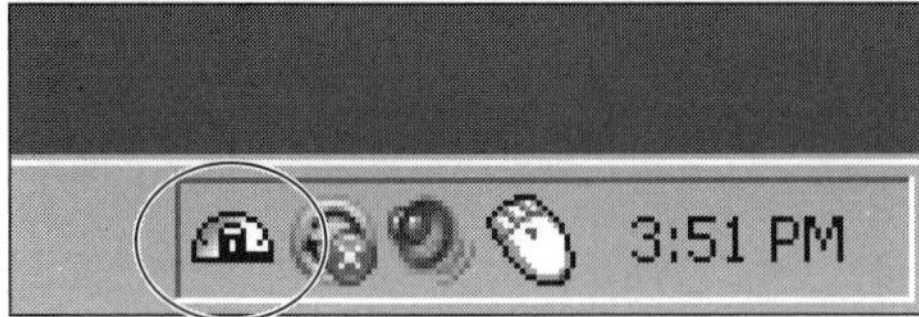

I The WAMP icon in the system tray

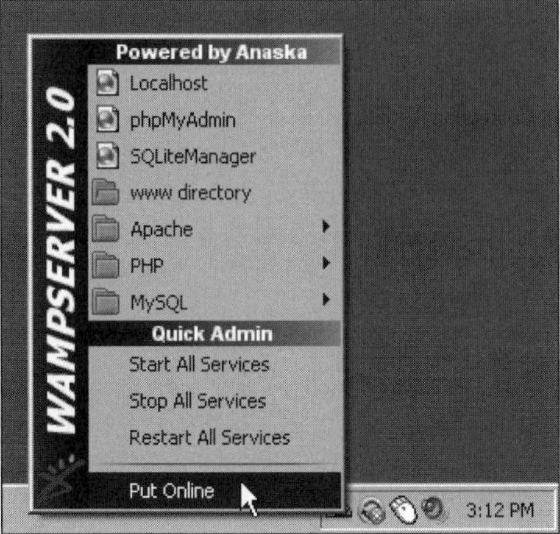

J Starting WAMP from the system tray

6. WAMP is now installed. To start it, click its icon—which looks like a parking meter I—in the system tray and select Put Online J.

TIP As in *nix systems, MySQL installs an initial user named `root` that has superuser powers to do pretty much everything to MySQL databases. When you install WAMP, that superuser has no password by default. If you intend to use your Windows computer as a public-facing server, or simply want to make the WAMP installation more secure, create a password by following instructions found at `udopage.com/developers/setting-up-passwords-for-wamp.php`.

What about *nix Operating Systems?

Many Drupal *administrators* develop their sites on a computer running the Mac or Windows operating system, then move them to managed, remote servers running some flavor of *nix. These servers almost always already have an AMP stack installed and running: Without them, they couldn't support a web hosting business!

But what if you want to develop on a *nix computer that's not running an AMP stack?

If you're running the Ubuntu or Debian distribution, you can use the Acquia Drupal .deb package available from **`acquia.com/downloads`**. (It includes Acquia Drupal as well as an AMP stack: See the sidebar "Understanding Acquia Drupal" for details.) Otherwise, the best solution is to install the AMP stack that's specific to your operating system's distribution, using its native package manager. See your operating system's documentation for more information. A second option is the one-size-fits-all solution XAMPP, which is available for a variety of platforms at **`apachefriends.org/en/xampp.html`**. Note that XAMPP's *developers* state that the default configuration is *not secure enough for a production environment*. However, it's both appropriate and fitting for developing a site that will later be moved to a secured server, and can itself be *hardened* (made more secure) by following instructions on the XAMPP web site.

Downloading and Unpacking Drupal

Once you have an AMP stack running, the next step is to download and unpack the Drupal package, and configure your AMP stack so it knows where Drupal is installed.

To download Drupal to a Mac or Windows computer:

1. Visit **drupal.org** in a web browser. There are several links that lead to the free, downloadable Drupal package, for example the "Drupal core" link in the right column. I prefer to go directly to the Drupal project's page at **drupal.org/project/drupal**.
2. Follow the "download" links until you find the latest version of Drupal 7 that doesn't end in "-dev." (Those are development versions, intended more for programmers than site administrators.)
3. Find the downloaded file, which will have a name similar to drupal-7.0.tar.gz, and double-click it to uncompress it. The result is a folder containing all the files you need to run Drupal **A**.

TIP You can rename your Drupal folder to anything you want, as long as your operating system and AMP stack allow it. (Don't use any names with periods in them.)

TIP Should you decide to change where you installed Drupal, move the entire folder. The Drupal installation contains a "hidden" file (`.htaccess`) that doesn't show up in the Finder on Mac OS X and therefore won't be copied if you simply select the folder's contents and move them elsewhere.

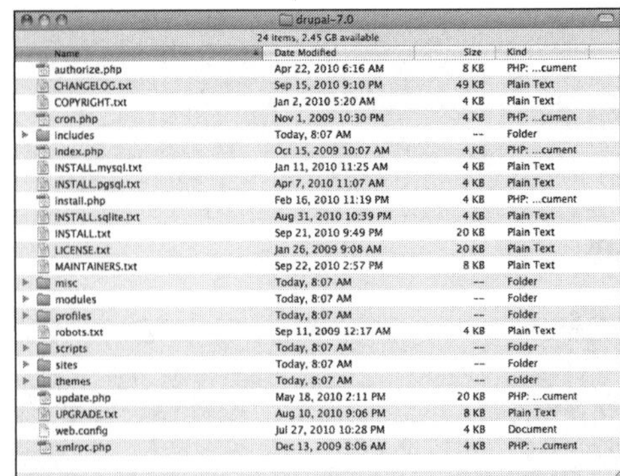

A Drupal, after expanding the downloaded file

Help! I Can't Uncompress the File!

Drupal comes as a compressed archive in the gzip format, which many versions of Windows don't understand without a helper application. Some programs that will let you uncompress gzip files include:

- WinImp (**technelysium.com.au/winimp.html**)
- StuffIt Expander (**stuffit.com/win-expander.html**)
- WinAce (**winace.com**)
- WinZip (**winzip.com**)

Some of these programs require payment, while others require you to join the company's marketing email list. If you don't like any of them, you can always just install Drupal using the Acquia Drupal stack installer for Windows (DAMP), which comes as a Windows executable file (.exe): See the sidebar "But I Want to Do This the Easy Way!" earlier in this chapter for details.

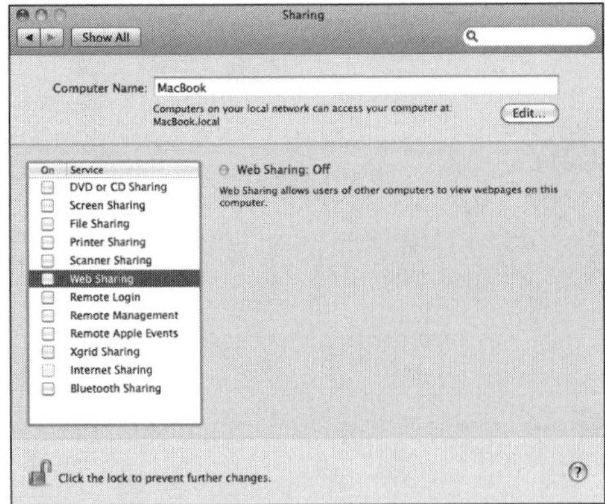

B Turning off Web Sharing

C The MAMP icon

To configure MAMP for Drupal on a Mac:

1. Mac OS X Web Sharing could cause conflicts with MAMP. To turn it off, choose Apple menu > System Preferences, click the Sharing icon, and ensure that the Web Sharing check box is not selected **B**.
2. If MAMP isn't already running, start it by double-clicking the MAMP icon in the **/Applications/MAMP** folder **C**. If you see a dialog box that warns you about MAMP being an application downloaded from the Internet, click Open.

   Two things happen: The MAMP application launches **D**, and a browser window opens with further information about both MAMP and your site. For now, ignore the browser window to focus only on the application, as that's where all the server-configuration settings are.
3. Click the Preferences button. A dialog box with four tabs opens: Start/Stop, Ports, PHP, and Apache.
4. Click the Apache tab **E**.

continues on next page

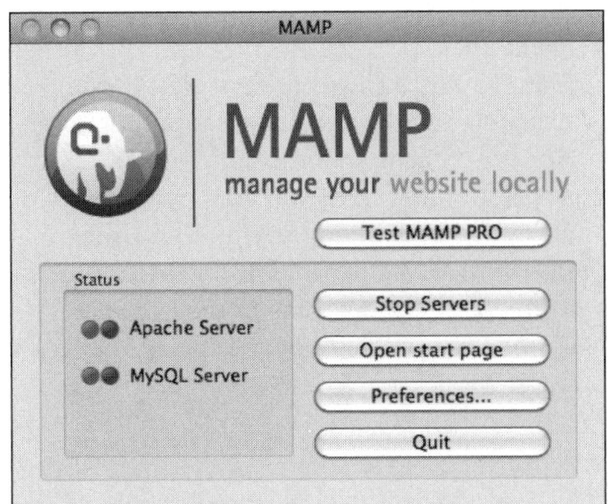

D The MAMP application

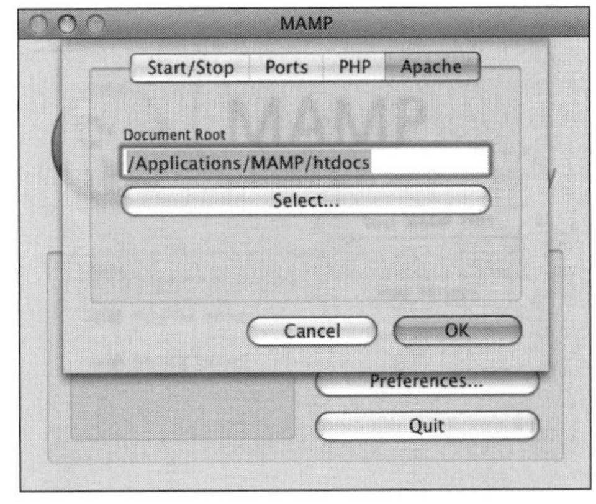

E MAMP's preferences dialog box, with the Apache tab selected, before choosing the new Drupal location

5. Click Select, navigate to the location of your Drupal folder, and click Open **F**. In the example, we've renamed our Drupal folder **`drupalvqs-site`** and moved it to the **`/Users/`*`username`*`/Sites`** folder.

6. **Recommended:** In MAMP, click Preferences, click the Ports tab, then click "Set to default Apache and MySQL ports" **G**. You'll need to enter your Mac OS X password when you start or stop the servers. However, if you leave the ports on their default MAMP settings, you'll need to type **`:8888`** at the end of every URL on your site, which can be much more intrusive.

TIP **The folder that serves documents to the web through Apache is called `DocumentRoot` or (colloquially) docroot.**

TIP **By default, MAMP sets `DocumentRoot` as `/Applications/MAMP/htdocs`, a folder inside the MAMP application itself. I recommend changing the `DocumentRoot` because most backup programs ignore the enormous Applications folder, which means you're likely to lose all your Drupal files if your hard drive fails.**

TIP **I prefer to use the `Sites` folder as my `DocumentRoot`, which is set up for just this purpose—and then make sure my backup program knows to look there. The `Documents` folder is also a good candidate, because most backup programs save files that are in there by default.**

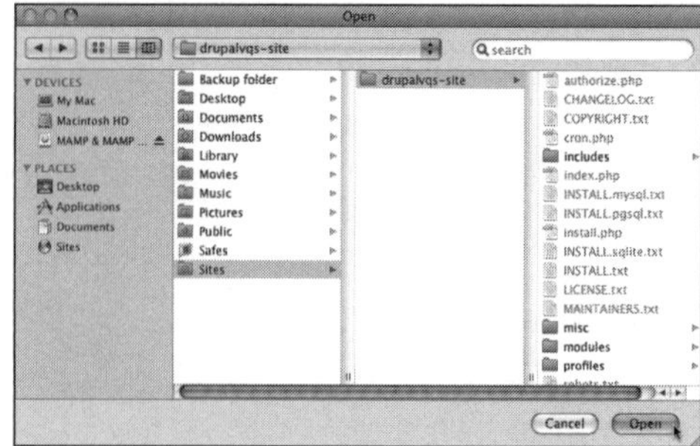

F Showing Apache where to find your Drupal installation

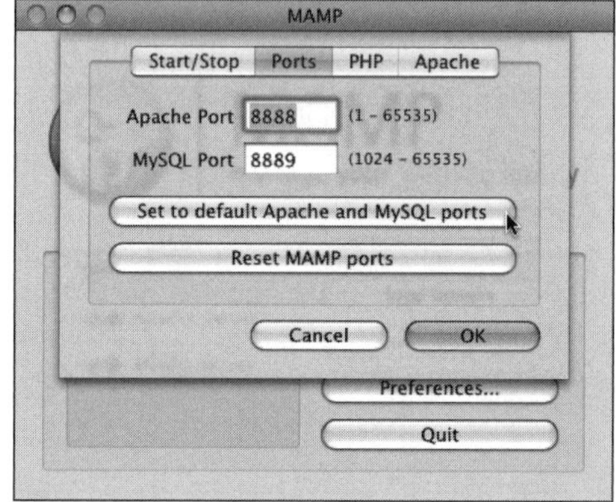

G Changing Apache and MySQL ports in MAMP

Couldn't I Just Use Mac OS X's Built-In Unix Programs?

Mac OS X is a Unix-based system, so you might be tempted to just tie together its Apache, SQLite (or downloaded MySQL), and PHP parts to create your own AMP stack. Unfortunately, doing so can interfere with Mac OS X's Web Sharing and other systems. It can be done; but in my (somewhat painful) experience, MAMP is by far the easier way to go.

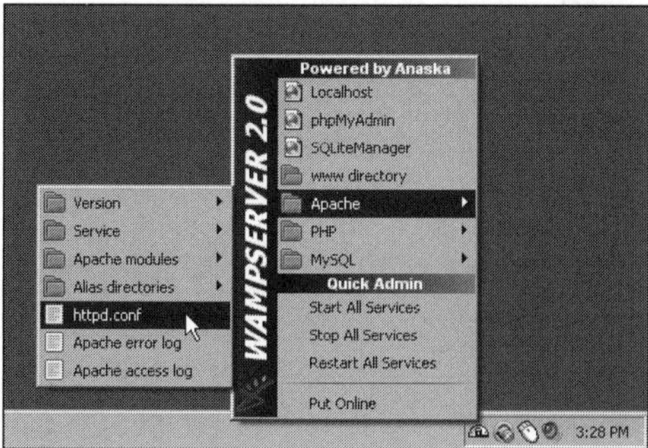

H Opening WAMP's `httpd.conf` configuration file in Notepad

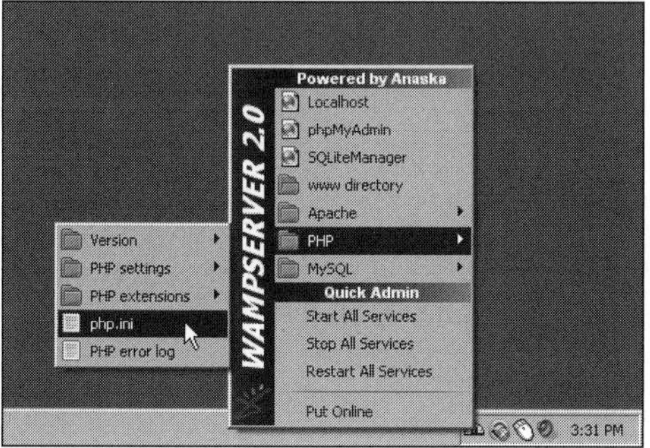

I Opening WAMP's `php.ini` configuration file in Notepad

To configure WAMP for Drupal on a Windows computer:

1. Click the WAMP icon in the system tray, then choose Apache > httpd.conf **H**. The `httpd.conf` file opens in Notepad.
2. Edit the line that begins with `DocumentRoot` to reflect where you put your Drupal files. This is the `DocumentRoot`, which by default is `c:/wamp/bin/apache/`*`apache-version-number`*. I recommend that you change that to somewhere you're sure your backup software will see it. The `My Documents` folder is a good choice.
3. By default, WAMP's PHP settings limit file uploads to be no larger than a paltry 2 MB, which will cause problems when you try to run Drupal. Change it by clicking the WAMP icon in the system tray, then choosing PHP > php.ini **I**. In the file that opens in Notepad, change the `upload_max_filesize` line to a larger number; I recommend at least 64 MB.

To transfer Drupal to a *nix server:

Now that you have the downloaded Drupal package on your local machine, you need to move it to your server, using one of several methods:

- Use a graphical file transfer protocol (FTP) program, such as Cyberduck for Mac (`cyberduck.ch`), WinSCP for Windows (`winscp.net`), or FileZilla for both platforms (`filezilla-project.org`). These programs all have familiar drag-and-drop interfaces.

continues on next page

- Use a text-based terminal program: One included with Mac OS X is at **/Applications/Utilities/Terminal**; on Windows, choose Start menu > Run, then type **cmd**. Connect to your *nix server by either typing **telnet** ***user@domain-name*** or **ssh** ***user@domain-name*** **J**. Then navigate to the directory where you want to install Drupal and type **wget** ***URL-to-drupal-package***. For the Drupal 7.0 version, for example, that's **wget http://ftp.drupal.org/files/projects/drupal-7.0.tar.gz**. (**Table 1.1** lists some useful *nix commands, and **K** shows a sample *nix navigation session.)

You are now ready to unpack the Drupal package.

To unpack Drupal on a *nix server:

1. Navigate to the directory where you downloaded Drupal.
2. Type **tar -xzf** ***name-of-file***. If you want to see a list of files as they're being unpacked, type **tar -xzvf** ***name-of-file*** instead.

   Drupal is now installed in a newly created directory at the same level as the .tar.gz file.
3. **Optional:** Delete the downloaded package by typing **rm** ***name-of-file***.
4. **Optional:** Rename the Drupal directory using the **mv** command, for example, **mv drupal-7.0 drupalvqs-site**.

TIP Most *nix systems can complete filenames automatically: Just type the first few letters of your downloaded file, then press Tab and *nix will fill in the rest—as long as there's no other item in that directory that starts with the same few letters.

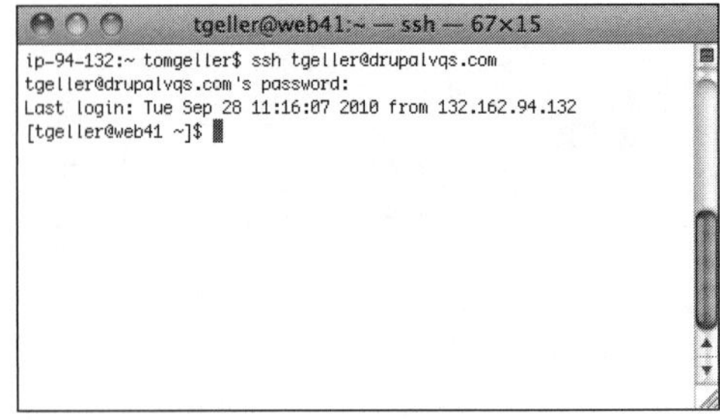

J Using **ssh** to connect to a *nix server

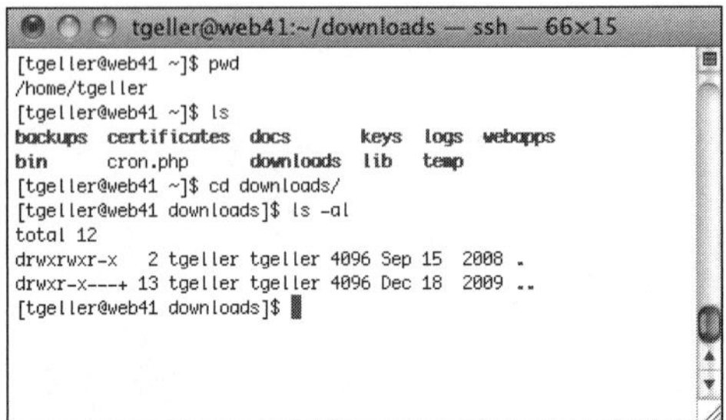

K Navigating in *nix; the parts after the "$" were typed by the user

TABLE 1.1 *nix Commands

*nix Command	What it Does
pwd	Shows your current location
ls	Lists items in your current location, in a basic format
ls -al	Lists all items, including invisible ones, with attributes
mv ***source destination***	Changes the location and/or name of a file or directory
cd ***directory-name***	Moves into a directory that's at the same level as your current location
cd ..	Moves to the directory one level up
cd ***/path/to/location***	Moves to a specific location

Understanding *nix Commands

*nix has notoriously obscure commands, and its text-only interface can be daunting if you've only ever used Windows or Mac OS X. But it packs a real wallop into just a few keystrokes, so learning a little *nix is well worth the time.

Some commands stand by themselves, such as **pwd** (which originally stood for "print working directory"). Most have additional options: **ls -al** means "list all files (including invisible ones) in a long format." Some require additional parts. For example, **cp** (copy) requires a source and destination, such as **cp** ***original.txt copy.txt***.

For detailed help using a specific command, type **man** ***command***. Help in another form is sometimes available by typing **info** ***command***, and you might find abbreviated help by typing ***command*** **--help**. To find a command based on its description, type **apropos** ***description***. (For example, **apropos copy** returns a list of several commands, including **cp**.) Not every command works on every version of *nix.

*nix's interface also employs dozens of shortcuts, such as the double period that means "the directory one level above where I am now." For a guide to some of them, check out the book *Unix: Visual QuickStart Guide, 4th Edition* (Peachpit Press, 2009).

Understanding Acquia Drupal

Until September 2008, general-purpose Drupal was mostly available only in one configuration, from **drupal.org**. That all changed when Acquia (**acquia.com**), a company co-founded by Drupal originator *Dries Buytaert,* released a commercially supported version called Acquia Drupal. It's a superset of the Drupal project's core Drupal with additional modules that (among other things):

- Open a communication channel between your installation of Drupal and Acquia's monitoring, search, and other services
- Make administration easier
- Improve support for graphics
- Give site visitors additional capabilities
- Permit construction and display of complex content structures
- Support other contributed modules

Acquia Drupal also includes some additional themes (graphical skins) for Drupal. Like the core Drupal *distribution,* Acquia Drupal is free and open-source software, and is made available under the GNU Public License.

To download Acquia Drupal, go to **acquia.com/downloads**; for more details on its contents, see **acquia.com/products-services/acquia-drupal**.

This book assumes you're using core Drupal unless otherwise specified.

Creating the MySQL Database Using phpMyAdmin

The Drupal files themselves don't contain any of the posts, comments, or settings of your web site. Instead, all text-based content passes through Drupal into a database, and Drupal retrieves that content from the database when requested. In fact, you could say that Drupal is only an attractive and convenient front end to that database; remove the database, and the site disappears.

Drupal can connect with databases in virtually any database program, but by far the most commonly used one is MySQL. The easiest way to manage a MySQL database is through the free program phpMyAdmin, which is part of both MAMP and WAMP installations.

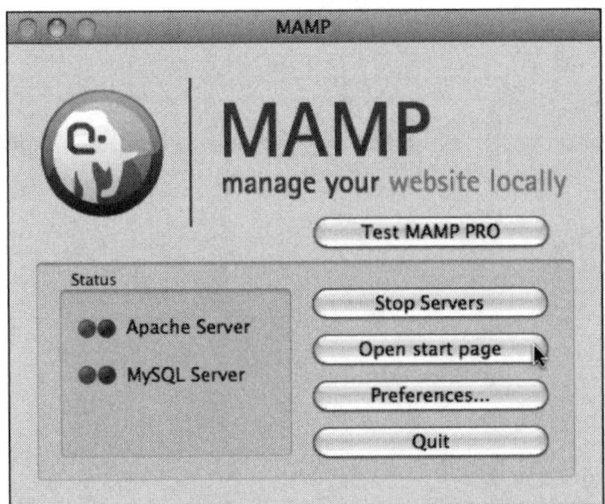

Ⓐ Launching MAMP's start page in a web browser

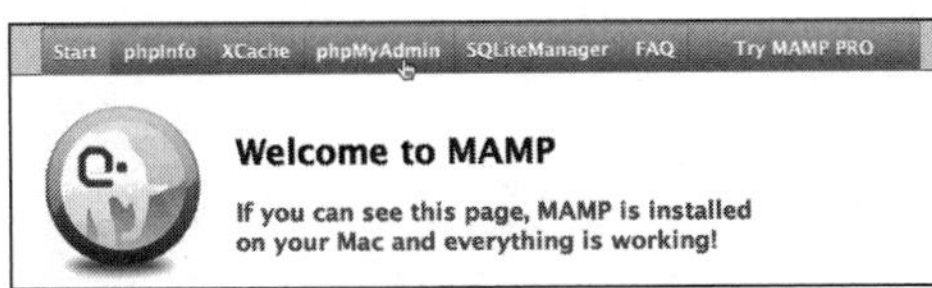

Ⓑ The link that leads to the phpMyAdmin screen

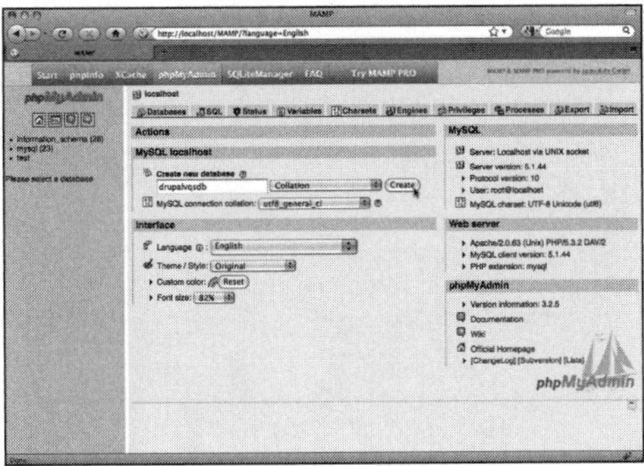

Ⓒ Creating a Drupal database named **`drupalvqsdb`**

To create Drupal's database on Mac OS X using MAMP:

1. If MAMP isn't already running, start it by double-clicking the MAMP icon in the **`/Applications/MAMP`** folder.
2. In the main MAMP screen, click the "Open start page" button Ⓐ to open a page in your browser window.
3. On the resulting web page, click the phpMyAdmin link Ⓑ.
4. On the phpMyAdmin screen, type a name for your database in the "Create new database" text box and click Create Ⓒ. In our example, we named the database **`drupalvqsdb`**.

   A screen appears with the notice "Database drupalvqsdb has been created."

TIP To be safe, use no more than 16 characters for your database name. Database names might be case-sensitive, depending on the operating system. Most characters are permitted, although you should avoid underscores and quotation marks in all their forms. Keep it simple by using only lowercase letters.

TIP Remember your database name! You'll need it to install Drupal. If you ever need a reminder, relaunch the phpMyAdmin screen and click the Databases tab at the top.

To create Drupal's database on Windows using WAMP:

1. Click the WAMP icon in the system tray and choose phpMyAdmin **D**.
2. On the phpMyAdmin screen, type a name for your database in the "Create new database" text box and click Create **E**. In our example, we named the database **`drupalvqsdb`**.

   A screen appears with the notice "Database drupalvqsdb has been created."

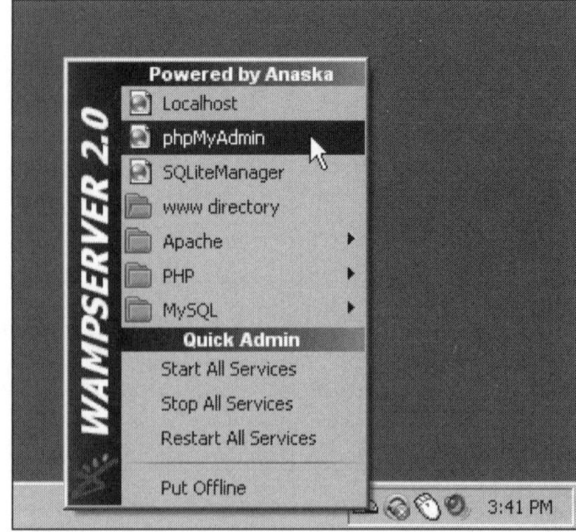

D Launching the MySQL control program, phpMyAdmin

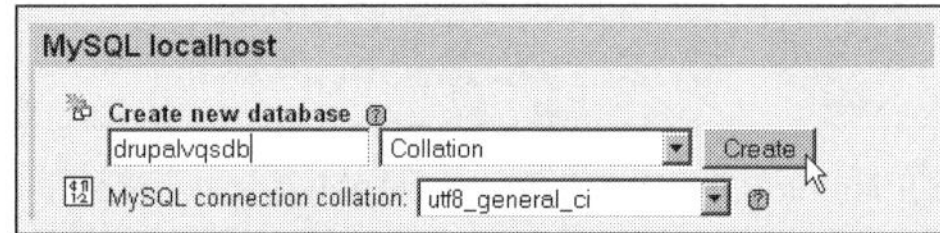

E Creating a Drupal database named **`drupalvqsdb`**

To create Drupal's database on *nix using the command-line interface:

1. Type **`mysqladmin -u root -p create`** ***`database-name`***. Follow the prompts to complete the process.
2. If you get the response **`mysqladmin: command not found`**, you'll need to locate the mysqladmin application on your *nix computer in one of the following ways:
   - Typing **`which mysqladmin`**
   - Typing **`locate mysqladmin`**
   - Typing **`find / -name mysqladmin`**

   You might have to find the correct instance of **`mysqladmin`** from among a long list.

TIP Many Internet service providers don't give you direct access to MySQL tools, and instead require you to create databases through web-based interfaces such as phpMyAdmin. Contact your service provider if you have any problems with this step.

Installing Drupal

After all you went through to prepare your computer, you'll be happy to discover that installing Drupal itself is—for the most part—surprisingly straightforward. A well-written web-based interface leads you through most of the process, and you're usually given hints to solve any problems that arise.

The only pieces of information you need in hand are:

- Your database name and password
- An email address to be associated with the site's first user

To install Drupal:

1. If you're installing on a local computer, make sure your AMP stack is running, with the Apache setting pointing at your Drupal folder.
2. Go to the site in a web browser:
   - If you're working on a local computer, the address is **`http://localhost`**. (If you're using MAMP and left the ports in their default configuration, however, the address is **`http://localhost:8888`**.)
   - If you're working on a remote computer, point your browser at the domain where you've installed Drupal (for example, **`www.example.com`**).

continues on next page

3. On the resulting page, you have a choice of whether to install Drupal "with commonly used features pre-configured," or in a stripped-down (minimal) version **A**. In fact, both install exactly the same software, but with different options enabled. Unless you have a particular reason to install the minimal version, I recommend that you go with the default, feature-filled version. Click "Save and continue."

4. The next page gives you the opportunity to install a version of Drupal with its interface in a language other than English, and instructions on how to do so. (The process involves finding, downloading, and installing a translation package.) We'll assume English is your preferred language; click "Save and continue."

5. If there are any problems with your installation, you'll see a screen labeled "Requirements problem," detailing the issue along with the status of several systems on which Drupal relies. (In **B**, you see the error message you'd get if a necessary file had been deleted.) You might also see non-critical warnings, for example if your PHP memory limit was set so low that problems would probably happen eventually. After correcting the errors, click the "proceed with the installation" link at the bottom of the page.

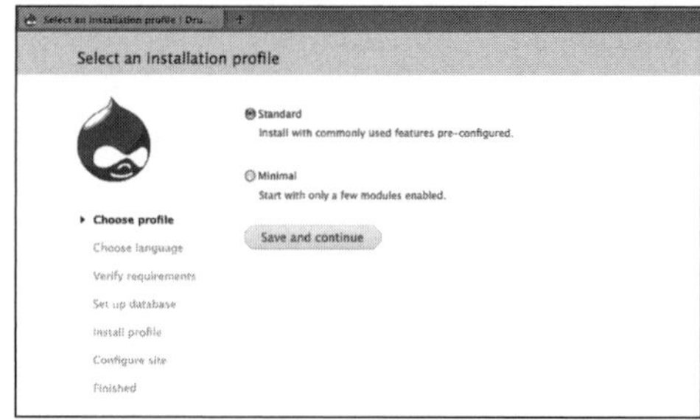

A Selecting either the full-featured or minimal Drupal installation

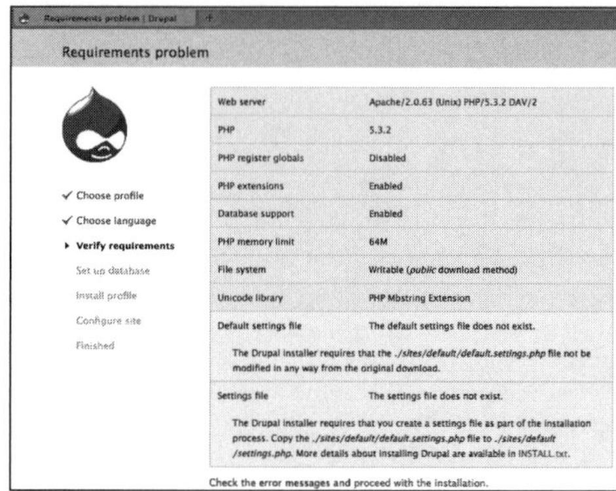

B Notification of problems during installation

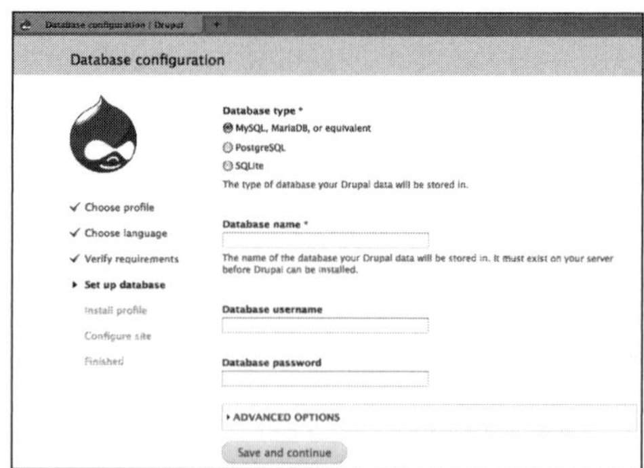

C Configuring Drupal to use the database you created earlier

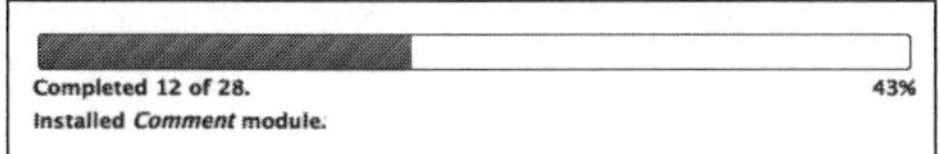

D Drupal's installation progress bar

All necessary changes to ./sites/default and ./sites/default/settings.php have been made. They have been set to read-only for security.
SITE INFORMATION
Site name *
My Drupal Site
Site e-mail address *
admin@example.com
Automated e-mails, such as registration information, will be sent from this address. Use an address ending in your site's domain to help prevent these e-mails from being flagged as spam.
SITE MAINTENANCE ACCOUNT
Username *
admin
Spaces are allowed; punctuation is not allowed except for periods, hyphens, and underscores.
E-mail address *
admin@example.com
Password *
Password strength: Strong
Confirm password *
Passwords match: yes
To make your password stronger:
• Add punctuation
SERVER SETTINGS
Default country
United States
Select the default country for the site.
Default time zone
America/New York: Wednesday, September 29, 2010 - 15:16 -0400
By default, dates in this site will be displayed in the chosen time zone.
UPDATE NOTIFICATIONS
Check for updates automatically
Receive e-mail notifications
The system will notify you when updates and important security releases are available for installed components. Anonymous information about your site is sent to Drupal.org.
Save and continue

E Drupal's initial configuration screen, where you name your site and create the initial administrative user

6. When there are no other show-stopping problems, you'll see the database configuration page **C**. Enter the required information. If you didn't change the database username or password as was described in "To install MAMP on a Mac" or "To install WAMP on a Windows computer," the database username is **`root`** in both MAMP and WAMP; the default database password is **`root`** on MAMP, and WAMP has no default password.
7. You'll generally only need to change the advanced options in unusual situations. Talk to your Internet service provider if you can't get past this step.
8. When finished, click "Save and continue."

   A progress bar appears **D**, typically just for a few seconds.
9. If all goes well, you'll see the "Configure site" screen **E**. Your Drupal site is now installed, but if you don't fill out the necessary fields in this form, you'll be locked out and unable to administer it. (Should you accidentally close this screen, you can return to it by going to ***`domain-name`*****`/install.php?profile=standard&locale=en`** in a web browser.)

continues on next page

10. Fill out the "Configure site" form. The user you create here is your Drupal site's *superuser*, able to perform all administrative tasks; the email address you enter is where important site information will be sent. Make sure it's correct! You'll later be able to change all this information through Drupal if you want by going to **http://*domain-name*/user/1** and **http://*domain-name*/admin/config/system/site-information**.

11. Click "Save and continue" for a confirmation that all went well **F**. Click the "Visit your new site" link to start administering it **G**. You're now logged in to your new Drupal site as the superuser. Congratulations!

TIP Drupal 7 introduced a new visual theme (called Seven) that appears when you perform administrative tasks. That's what you saw when installing Drupal; G is the theme that visitors to your site see, and that appears when you're doing non-administrative tasks. You'll learn how to change these themes in the section "Selecting a Visual Theme" in Chapter 2.

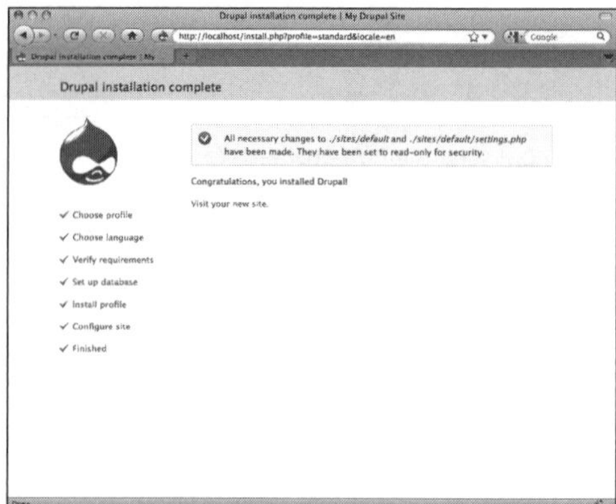

F Drupal, installed and ready to go

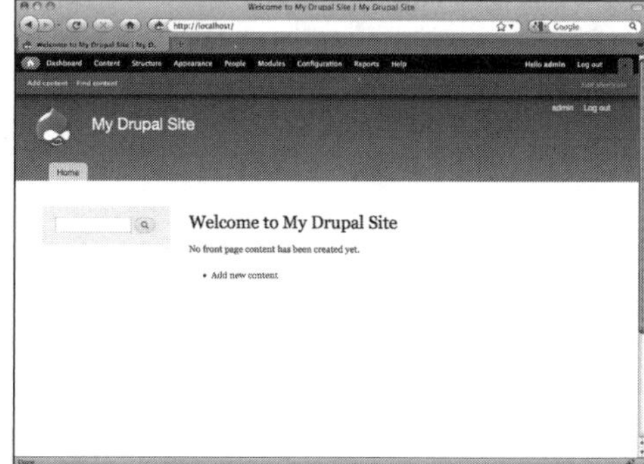

G Your new site's home page as it appears when logged in as the superuser

What Is This "localhost" I Keep Reading About?

You might have noticed that the term *localhost* keeps popping up. That's Apache's way of saying, "The domain of the machine you're currently using." So entering **http://localhost** into a browser looks for a site that's running on the same computer as your browser, whereas **www.example.com** will go out onto the Internet to find **example.com**.

Establishing Your Drupal Site

Now that you've installed Drupal, you may find yourself asking, "What now?" We're going to take it step by step, starting with the tasks you probably want to do right away, and coming back to other administration tasks as we go through the book. But first you'll learn how to:

- Use Drupal's administrative interface
- Turn on features
- Create pages
- Change your site's basic information
- Change the overall look of your site through built-in and downloaded *themes*
- Back up and restore your site
- Get help from the Drupal community or from Drupal's built-in help

In This Chapter

Using the New Administrative Interfaces in Drupal 7

Version 7 of Drupal introduced several features to ease administrators' jobs.

The first is two new themes. One is called Seven, which appears whenever you see a page for administering Drupal and favors clarity over flash **A**. (You saw Seven during the installation process.) On other pages, Bartik is the new default theme **B**.

The second feature is an *administrative overlay* that appears in front of the page you're affecting and helps administrators differentiate between pages that the public sees and those that only administrators see. This pretty effect appears whenever you follow a click path to an administrative page: for example, by clicking Modules. It's possible to bypass the overlay by typing an administrative URL directly in to your web browser's address bar or by disabling the Overlay *module*.

Also new in Drupal 7 are a *Toolbar* and *Shortcut bar.* They float at the top of your browser window whenever you're logged in as a user who's been granted permission to see them. (Those permissions are in the Shortcut and Toolbar groups on the Permissions page: To learn how to set them, see the section "To change user access permissions" in Chapter 7, "Wrangling Users.")

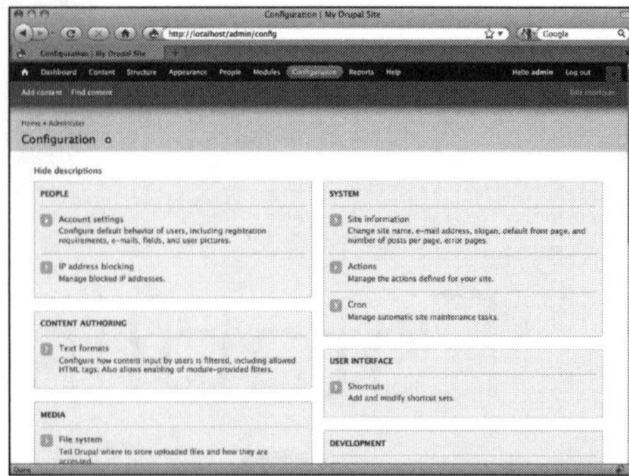

A Seven, Drupal 7's default administration theme

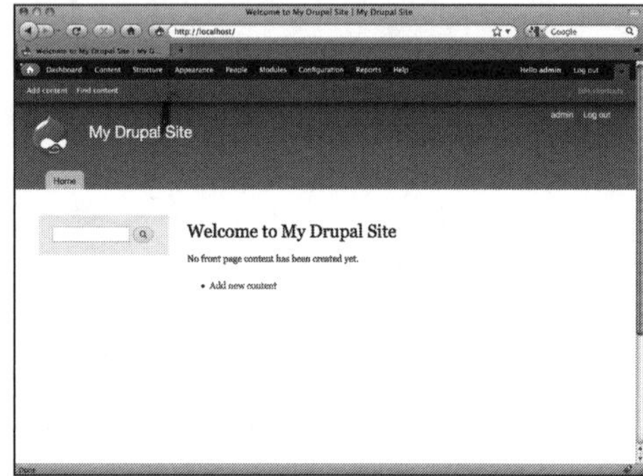

B Bartik, Drupal 7's default general-purpose theme

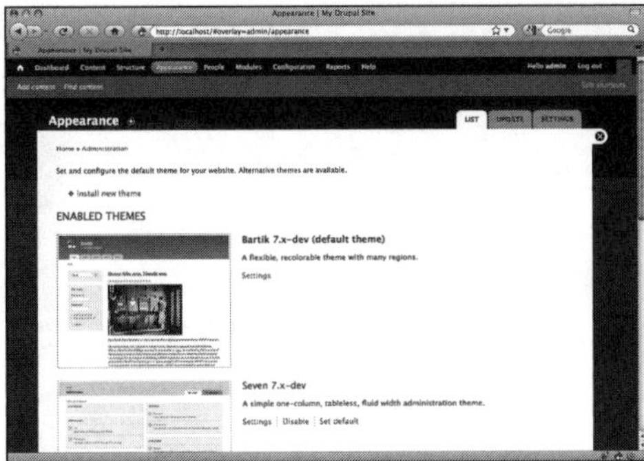

C The Appearance administration page

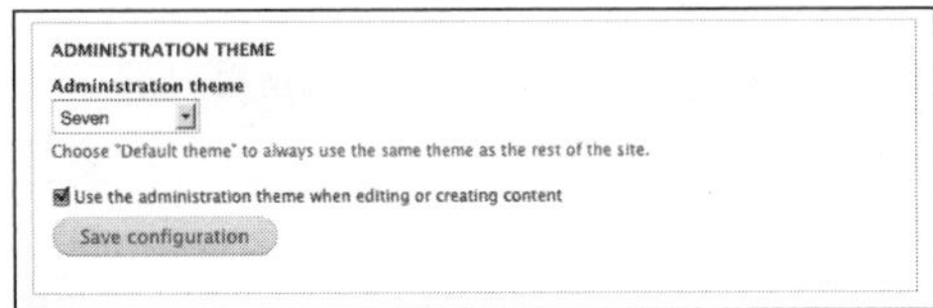

D The setting for changing the administration theme

Throughout this book are directions to go to certain locations by clicking something in the Toolbar. However, you can also go to those places by typing the destination URL directly in your web browser's address bar.

Drupal now provides a *dashboard* you can customize to give you fast access to common tasks (such as monitoring recent *comments*).

To change the administration theme:

1. Click Appearance in the Toolbar. You'll see the Appearance administration page **C**.
2. Scroll to the "Administration theme" section at the bottom of the page **D**.
3. Select the theme you want for the administration theme from the pop-up menu. If you want it to be the same as the theme on all other pages, choose "Default theme." You also have the option of showing this theme whenever you edit or create content. Click "Save configuration."

TIP The benefits of having a separate administration theme become obvious if your main theme has a narrow content area or a lot of unusual customizations, which could make some administrative controls unavailable.

To see pages with the administrative overlay:

1. Go to any administrative page, for example by clicking Modules in the Toolbar **E**.
2. To remove the administrative overlay and return to the page underneath it, click the **x** in its upper-right corner **F**.

TIP **When you see the administrative overlay, the page underneath it is coded into the URL showing in your browser's address bar. Let's say, for example, that you're on the page `http://`*`domain-name`*`/article-about-bears` and click the Modules link in the Toolbar. The resulting URL is `http://`*`domain-name`*`/article-about-bears#overlay=admin/modules`.**

To see pages without the administrative overlay:

Reach an administrative page by typing its URL directly in your browser's address bar, for example **`http://localhost/admin/modules`** **G**.

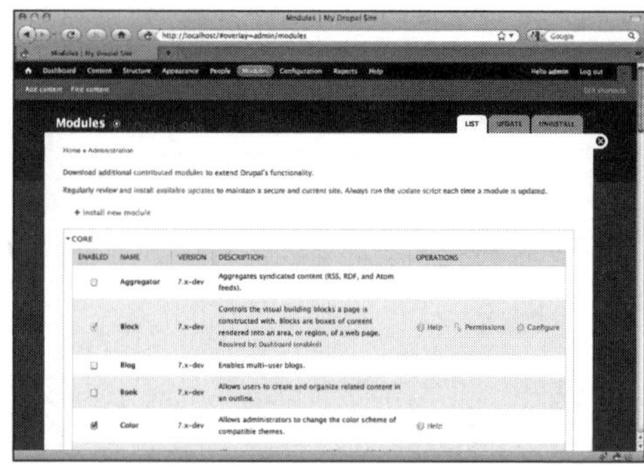

E The Modules page with the administrative overlay

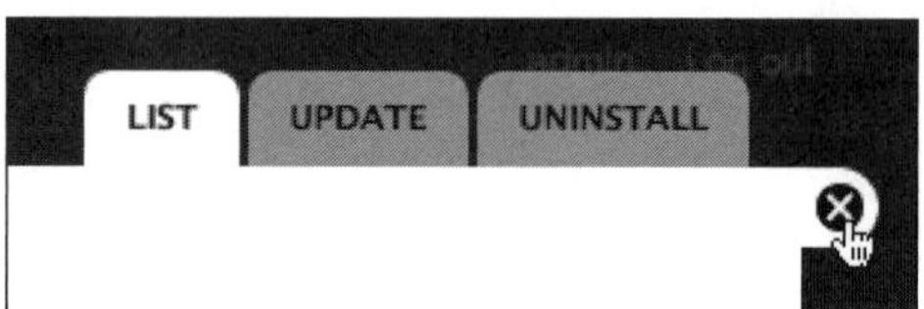

F Removing the administrative overlay

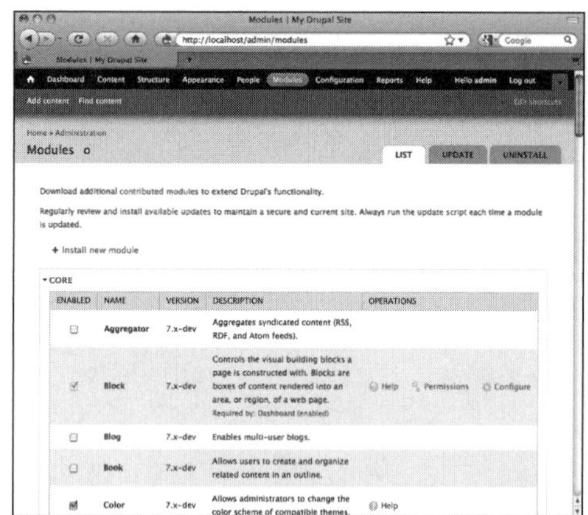

G The Modules page, as seen when you type its URL in your web browser's address bar

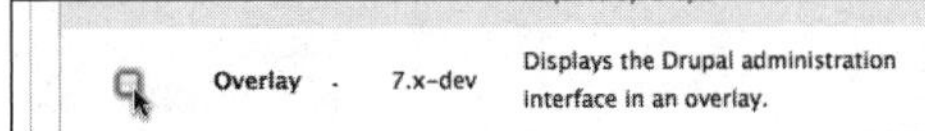

H The check box on the Modules page where you can disable the administrative overlay

To turn off the administrative overlay entirely:

1. Click Modules in the Toolbar.
2. Scroll down to deselect the Overlay check box **H**.
3. Scroll to the bottom of the page and click "Save configuration." The administrative overlay will remain off until you enable it again.

TIP You can switch between seeing and not seeing the administrative overlay by removing the path to the underlying page *and* the `#overlay=` in the URL. So for the Modules pages shown in E and G, the URLs are `http://`*`domain-name`*`/article-about-bears#overlay=admin/modules` and `http://localhost/admin/modules` respectively. Conversely, you can see the administrative overlay by adding that text. The content is the same in both cases.

To change which items appear in the Shortcut bar:

There are two ways to add items to the Shortcut bar. *Either:*

- Navigate to the administrative page for which you'd like a shortcut in the Shortcut bar, then click the + sign icon next to the page's name **I**. The shortcut's text will be the same as the page's name—in this case, "Content types."

or

- Click "Edit shortcuts" in the right side of the Shortcut bar itself to show the "Edit shortcuts" page **J**. Then click "Add shortcut," type the name and path of the shortcut you'd like to add (without the **`http://`*`domain-name`*`/`** or ***`underlying-page-URL`*`#overlay=admin`** parts), and click Save **K**.

TIP When you link to administrative pages in the Shortcut bar, those links will always show the resulting pages with the administrative overlay, as long as the Overlay module is enabled.

TIP You can set up multiple Shortcut bars, each with its own set of shortcuts, by clicking Configuration > Shortcuts.

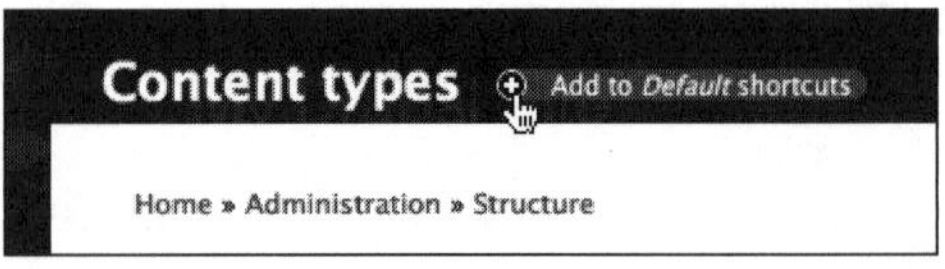

I Adding a link to the Shortcut Bar from (nearly) any page in Drupal

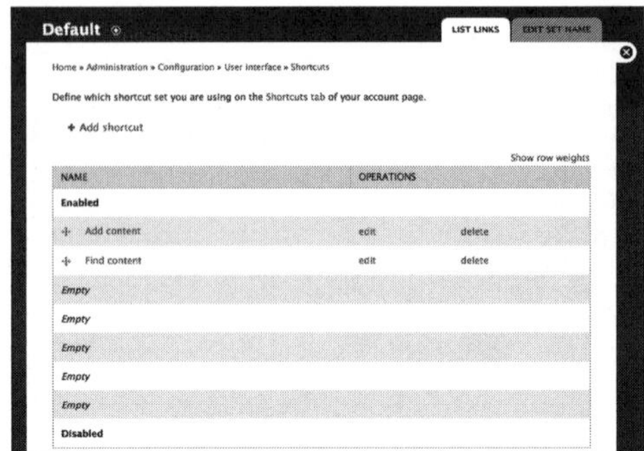

J The administration page for adding links to the Default Shortcut bar

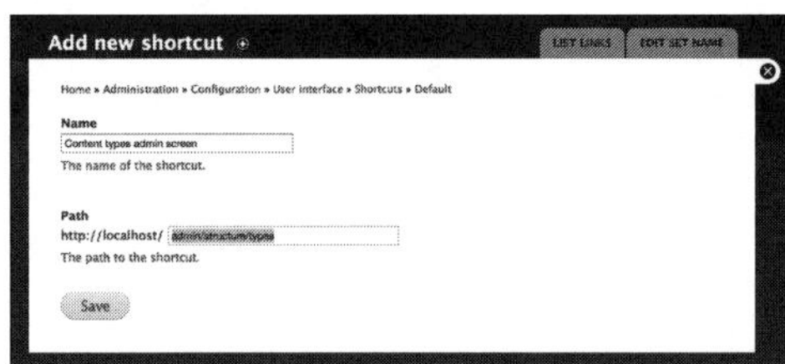

K Adding a link to the Shortcut bar by typing in the target page's URL

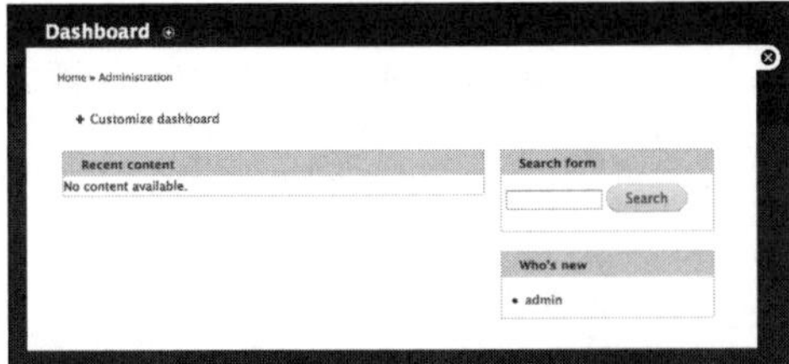

L The Dashboard

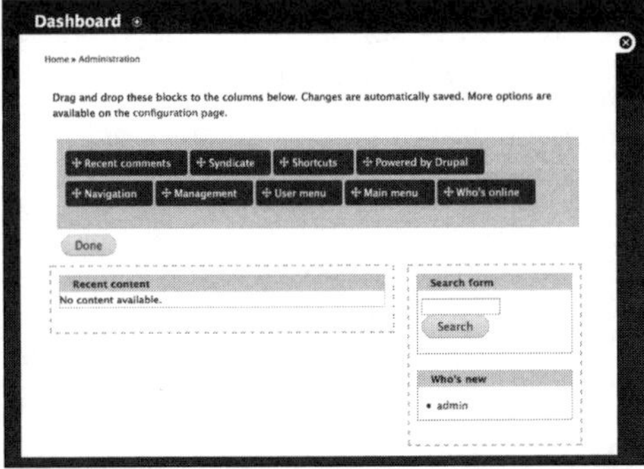

M The Dashboard, ready to customize

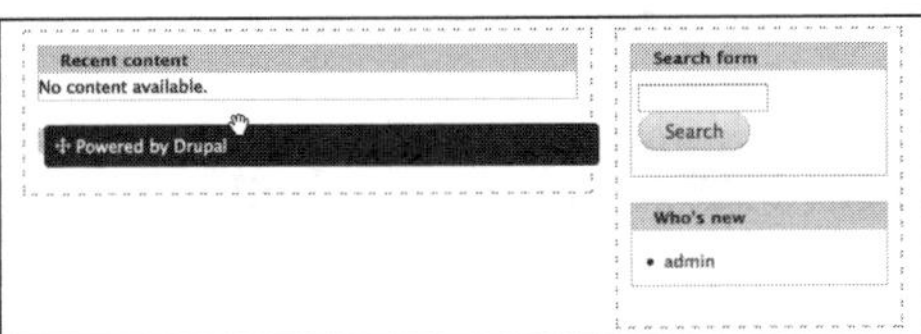

N Adding an item to the Dashboard

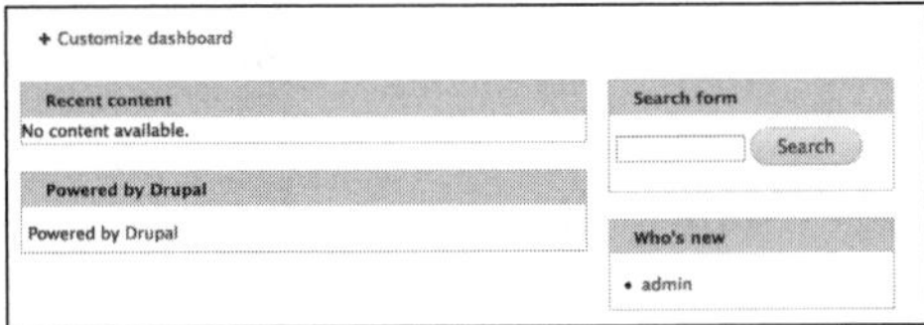

O The newly changed section of the Dashboard

To customize the Dashboard:

1. Display the Dashboard by clicking Dashboard in the Toolbar **L**.
2. Click the "Customize dashboard" link. Dotted lines appear around areas where you can place Dashboard items that are shown in a gray area near the top of the screen **M**.
3. Drag any of the Dashboard items into the areas delimited by dotted lines **N**. To remove a Dashboard item, drag it back into the shaded gray area.
4. When you've arranged all the Dashboard items you want in the desired areas, click Done. The Dashboard now appears with the items in place and ready for use **O**.

TIP Dashboard items are actually just *blocks*. For more about blocks, see "Laying Out Your Site with Blocks" in Chapter 6, "Improving Access to Content."

TIP Many of the Dashboard items are dynamic: That is, they change depending on what's on your site. (The *Who's online* item is a good example.)

Turning on Built-In Features

Drupal comes well-configured fresh out of the box: You don't have to change it much to create a simple but effective site. In fact, you've already learned all you really need!

But for simplicity's sake, some features of Drupal are disabled by default.

This section tells you how to turn on those built-in features, called *modules*.

To turn on built-in features:

1. Go to the Modules page by clicking Modules in the Toolbar **A**.

   Modules are self-contained packages of software that give Drupal its functionality. Some are required by Drupal. Others are optional; by default, Drupal comes with some of these optional modules enabled. There are also hundreds of additional modules available for free download at **`drupal.org/project/modules`**. For more information about them, see Chapter 9, "Extending Drupal with Modules."

2. Select the check box next to the feature you want to enable.

3. Scroll to the bottom of the page and click "Save configuration."

4. Most modules come with one or more administration pages that appear after you enable the module. The quickest way to find them is to click the Configure link on the Modules page next to the new module.

TIP Another place to find documentation for downloaded modules is among the modules' files themselves, particularly those named `README.TXT` and `INSTALL.TXT`.

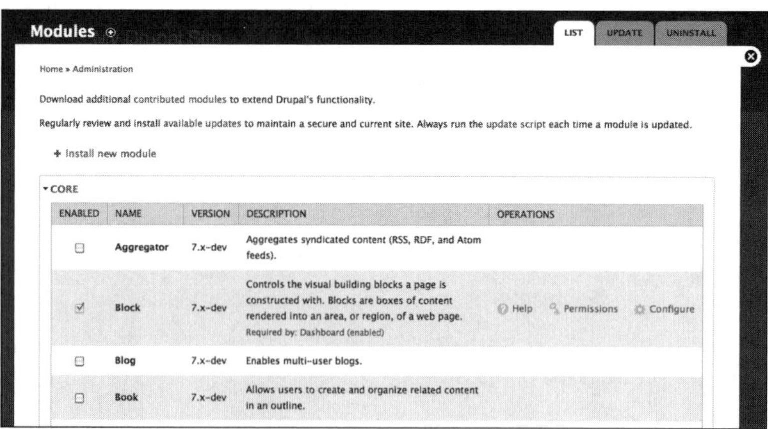

A The Modules administration page

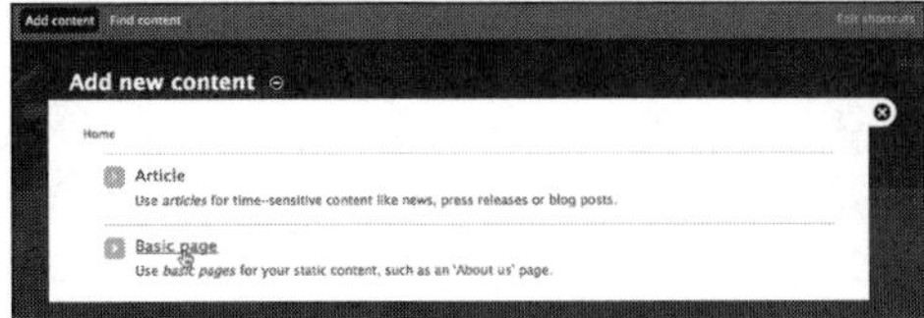

A Choosing whether to create an article or a basic page

Giving Your Site Its Identity

Your newly installed Drupal site is like a newborn baby: full of possibilities and just waiting for shaping influences. Its design, like human DNA, determines *what* it can be, in a huge range from a simple "brochure" site to a complex customer-relations management system. As with a baby, the actions you take from the beginning of your site's "life" can have profound effects on its direction.

But your new Drupal site is unlike a baby in many ways, and two are of particular interest. First, your Drupal site won't naturally grow without your involvement. Second, your actions are usually reversible—although you might have to untangle a series of steps to correct earlier errors.

This section shows you how to give your site its own personality right from the beginning. For some of you, this is all you'll need: By the end of this section, you'll have a functioning (albeit simple) multipage site that contains your name and some content.

To create your site's home (front) page:

1. Go to the Add content page by clicking "Add content" in the Shortcut bar.
2. Click the "Basic page" link **A**.

   The section "Gaining More Control of Individual Nodes" in Chapter 3, "Creating and Managing Content," discusses differences between the article and basic page *content types*.

continues on next page

3. Enter title and body content into the Title and Body *fields* **B**. Here you can also add a summary by clicking the "Edit summary" link. The summary is used to describe content, and appears in various places where a brief description is more useful than the full body. (For more about summaries, see "Gaining More Control of Individual Nodes" in Chapter 3.)
4. Scroll down on the form and click "Publishing options." Although it looks somewhat like a link to another page, it's actually a control called a tab: Clicking it reveals a new group of settings without taking you away from the current page.
5. Select the "Promoted to front page" check box **C**.
6. Click Save at the bottom of the form to see the completed page **D**. Near the page's title are two tabs: View (which is selected) and Edit. You can edit the page at any time by clicking the Edit tab.
7. To confirm that the content you just entered is on the front page, you can:
   - Click the site's logo.
   - Click the site's title ("My Drupal Site" in this case).
   - Click the little "Home" icon in the Toolbar.
   - Type **`http://domain-name`** in your web browser.

   Doing so returns you to the front page to see a screen similar to **D** but without the View and Edit tabs. (If you entered a summary, you'd see it here instead of the contents of the Body field.) To edit the content again, click its title, then click the Edit tab.

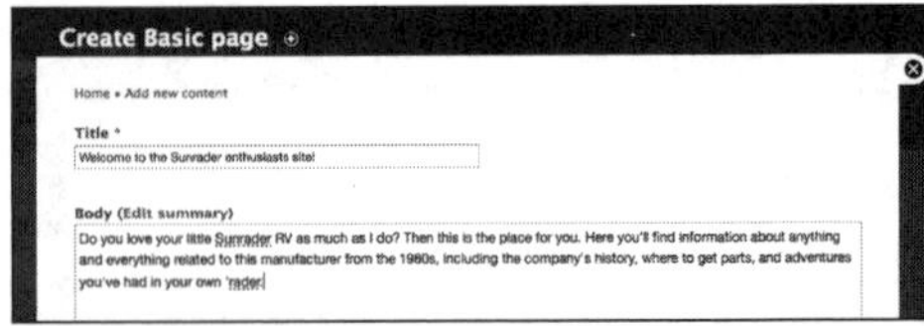

B Creating a page's content

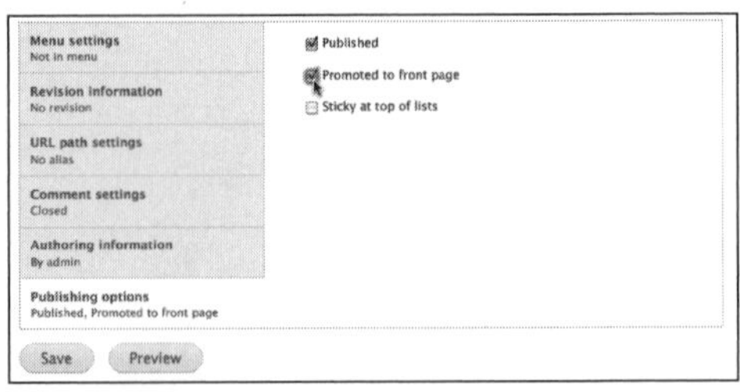

C Making the page's content part of your site's front page

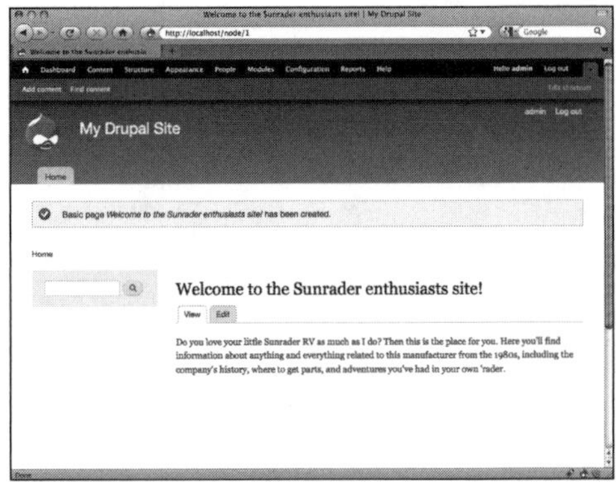

D The published page

How Can a Page Contain a *Page*? And What's a Node?

The word *page* has two different meanings in Drupal. In one sense it means anything within boundaries of your browser's window. But in the other, it means a *node* of the *basic page* content type.

When you clicked "Create content" to make that first front page, Drupal presented you with the choice of creating a basic page or an article. These are the two content types that are available in Drupal by default. Another example of a content type is *blog entry*, which becomes available when you turn on the Blog module. (You'll see how to do that in Chapter 3.) Other content types appear when you download and install other modules, or when you specifically create them.

Whichever content type you choose—basic page, article, or something else—the resulting unit of content is stored as a *node* in Drupal. Its contents appear on its standalone page at **http://*domain-name*/node/*node-identifier***. (In our example, that was **http://localhost/node/1**.) A node typically appears in the *content region* (generally in the middle of the page), surrounded by other page parts such as the header and footer.

The node can appear elsewhere in the site, though, sometimes grouped together with other nodes. That's the case on the front page, where you'll see all nodes that have the "Promoted to front page" setting selected. In such cases, you can always return to that node's standalone page to view and edit it by clicking its title or entering its URL in your web browser.

To change your site's basic information:

1. Go to the site information page by clicking Configuration > Site Information in the Toolbar.
2. You see a page that looks similar to one that appeared during the installation process. Here you can:
   - Change the site's name. The name appears most prominently at the top of every page, but also in such places as administrative emails and in the Title Bar of many browsers.
   - Change the site's slogan. The slogan appears in some themes below the site's name at the top of the page and in the Title Bar of the browser when looking at the home page. You'll learn more about the site slogan in the section "Selecting a Visual Theme" later in this chapter.
   - Change the administration email address. Emails sent automatically by Drupal will appear to come from this address. By default it's the same as the one for the administrative *super-user*—that is, the user created when you first installed Drupal.
   - Change the number of posts that appear on the front page. This number determines how many "Promoted to front page" *nodes* show on the front page at one time. When there are more than that number, links at the bottom of the page (known as a *pager*) will let visitors see older nodes.

continues on next page

- Redirect visitors to alternative target pages. You can do this:
  - For the front page ("Default front page")
  - When they're denied access to content ("Default 403 (access denied) page")
  - When they try to go to a page that doesn't exist ("Default 404 (not found) page")

  These pages can be anywhere on your site as long as they have valid URLs, including nodes (such as **`node/1`**) or a system page (such as **`user`**).

3. When you've finished making your changes, click "Save configuration." In our example, we've changed the site's name to "Sunrader Fans" and added a slogan **E**.

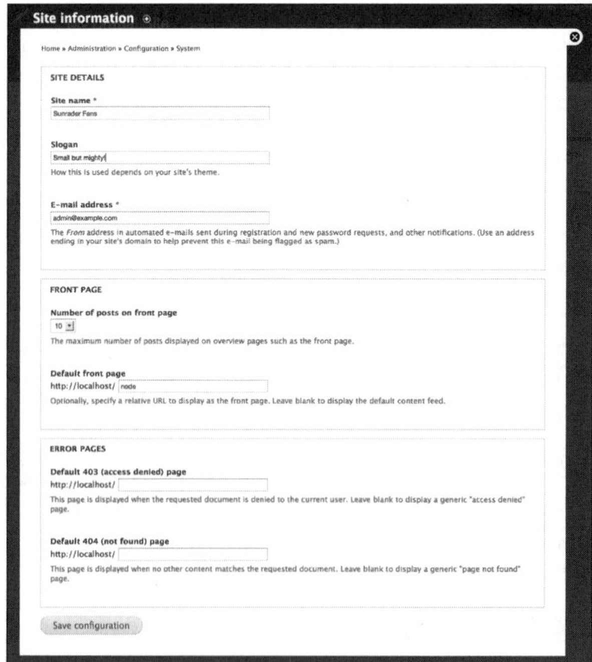

E The "Site information" page

Selecting a Visual Theme

Traditionally, a web site's creator tackles visual design very early in the process. Often the design comes even before the content, which then has to be developed to fit its constraints.

But as a *content* management system, Drupal puts more importance on content—that is, the information that you put in nodes. A *theme* tells Drupal how to display that content. You can change themes, even when your site has thousands of nodes, and your site will still (mostly) work as expected.

A Drupal theme typically includes five parts:

- *Style files* define such matters as typography and layout. They are CSS (Cascading Style Sheets) and end in *.css*.
- *Programming files* give the theme logic so that, for example, a catalog page looks different from a user's profile. They are written in PHP and end in *.php*.
- *Graphics files* typically appear as patterned backgrounds, icons, and splash images. They can be in any format understood by web browsers, most commonly with filenames ending in *.jpg*, *.gif*, and *.png*.
- A *metadata text file* ending in *.info* contains the information that Drupal uses to keep track of such matters as theme name, version, description, and referenced files.
- *Script files* containing code to enhance the features of a theme in a dynamic way. These JavaScript files end in *.js*.

Of these five parts, only the .info file is really required to create a new theme. The rest are added as needed.

continues on next page

Core Drupal includes four themes in the **themes** folder. Many additional free and for-purchase themes are available for download from **drupal.org/project/themes** and elsewhere, and anyone with ambition and some CSS knowledge can design a theme from scratch.

This section discusses only the basics of enabling, selecting, and installing themes. Chapter 8, "Customizing Drupal's Look and Feel," provides further details.

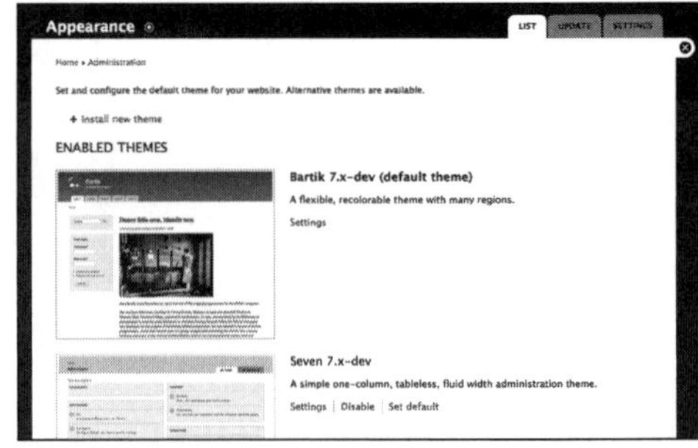

A The theme selection page

To use a built-in core theme:

1. Go to the Appearance administration page by clicking Appearance in the Toolbar. You will see a list of available themes **A**.
2. Click the "Set default" link next to the theme you want to use.

   A section at the bottom of this page lists disabled themes, which are in your Drupal folder but unavailable for any purpose until you enable them. To enable a theme, click the Enable link next to it. To enable a disabled theme *and* make it the active theme, click its "Enable and set default" link.
3. Click "Save configuration." To see the new theme, go to a content page.

TIP Changing the theme in this manner only affects content pages, *not* administrative pages. For that, see the section "To change the administration theme" earlier in this chapter.

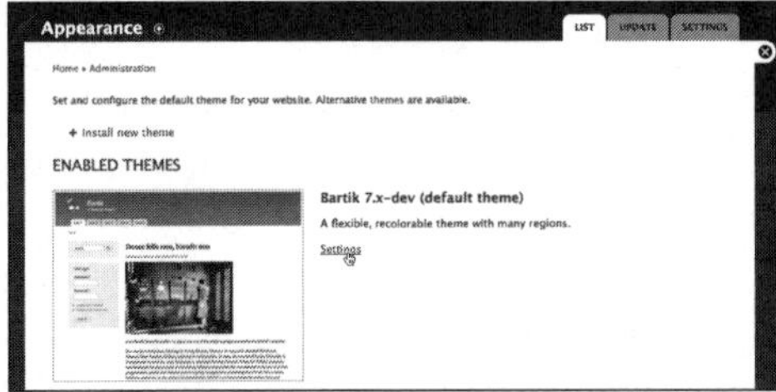

B Changing settings for the Garland theme

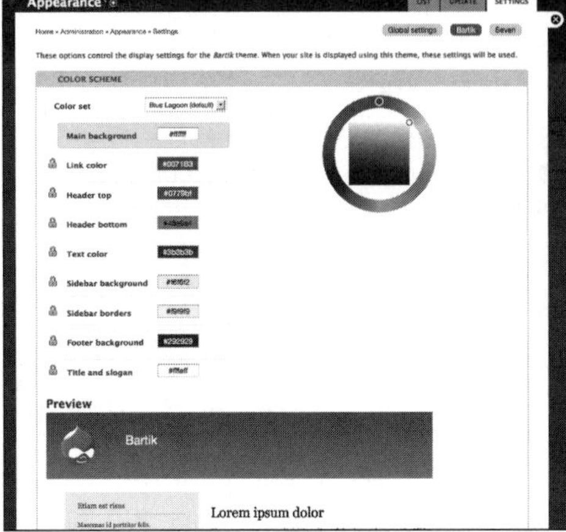

C Color settings for the Bartik theme, with the Blue Lagoon color set selected

To change a theme's settings:

1. Go to the Appearance page by clicking Appearance in the Toolbar.
2. Click the Settings link to the right of the theme you want to change **B** to go to that theme's settings page, *or* click the Settings tab in the upper-right corner of the screen, then click the name of your theme below that tab in the resulting page.
3. Available settings vary from theme to theme. One nice feature of Bartik is that it's *recolorable*—that is, you can choose colors for several interface elements. (Few themes have this feature.)
   - To select a group of colors designed to look harmonious together, choose an option from the "Color set" pop-up menu.
   - To change the color of an individual interface element, click its field then either type the hexadecimal value of the color or click the desired color in the color wheel.

   The preview immediately changes to reflect your choices **C**.

continues on next page

4. The "Toggle display" section further down on the screen **D** lets you show or hide various theme features:

   - The logo is the picture that usually appears in the screen's upper-left corner. This check box turns its display on or off: See the logo image settings in step 5 to learn how to change the logo.
   - The site name and site slogan are set on the "Site information" screen. See the earlier section "To change your site's basic information" for details.
   - The "User pictures in posts" and "User pictures in comments" check boxes are unavailable until you've turned on the "Enable user pictures" setting on the "Account settings" page at **http://*domain-name*/admin/config/people/accounts.** For more details, see Chapter 7.
   - The "User verification status in comments" check box comes into play when you allow *anonymous users*—that is, those who haven't logged into Drupal—to leave comments in response to node content. (Learn how to allow that in the section "To change user access permissions" in Chapter 7.) If you leave this box selected, comments left by users who include their name and contact information will be accompanied by the text "not verified."
   - The "Main menu" and "Secondary menu" check boxes define whether the two menus appear. In Bartik and most other themes, they're in the upper-right corner.

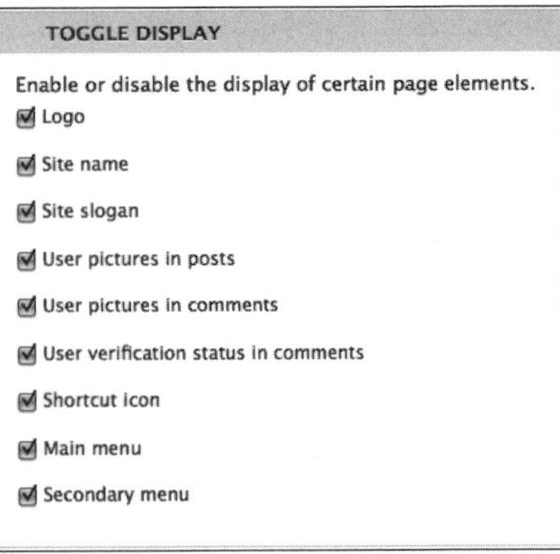

TOGGLE DISPLAY
Enable or disable the display of certain page elements.
Logo
Site name
Site slogan
User pictures in posts
User pictures in comments
User verification status in comments
Shortcut icon
Main menu
Secondary menu

D The "Toggle display" section of the theme settings screen

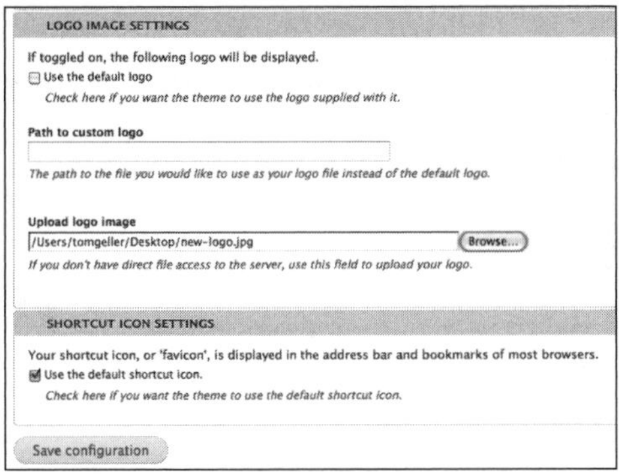

Accepting the default shortcut icon on the theme settings screen while uploading a custom logo

What's All This about Global Settings?

If you clicked the Settings tab on the Appearance screen, you might have noticed the enigmatic phrase "Global settings." Clicking it brings you to a settings screen very similar to the one you were editing. So what's the difference?

The global settings screen is a place to set theme *defaults*; that is, what you see when you first visit the settings screen for a specific theme. You can ignore it if you plan to use only one theme on your site. But it comes into play if you plan to experiment with several different themes. Having intelligent defaults in place prevents you from having to re-create the same settings time after time.

5. The "Logo image settings" and "Shortcut icon settings" sections define what images these items use. By default, Drupal uses whatever image was included with the theme, but you can change it by deselecting the relevant check box.

   There are two ways to indicate an image file:

   - Upload the file manually to somewhere on the Internet. A typical place is inside your site's theme folder, such as at **/sites/default/themes/*theme-name*** or **/sites/all/themes/*theme-name***. (Don't ever add or change files to the **/themes** folder; you'll lose such changes when you eventually update Drupal.) Then, tell Drupal where to find it by typing its path in the "Path to custom logo" or "Path to custom icon" field (for example, **sites/default/themes/*theme-name*/new-logo.jpg**).

   or

   - Upload it by clicking the appropriate Browse button and selecting your image.

6. When you've made all your desired changes, click "Save configuration."

To find, download, install, and enable an alternative theme:

1. Go to a site where downloadable themes are available. By far the most common source for free themes is **drupal.org/project/themes**. Theme Garden (**themegarden.org**) links to many of the themes found on the **drupal.org** site and lets you try them out before downloading them. A web search for "drupal themes" turns up several other free theme sources, along with suppliers of commercial themes.
2. Select a theme. *Either*:
   - Download the theme to your computer.

   or

   - Copy the URL where the theme is located. To do so, press the Control key while clicking the download link (on Mac) or right-click the download link (on a computer with a two-button mouse). Then select "Copy link location."
3. On your site, go to the Appearance page by clicking Appearance in the Toolbar.
4. Click the "Install new theme" link, which leads you to a screen where you can either paste the URL you copied earlier, or click Browse and upload the theme you downloaded **F**.
5. Click Install. Your theme is now installed and appears on the Appearance page.

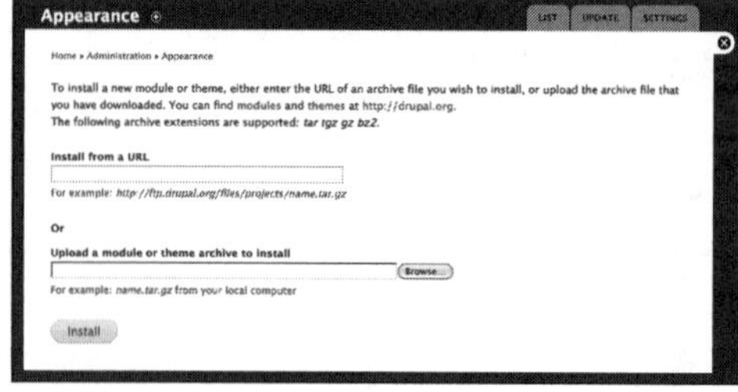

F The theme installation screen

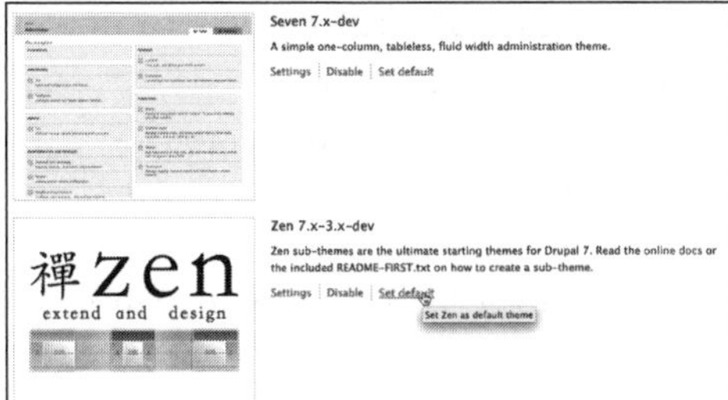

G Enabling the newly installed Zen theme and setting it as the default

6. To set your theme as the one seen by visitors to your site, return to the Appearance page by clicking Appearance in the Toolbar. Then click Enable to simply make the theme available, or click "Enable and set default" to make it both available and the active theme **G**.

TIP Make sure you've downloaded a theme designed for the Drupal version you're using. Drupal 6 (and earlier) themes won't work on a Drupal 7 installation.

TIP Instead of using Drupal's "Install new theme" link, you can also install the theme by downloading it, uncompressing it, and placing the resulting package in the `/sites/default/themes`, `/sites/all/themes`, or site-specific folder of your Drupal installation. (That's how theme installation worked in the previous versions of Drupal.)

Understanding the sites Folder

The **`sites`** folder in your Drupal installation is intended to contain all the files that are specific to your site. (When you install a new theme, for example, Drupal puts it in **`/sites/all/themes`**.) That structure makes updating Drupal easy: When a new version comes out (as happens every month or so), the only directory you need to move to the new installation is the **`sites`** folder. For more details on updating, see the "To update Drupal" section later in this chapter.

One installation of Drupal can run multiple sites. (We won't discuss such multisite installations in this book; for tutorials on the subject, see **`drupal.org/node/43816`**.) The **`sites`** folder reflects that by containing two folders, named **`all`** and **`default`**. To run a multisite installation, you'd basically add other folders, each one indicating a different site and containing different files.

Modules and themes put in the **`all`** folder are available to all sites in a multisite installation; those in another folder are available only to the site associated with that folder.

When you install modules and themes using Drupal's own installation process, they automatically go into the **`all`** folder. But you could manually put files into other folders within the **`sites`** folder by downloading, uncompressing, and moving them there. You'd first need to create folders named **`modules`** or **`themes`** in those folders, however.

In any case, one thing bears repeating: *Never* add or change files outside of the **`sites`** folder, because you'll lose them when you update Drupal. That way lies madness.

Monitoring Your Drupal Site

Like a living thing, your Drupal site requires attention to stay in tip-top health. *Developers* correct newly discovered *code* flaws; resources your site relies on move or disappear; hardware fails; and online vandals, as always, try ever more devious ways to attack. Regular maintenance procedures ensure that you're both protected from danger and able to recover when disaster strikes.

Maintenance requires both attention and action. Fortunately, Drupal includes reports that make monitoring easy; unfortunately, some maintenance actions are a bit tricky. But done periodically, they're an effective defense against the thousand natural shocks that Drupal is heir to.

To correct most routine Drupal system issues:

1. To see a list of items that Drupal automatically checks, click Reports in the Toolbar and then click "Status report" **A**. The list on this page may grow as you enable more modules.
2. Examine the page for errors—that is, any items highlighted with a contrasting background color.

   Those with a non-critical issue display with a blue background; those that are likely to cause problems display with a red background.

   In any case, links in the descriptive text lead you to a page on your Drupal site where you can correct the error or to a help resource that will guide you to its resolution.

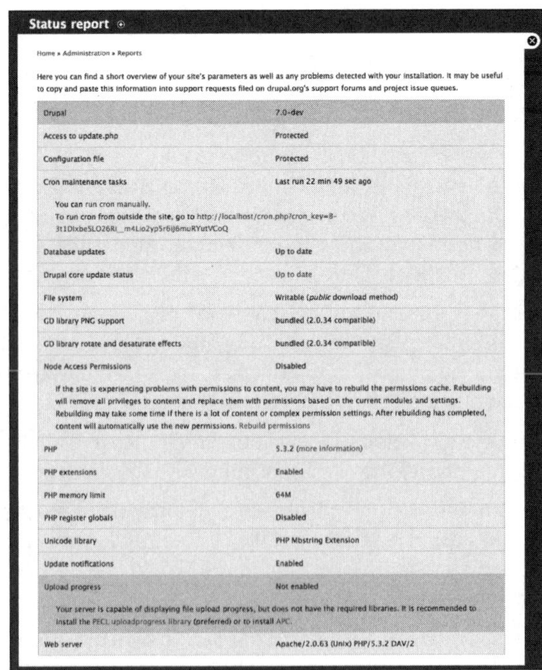

A Drupal's "Status report" screen

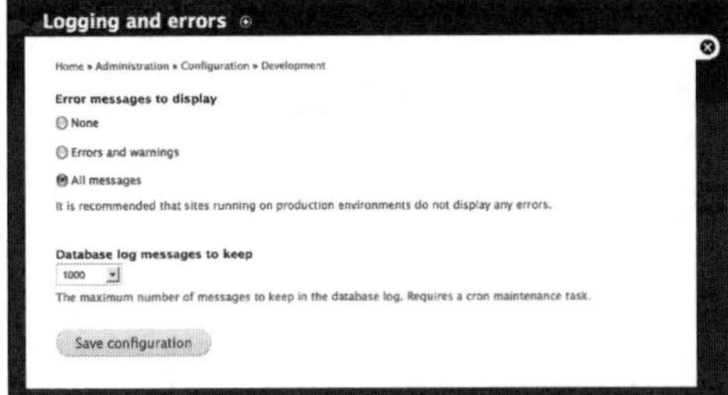

B Database logging options

C Recent log messages

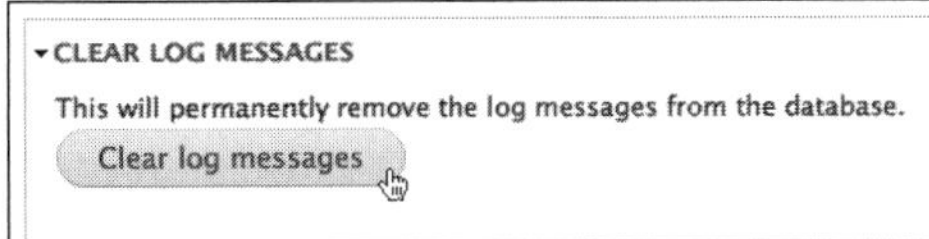

D Clearing the database log

To track system activity on your Drupal site:

1. By default, Drupal's database logging (dblog) system keeps track of various activities on your Drupal site, such as user logins, content additions, page-access problems, and PHP errors.

   You can reduce the amount of tracking activity and change the number of log entries that Drupal saves by clicking Configuration in the Toolbar and then clicking "Logging and errors" **B**.

   After you've made your changes, click "Save configuration."

2. You can see a complete list of log entries by clicking Reports in the Toolbar and then clicking "Recent log messages." Entries appear from newest to oldest **C**.

3. Removing all messages from the database log and starting with a clean slate is sometimes useful—for example, if you want to track errors over a specific period of time, or to debug a problem without getting noise from previous attempts to solve it. To clear the log, first click the "Clear log messages" link or its disclosure triangle **D**. Then click the newly revealed "Clear log messages" button.

continues on next page

4. You can hide database log messages you don't want to see, thereby focusing on, for example, emergency-level system messages. To do so, click the "Filter log messages" link, or its disclosure triangle, to reveal the filter controls. Then select both the types and the severity levels of messages you want to see. To select multiple items, press the Command key (Mac) or Control key (Windows) while clicking. When you've made your selections, click the Filter button **E**.

5. Drupal also offers two summary pages to quickly check common access problems:

   - To see a list of pages that visitors have tried to access without permission, click Reports in the Toolbar and then click "Top 'access denied' errors" **F**.
   - To see a list of nonexistent pages that visitors have tried to access, click Reports in the Toolbar and then click "Top 'page not found' errors."

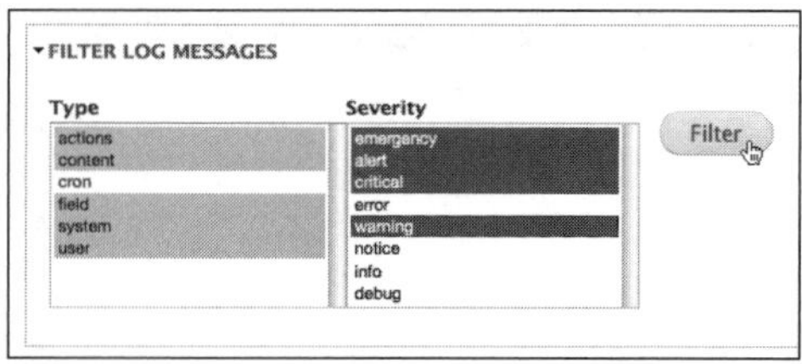

E Narrowing the list of database log messages to show only certain types and severity levels

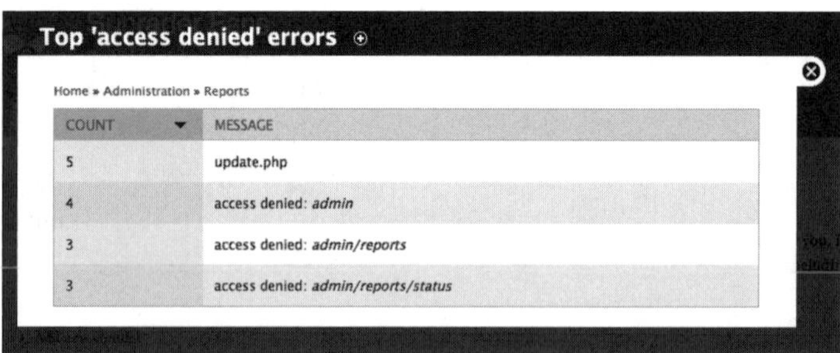

F The access denied page, with pages that have the most failed attempts topping the list

Packaging Your Drupal Site

So—you've created the perfect Drupal site on your laptop. It's time to go live!

Moving your Drupal site to a server takes two steps:

- Move the files.
- Move the database.

Learning how to move your site also teaches you another valuable skill: how to back up and restore your site in case of emergency. In either case, the procedures aren't difficult. However, the cost for failure is high.

A backup that you can't use is as bad as no backup at all. Therefore, try restoring your site from backup once in a while—preferably on a test site, not your live site—to make sure that everything works properly. It's better to discover something amiss when you're calm and unhurried than when your site is down and users are clamoring for its return.

Finally, this section also includes information about updating Drupal—a process you'll find yourself doing about once a month. It's a bit of a pain, but your site getting cracked because you didn't install the latest security patch is far worse.

To back up your Drupal installation's files:

1. Backing up your Drupal site is a two-step process. The first step is to put a copy of your Drupal files in a safe and accessible place:
   - **On Mac or Windows:** Click once on the folder containing your Drupal files, then press Command-C (Control-C) to make the copy. Navigate to where you want to save the copy, then press Command-V (Control-V) to paste it in its new location.
   - **On *nix:** Use the command **`tar -cvzf`** ***`target-file source-directory`*** to create a compressed, single-file *tarball* archive of your site. (For help using *nix commands, see the "To transfer Drupal to a *nix server" section in Chapter 1, "Getting Drupal Up and Running.")
   - If your files are on a remote server and you want to store them on a local computer: First create a tarball, as described in the preceding step; then use an FTP or SCP program to transfer the file between the two.
2. **Optional:** Compress the backup you just created to save space:
   - **On Mac:** Press the Control key while clicking the folder, then choose "Compress *foldername*" from the pop-up menu.
   - **On Windows:** Select the file, right-click, and from the contextual menu choose Send To > Compressed (zipped) folder.
   - **On *nix:** The files were compressed in step 1 when you created the tarball.
3. Label and store the backup.

   Too many people forget this step and end up with a bunch of mysterious files labeled *backup* in random folders. I use the pattern ***`YYYYMMDD-sitename`***. For example, a copy of the site **`drupalvqs`** saved on December 10, 2010 would have the name **`20101210-drupalvqs`**. A nice side effect of this convention is that files appear sorted chronologically, so it's easy to find the most recent backup.

TIP In reality, you don't need to back up your entire Drupal installation. You could make do with just the `sites` folder, which includes all the files, modules, and themes that are specific to your site. However, I still prefer to make a full backup once in a while. Doing so removes the possibility of incompatibilities between my old modules and the newly downloaded version of Drupal. Such incompatibilities are rare, but it's better to be safe than sorry when disk space is so cheap!

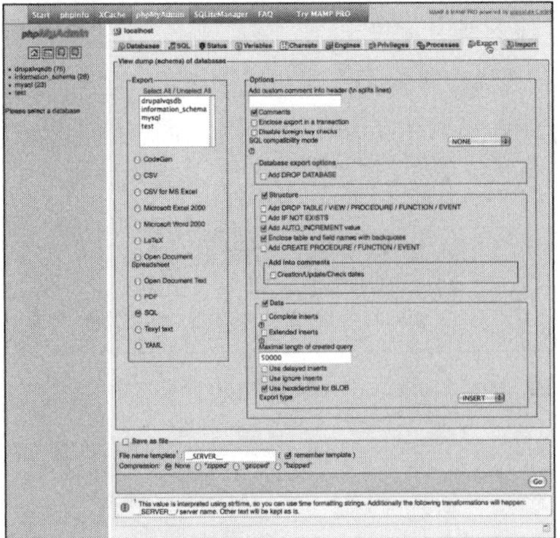

A The phpMyAdmin Export screen

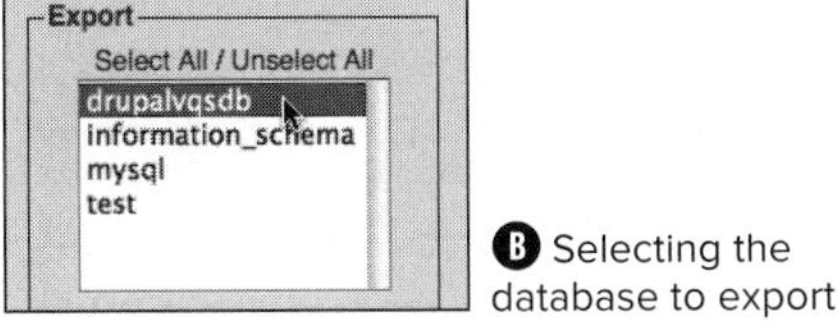

B Selecting the database to export

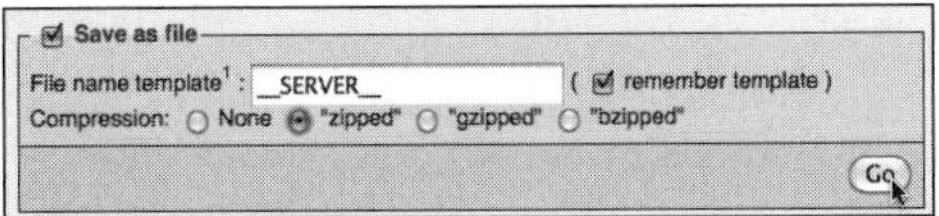

C Exporting your Drupal site's database to a file in `.zip` format

To back up your Drupal site's database using phpMyAdmin:

1. Launch phpMyAdmin, as described in the "Creating the MySQL Database Using phpMyAdmin" section in Chapter 1.

   Your Internet hosting provider might require you to use some other procedure; contact its support department if so.

2. Click the Export link to go to phpMyAdmin's Export screen **A**.

3. Click the name of your database—in this example, **`drupalvqsdb`** **B**.

   If you don't see the name of your database, you probably don't have export permissions; ask your system administrator for this permission.

4. Select the "Save as file" check box at the bottom of the screen. You can optionally name the file and choose to download the file in compressed format (doing this saves time). Then click the Go button **C**.

   If you later have difficulty importing your database, you might need to change one of the other settings on this page. They're too numerous to detail here: Talk with your system administrator for recommendations.

   The database will download to your web browser's default download location.

To restore your Drupal site from backup:

1. Find the most recent backup of your Drupal installation files. If the files are in a compressed package, uncompress it.
2. Delete your old Drupal installation files, if necessary.
3. Move the uncompressed backup folder to the former location of your old Drupal installation. Be sure to move the entire folder, not just its contents. It contains a hidden file (`.htaccess`) that you'll miss by just copying the visible files.
4. You now need to *drop* (delete) your site's old database. Launch phpMyAdmin, as described in the previous section, "To back up your Drupal site's database using phpMyAdmin."
5. Click the Databases link in phpMyAdmin to see a list of available databases.
6. Select the check box next to your database **D**.
7. Scroll to the bottom of the screen and click the icon with a red X through it to the right of the text "With selected." You'll see a warning that asks you whether you really want to destroy your database. Click Yes.
8. Now it's time to import the backup database. In phpMyAdmin, click the Import tab at the top of the screen to see the Import screen **E**.
9. Click the Browse button, then find and select your backup database file through the file selection dialog box.

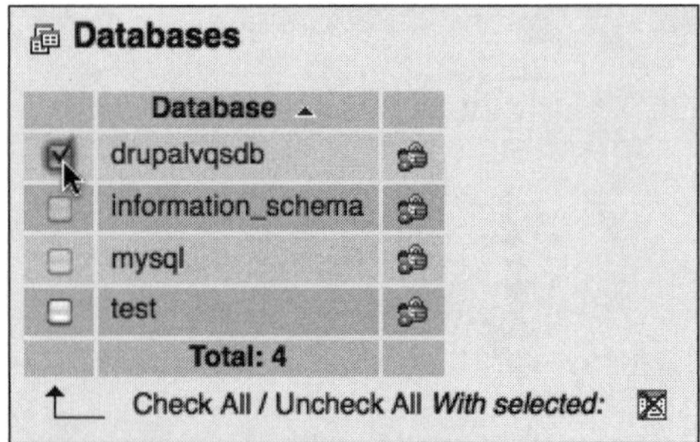

D Selecting a database to drop

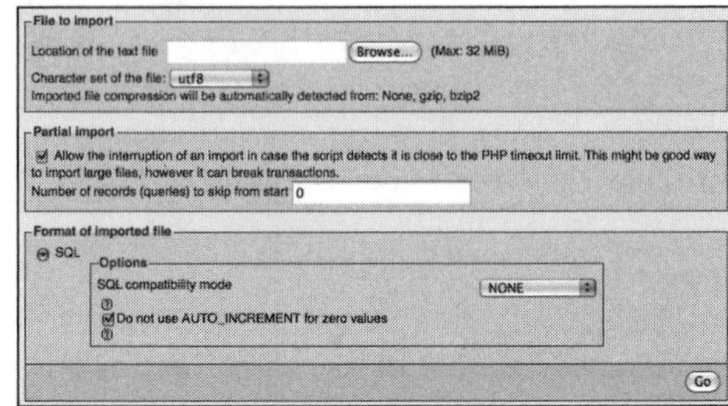

E The phpMyAdmin Import screen

```
$databases['default']['default'] = array(
    'driver' => 'mysql',
    'database' => 'drupalvqsdb',
    'username' => 'root',
    'password' => 'root',
    'host' => 'localhost',
    'prefix' => '',
  );
```

F The section of **settings.php** you may need to change when you move your Drupal site

Help! I Couldn't Import My Database!

Hoo-boy. As you might have guessed from the complexity of the database import/export screens, this is an area rich with potential problems. Some Internet hosting providers don't allow you to create databases directly, for example; in that situation you'd have to modify the instructions a fair amount.

One common error is that phpMyAdmin on a Windows computer won't let you import databases larger than 2 MB. To fix that, see the section "To configure WAMP for Drupal on a Windows computer" in Chapter 1. Another solution is to use the program BigDump, available from **http://ozerov.de/bigdump.php**.

You can find further database help at **http://drupal.org/node/81995**.

10. Click Go.

    There will be a pause while phpMyAdmin imports the file. You won't see any changes until it's finished, but don't worry if it takes a few minutes. When finished, you'll see a message that "Import has been successfully finished."

11. Your site is now restored: To be sure, go to it in a web browser. You'll probably find that you've been logged out. Log in again if necessary.

TIP These instructions assume that you don't need to back up your current installation before restoring from backup. If you do, follow the backup procedure first before deleting your current files and database.

To move your Drupal site to another computer:

1. Back up your site's files and database.
2. Restore the site in its new location by copying those files and importing that database.
3. In the Drupal installation that's in its new location, open the file at **/sites/default/settings.php** with a text editor.
4. Find the section that begins with **$databases = array**, which is at or around line 181 F.
5. Change the information as needed for the new location. (Often the database user name or password will be different for your remote database server.)

TIP You might have noticed that this file actually contains your database's user name *and password* in plain text. Don't leave it in an accessible place!

To update Drupal:

1. Go to the updates page by clicking Reports in the Toolbar and then clicking "Available updates."

   On the resulting page, warning icons tell you whether you should update modules, themes, or Drupal itself. (In this chapter we'll only discuss how to update Drupal itself. To learn how to update individual modules or themes, see Chapter 9.)

2. Each update includes a description with several links, most of them informational. To download the latest version, click the Download link or use the *nix **wget** command.

   (For help downloading the package, see the "To download Drupal to a Mac or Windows computer" and "To transfer Drupal to a *nix server" sections in Chapter 1.)

3. **For Mac or Windows:** Double-click the downloaded package to uncompress it. On Windows, you'll need to install a utility as was discussed in the Chapter 1 sidebar "Help! I Can't Uncompress the File!"

   For *nix: Type **tar -xzvf *drupal-package***.

4. Take the site offline by clicking Configuration in the Toolbar and then clicking "Maintenance mode" **G**. Select the "Put site into maintenance mode" check box and click "Save configuration."

   Visitors attempting to reach your site now see the offline message you indicated.

5. Remove the **sites** folder from the newly uncompressed package.

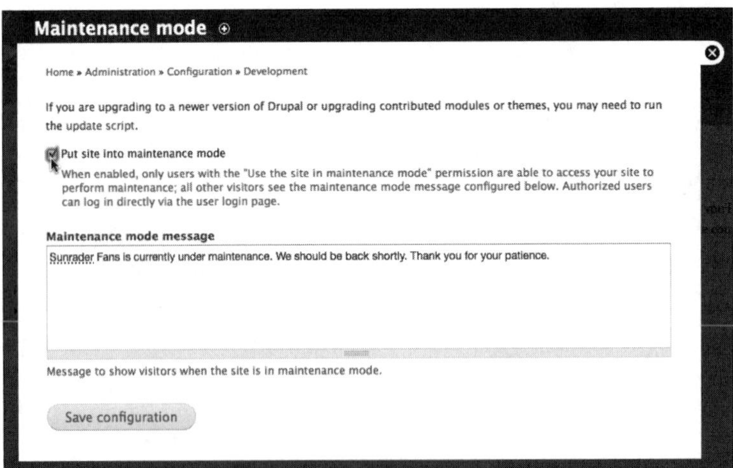

G Turning on your site's Maintenance mode to keep visitors away while you're working on it

6. Move or copy the **sites** folder from your old Drupal installation to the new one.

7. Next you'll remove your old installation and move the new installation (containing a copy of your old **sites** folder) into its place. First, move the old installation to another location. Then, give your new Drupal installation the same name as the old one and move it to the location of the old one.

   The new installation now has the same name and location as the old one did, and it contains the old one's **sites** folder.

8. Now it's time to update the Drupal database to make it compatible with changes in the code files. *Either:*

   ▸ Click the "update script" link on the Maintenance mode page.

   or

   ▸ Go to the update page by typing **http://*domain-name*/update.php** in your browser's address bar.

   In either case, you must be logged in as the user you created when you first installed Drupal (the superuser), or as a user that has been granted the "Administer software updates" permission. To learn about permissions, see Chapter 7.

9. A page describing the update process appears Ⓗ. Click Continue.

10. When the process is complete—usually within a few seconds—you get a message about what changes were made, along with links back to view and administer your site.

continues on next page

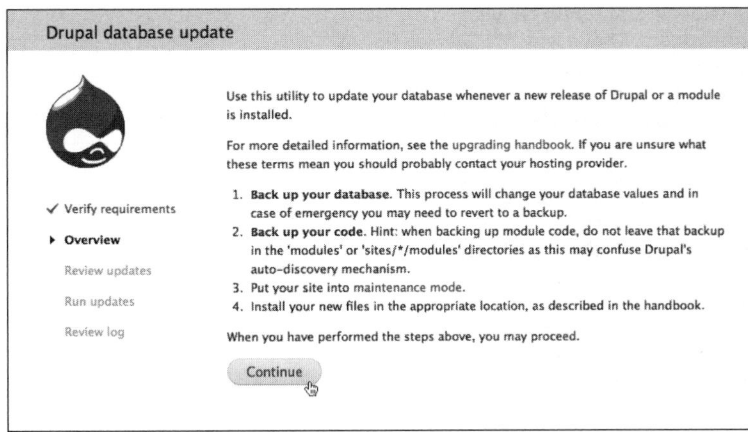

Ⓗ Starting the update process

11. Turn the site back on again by clicking Configuration in the Toolbar and then clicking "Maintenance mode." Then deselect the "Put site in maintenance mode" check box and click "Save configuration."

    Your Drupal installation is now up to date.

TIP There are actually a few different ways to update Drupal. The one shown here assumes that there's a place on your computer *outside* your current Drupal installation where you can set up the new installation, and that you can move and delete files at will. If that's not true for you—if, for example, you don't have access to anyplace on the server other than the inside of your Drupal installation's directory—then you'll have to adapt these instructions to fit your situation.

TIP If you've been administering Drupal correctly, you'll need to move only the `sites` folder; everything outside that folder is considered the Drupal core and will be replaced by the new Drupal installation. If you've made any changes outside of that folder, they'll be destroyed by the update. That's why Drupal developers constantly warn: "Don't hack core!" ("Core" is Drupal's central programming, which comprises the entire Drupal installation outside the `sites` folder.)

TIP Whenever updating your site, log in as the administrator in a browser, such as Firefox. Then after step 4, when the site is offline, visit it in another browser, such as Safari, *without* logging in, so that you see the "currently under maintenance" message. That serves as a reminder to put the site back online when you're finished; you wouldn't believe how often Drupal administrators forget to do that!

Creating and Managing Content

Now that you've installed and configured Drupal, you're like someone who's just walked out of a car dealership, keys in hand. You had to deal with some necessary-but-technical tasks, just as the new-car buyer had to deal with title and loan paperwork. Now it's time to get in and drive!

In this chapter, you'll learn how to:

- Create nodes of various kinds
- Adjust how those nodes appear and behave
- Handle books, blog posts, and news feeds
- Manage content en masse

Three other chapters help you further improve your site's content. Chapter 4, "Customizing Content," shows you how to work with images and create your own content types; Chapter 5, "Making Content Interactive," shows you how to let users talk to each other (and you) within your site; and Chapter 6, "Improving Access to Content," moves content beyond the boundaries of the nodes that contain it.

In This Chapter

Gaining More Control of Individual Nodes

Drupal lets you create two types of content by default: articles and basic pages. You can also create your own content types, as you'll learn in Chapter 4. All content types are available when you click the "Add new content" link.

Both articles and basic pages contain the following elements:

- Title: This is the only required field in most edit forms. It becomes the clickable link that lets visitors view the full node.
- Summary: A short description of the node, which will later appear in places where the full node would be unwieldy or inappropriate. The Summary section is like a blurb on a newspaper's front page: just long enough to get people interested in the story. If you leave the summary blank, a short section of the "Full text" field will appear in its place. On pages that show the full node, the summary does not appear. (To change how much text is taken from the "Full text" field to auto-create the summary, see Chapter 4.)
- Body: The node's main content.

Table 3.1 shows the main differences between articles and basic pages by default; however, controls near the bottom of each node's "edit form" let you change the commenting and front-page qualities on individual posts.

You see this edit form either when you first create a new node or when you edit an existing one. We'll show you how to do both, which will revisit a screen that will look familiar to you from the section "To create your site's home (front) page" in Chapter 2.

TABLE 3.1 Comparison of Article and Basic Page Content Types

Basic page	Article
Does not appear on front page	Displays Summary section on front page
Cannot add tags	Can add tags; Drupal generates a page for all articles with the same tag
Commenting disabled	Visitors can leave comments
No easy way to add a graphic	Includes an Image field to add a single graphic

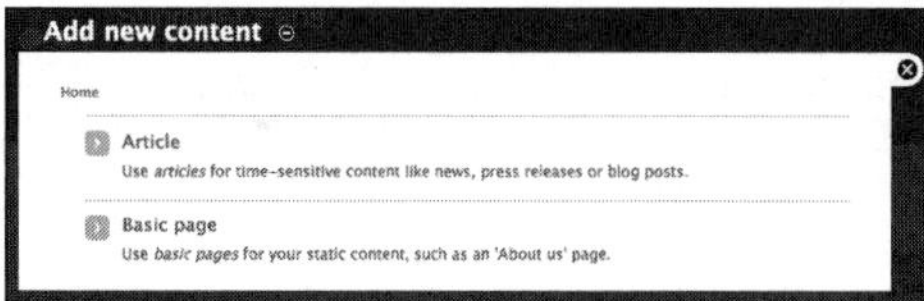

A Selecting a content type

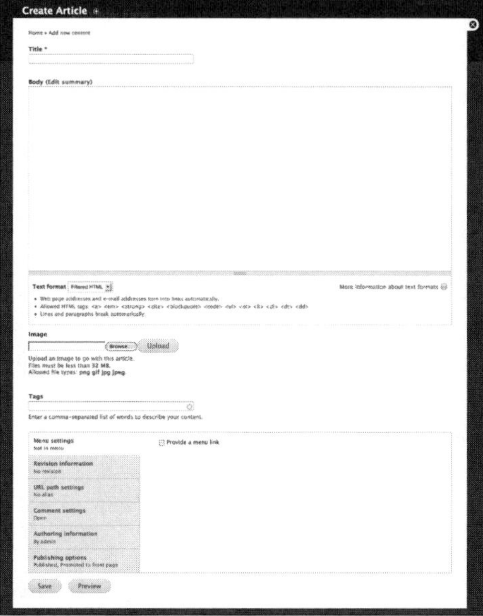

B A node edit form

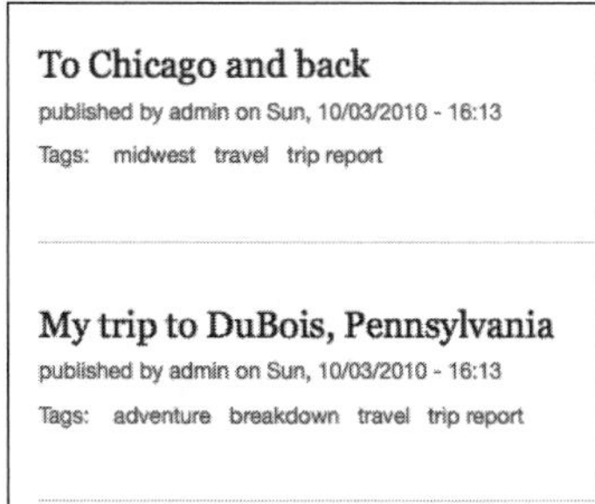

C A page of articles that have the "trip report" tag

To create a new node:

1. Click "Add content" in the Shortcut bar. You'll see a list of available content types **A**.
2. Click the content type you'd like to create.
3. Write the node's title in the Title field.
4. Fill in the other fields in the edit form **B**.
5. Change options as desired at the bottom of the edit form. They are divided into six categories:
   - Menu settings
   - Revision information
   - URL path settings
   - Comment settings
   - Authoring information
   - Publishing options

   The rest of this section tells you about those options in detail.
6. **Optional:** Click Preview to see what the node will look like without actually saving it.
7. Click Save.

TIP **Articles contain *tags*, which are words or short phrases separated by commas. Tags appear in various contexts and are linked to screens of similarly tagged nodes C. For more about tags, see the "Categorizing Content with Taxonomies" section in Chapter 5.**

To edit an existing node:

1. Select a node that you want to edit, either by finding it on your site or by following the instructions in the section, later in this chapter, "Finding, Editing, and Deleting Content."
2. Go to the node's edit form. *Either*:
   - Click the node's title, then click the Edit tab.

   or

   - Hover your mouse over the node, then click the little gear icon that appears in the upper-right corner and select Edit **D**. This icon only appears when the node is grouped with others, as occurs on the front page and elsewhere.

   You now see the same edit form as when you created the node, and you can edit and save it in the same way. (See "To create a new node" for further help.)

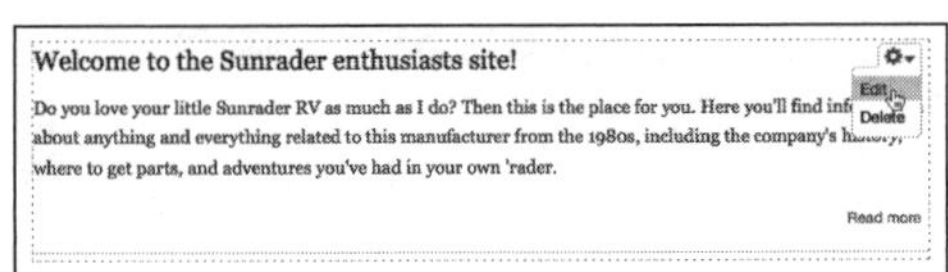

D Editing a node through its pop-up menu

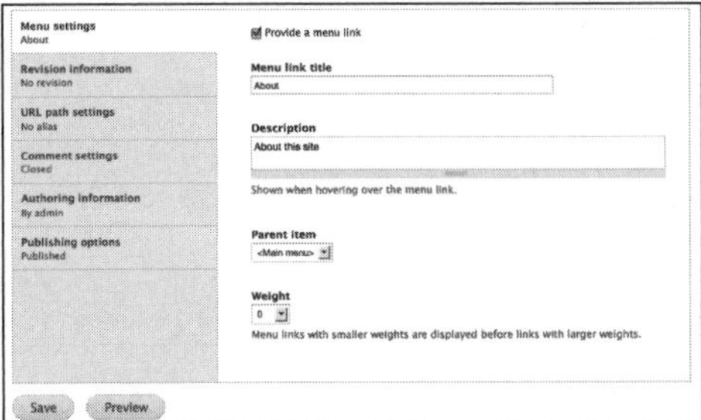

E Creating a menu item to lead visitors to a node

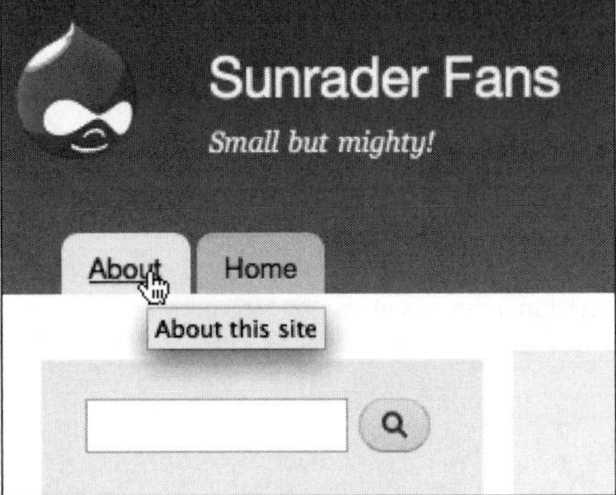

F A menu item in the Main menu

To create a menu item that links to a node:

1. Go to a node's edit form. Scroll to the bottom, to the "Menu settings" tab.
2. Select the "Provide a menu link" check box.
3. In the "Menu link title" field, type the text you would like to appear as the link. By way of confirmation, that text appears on the "Menu settings" tab to the left **E**. You can also add a Description, which appears when visitors hover their pointers over the menu item.
4. Click the "Parent item" pop-up menu to decide which menu this link should go in. By default, only the "Main menu" option is available, although there are actually several menus in Drupal. (The Main menu is generally at the top of the screen; in Drupal's default Bartik *theme*, items in the Main menu show up as tabs just below the logo.) To learn more about menus, see the section "Directing Traffic with Menus" in Chapter 6; to learn how to put links to nodes in other menus, see the section "Defining Custom Types of Content" in Chapter 4.
5. The Weight pop-up menu lets you determine the placement of this node within the selected "Parent item" menu. Numbers on this menu range from –50 to 50: To move an item toward the top of the menu, give it a lower number. (Chapter 6 will show you an easier way to organize menus.)
6. Click Save to create your link, which is shown in **F**.

TIP You can create your own menus to augment those that come with Drupal. You will learn how in Chapter 6.

To keep track of changes made to a node:

1. Go to a node's edit form. Scroll to the bottom and click the "Revision information" tab.
2. Click the "Create new revision" check box, and then in the "Revision log message" box type a summary of the changes you made **G**.
3. Click Save.

   Now you (and users who've gotten your permission, as is detailed in Chapter 7, "Wrangling Users") can see the node as it existed in past versions **H**.

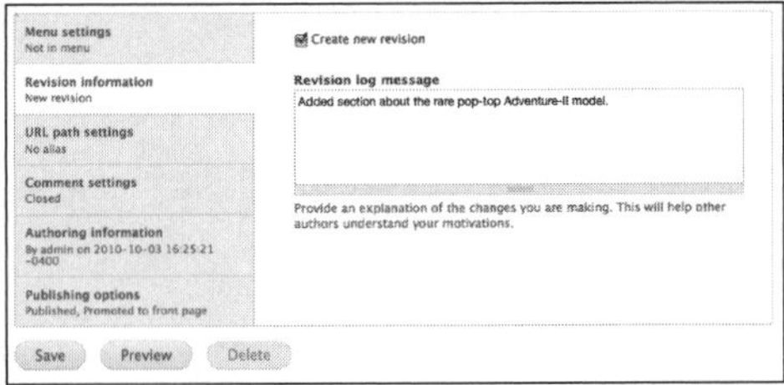

G Using a revision to keep track of changes to a node

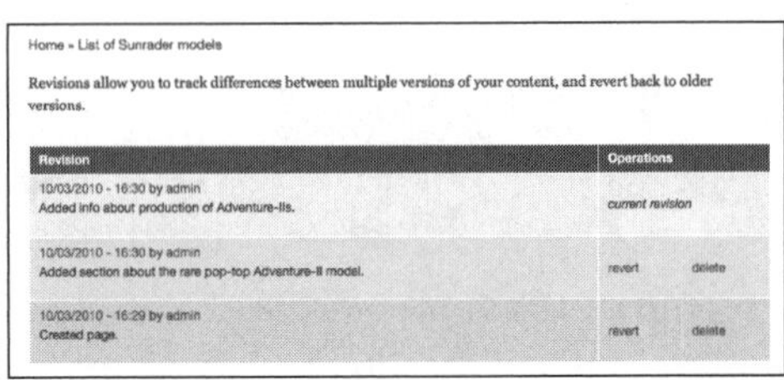

H A list of a node's past versions, annotated with revision log messages

What Is a Revision, and Why Should I Care?

By selecting the "Create new revision" check box, you're effectively making a backup of the node. Backups are good; they allow you to return to previous versions if an experiment goes wrong, and they can save your bacon when other problems occur (such as vandalism).

I can think of only two reasons why you wouldn't want to save revisions: first, to cover your tracks and hide past versions; second, for technical reasons related to disk space and database complexity. Except for rare circumstances, neither strikes me as terribly compelling.

When you first install Drupal, the revisions check box is turned off for both the article and page content types. I prefer them to be on by default so editors don't run the risk of forgetting to save a revision. Learn how in Chapter 4.

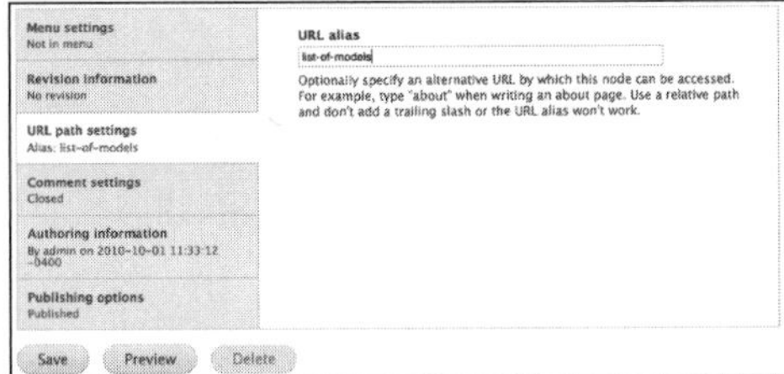

I Adding a URL alias to make access to the node more meaningful to people (and search engines)

To make a node's URL path more user-friendly:

1. Go to a node's edit form. Scroll to the bottom and click the "URL path settings" tab.
2. Type the desired URL path in the space provided **I**.

   The URL path is what appears after your domain's name. For example, if you type **`list-of-models`** here, and your domain is **`example.com`**, the resulting URL to reach this node will be **`http://example.com/list-of-models`**.
3. Click Save.

TIP **Drupal's natural URL path to (for example) the tenth node created on a site is `http://`*`domain-name`*`/10`. Visitors can reach the node through both URLs.**

TIP **Some characters, such as the ampersand (&), shouldn't be used directly in URLs. Drupal will automatically translate such characters into a code (`%2526` in this case) that makes it "legal," but the URL stops being user-friendly. Your best bet is to stick with letters, numbers, hyphens, and underscores when creating URL aliases.**

To permit users to leave comments in response to a node:

1. Go to a node's edit form. Scroll to the bottom and click the "Comment settings" tab.
2. Select the Open radio button **J**.
3. Click Save.

TIP **Nodes of the article content type are open to comments by default; those of the "basic page" content type are closed to comments by default.**

TIP **Unless you change commenting permissions (as you'll learn how to do in Chapter 7), only users who have logged in to your site (authenticated users) can add comments.**

TIP **You have considerable control over comment display and traffic. For details, see Chapter 4.**

J Permitting users to add comments in response to a node

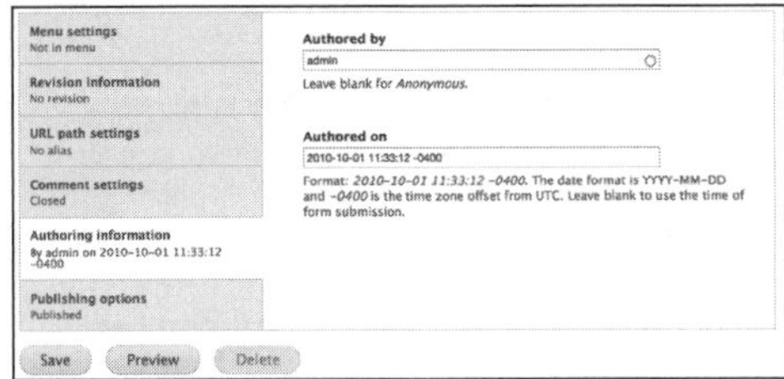

K The “Authoring information” section, as it appears on a previously created node

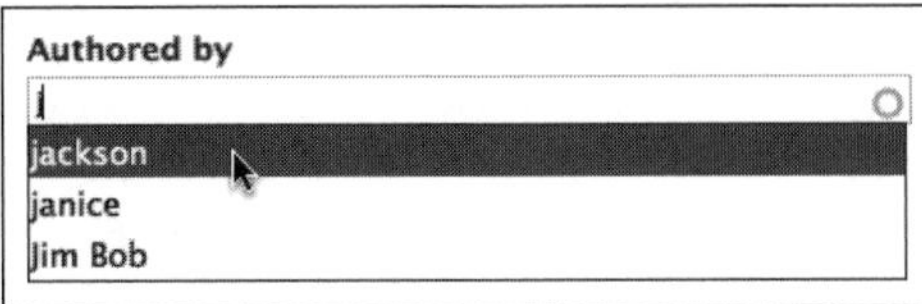

L Drupal’s autocomplete feature, suggesting user names from among your site’s authenticated users

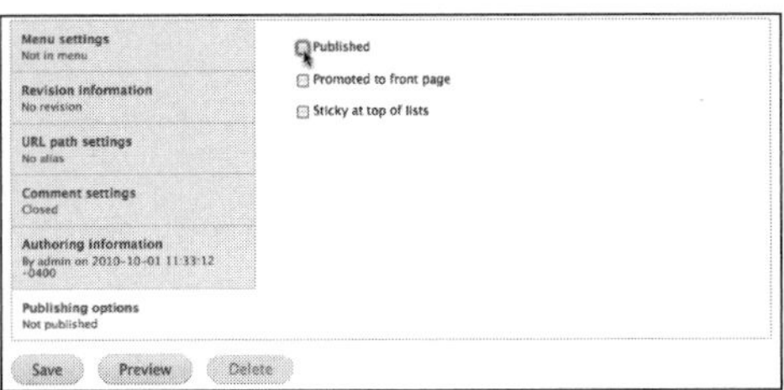

M The “Publishing options” tab’s three check box settings

To change the apparent author and date of a node:

1. Go to a node’s edit form. Scroll to the bottom and click the “Authoring information” tab.

   This tab contains two fields: “Authored by” and “Authored on.”

   - If this is a new node, the “Authored by” field will have your user name in it, and the “Authored on” field will be empty.
   - If this is an existing node, the fields will reflect the user name of the person who created it, and the time when it was created **K**.

2. To change the author, start typing a user name in the “Authored by” field. Using a Drupal feature called autocomplete, a list of user names that match the typed characters appears **L**. Click the one you want when it becomes available. (The user name must already exist; if you try to type in one that doesn’t exist, Drupal will refuse to save the change.)
3. To change the time the node was first posted, enter (or change) information in the “Authored on” field. Note the instructions beneath the field that specify the required format. To use the current date and time, delete all information in that field.
4. Click Save.

To hide a node without deleting it:

1. Go to a node’s edit form. Scroll to the bottom and click the “Publishing options” tab **M**.
2. Deselect the “Published” check box.
3. Click Save.

To promote a node to the front page:

1. Go to a node's edit form. Scroll to the bottom and click the "Publishing options" tab.
2. Select the "Promoted to front page" check box. (This check box is selected by default in article nodes.)
3. Click Save.

To make a node appear at the top of the page when grouped with other nodes:

1. Go to a node's edit form. Scroll to the bottom and click the "Publishing options" tab.
2. Click the "Sticky at top of lists" check box.

   This setting is particularly useful to draw attention to a node's content on the front page. All nodes with this setting appear above those without it, with the most recent at the top of each of those two groups. It's often used on the front page, where some content should remain near the top while timely information (such as news items or blog posts) appears beneath it.

   In some themes—including Drupal's default theme, Bartik—"sticky" items appear in a different style from other items **N**.

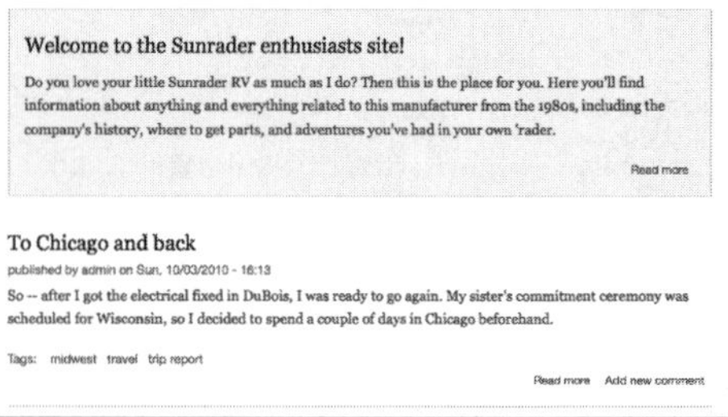

N A "sticky" item on the front page, followed by a non-sticky one

Creating Other Types of Content

Drupal's programmers and designers constantly dance on the line between complexity and ease of use. On one hand, administrators demand more and more features; on the other, some criticize Drupal for trying to do too much.

One part of their solution has been to include certain functions in Drupal but leave them turned off by default. To take advantage of them you first have to turn on modules, as discussed in the section "To turn on built-in features," in Chapter 2. The three types of content, and the modules you need to enable are:

- Blog posts: Let each user keep an online journal (Blog module)
- Books: Provide a structure that links nodes in an easy-to-read way (Book module)
- News feeds: Let your Drupal site display content from elsewhere on the Internet (Aggregator module)

The content these tools let you create is somewhat like the articles and basic pages you already know, but it's different in some ways. This section shows you how to create these new content types *and* understand the conceptual differences you need to master them.

To create blog posts:

1. Enable the Blog module.
2. Click "Add content" in the Shortcut bar and then click the newly added option, "Blog entry" **A**.
3. Fill out the node entry form, as outlined in the section "To create a new node" earlier in this chapter.

   The form looks exactly the same as the one for the article content type, except without the Image or Tags fields. Like an article (and unlike a basic page), a blog entry by default permits authenticated users to comment and is promoted to the front page.
4. Click Save.

A The new "Blog entry" content type, the result of turning on the Blog module

How Is a Blog Entry Any Different from an Article or Page?

At first glance, the blog entry content type seems unnecessary: Articles that don't have tags or images seem to be exactly the same as blog entries.

But blogs are different in one important way: Whenever a member of your site creates a blog entry, the entry adds itself to that member's personal blog page, which is available at **http://*domain-name*/blog/*user-ID***. Further, the page at **http://*domain-name*/blog** aggregates *all* blog entries on your site, giving visitors another way to stay informed with your members' commentary.

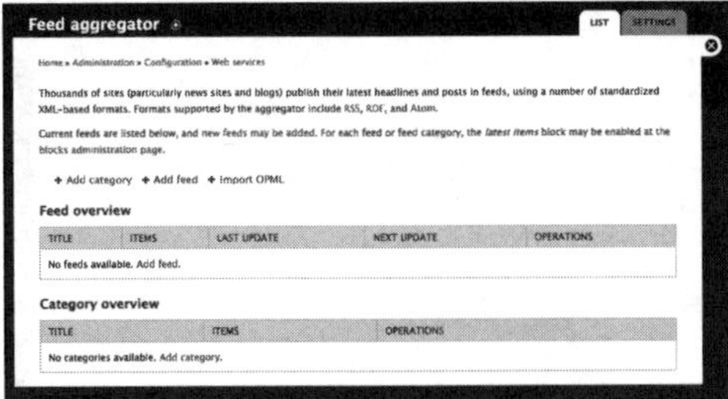

B The "Feed aggregator" page, showing no feeds added yet

To subscribe to content feeds from other sites:

1. Enable the Aggregator module.
2. Click Configuration in the Toolbar and then click "Feed aggregator" to open the "Feed aggregator" page **B**.

   The aggregator pulls news feeds you specify from around the Internet and aggregates them into a single page.

   This module adds the menu item "Feed aggregator" to the Navigation menu in the left sidebar of non-administrative pages.

   The "Feed aggregator" page eventually shows a list of all the news items from feeds aggregated on your site.
3. **Optional:** To add news feed categories, click the "Add category" link, provide the category's name (and description, if you'd like), and click Save. When you create or edit a news feed, you'll now have the option of adding it to a category, and later be able to display news feed items grouped by this category.

   If you plan to add several feeds to your site, it's a good idea to put them into categories. For this site, for example, we might choose to have a "Press releases" category for marketing information from RV manufacturers, and an "Industry news" category for feeds from independent sources.

continues on next page

4. Click the "Add feed" link.

   On the resulting page **C**, provide:

   - Title: This is the title for the feed and will display on pages, in blocks, and elsewhere throughout the site to identify the feed.
   - URL: This is the feed's URL, which needs to lead to a page with feed items in a format that Drupal understands. (For details, see the sidebar "How Do I Find News Feeds to Feature on My Site?")
   - Update interval: This is how frequently your site should receive news feed items. The shorter the update interval period, the more up-to-date, but also the more demands the process makes on your server (and the one providing the feed).
   - News items in block: This is the number of items that will appear in a sidebar, known as a *block*. You'll learn more about blocks in Chapter 6.
   - Categorize news items: These are the categories you want this news feed to belong to, if you created categories earlier. (If not, you can always edit the feed and add them later.) You can make this control appear either as check boxes or as a multiple-select list; step 9 shows you where that setting is.

5. Click Save.

6. Your site is now ready to receive news feed items, but you won't see them until the next "Update interval" period passes. To force your site to grab news feed items at any time, click List at the top of the "Feed aggregator" page, then click the "update items" link next to the news feed you set up **D**.

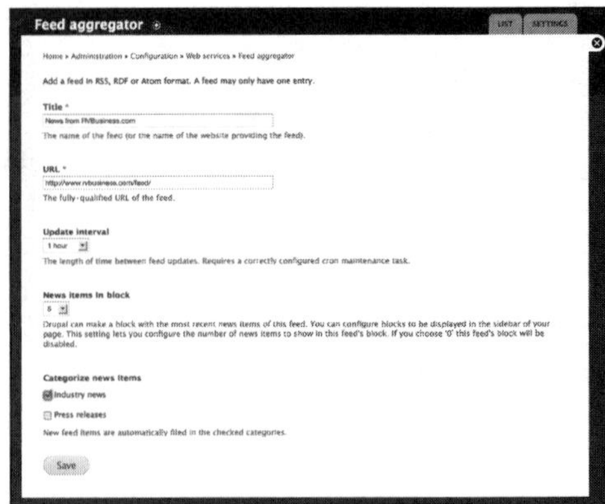

C Setting up Drupal to receive news feed items from `rvbusiness.com`

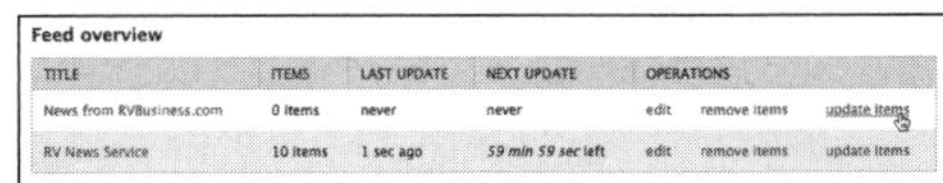

Feed overview

TITLE	ITEMS	LAST UPDATE	NEXT UPDATE	OPERATIONS		
News from RVBusiness.com	0 items	never	never	edit	remove items	update items
RV News Service	10 items	1 sec ago	*59 min 59 sec left*	edit	remove items	update items

D Updating items in the "News from RVBusiness" feed

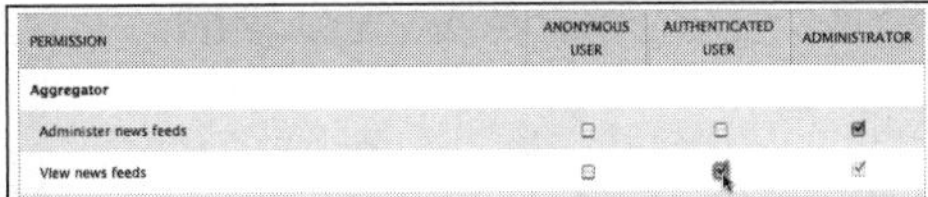

E Setting permissions to allow site members to view items from news feeds

F The link that leads to a page showing only news items from feeds in the "Industry news" category

7. By default, items from news feeds are visible only to site administrators, not to site members or anonymous visitors. To make them available to others:

   - Click People in the Toolbar. Then click the Permissions tab and scroll down to Aggregator > View news feeds.
   - Select the appropriate check boxes to give access to nonmembers (anonymous users) or site members (authenticated users) **E**.
   - Click "Save permissions."

   For more information about setting user permissions, see Chapter 7.

8. On any non-administrative page, click "Feed aggregator" in the Navigation menu in the left column, or go to **`http://`*`domain-name`*`/aggregator`**, to view all news feed items on one page.

   Note that these items are not nodes on your site; clicking an item's headline takes you to its source on someone else's web site.

   Under the "Feed aggregator" link are up to two additional links: Categories (if you set up categories) and Sources. Clicking those links allows you to drill down and see only news feed items from specific categories or sources **F**.

continues on next page

9. To change general settings affecting all news feeds that you aggregate on your site, click the Settings tab on the "Feed aggregator" page.

   The Aggregator settings page **G** gives you controls to:

   - Say which HTML tags are permitted in feeds as they appear on your site. This is an important filter to prevent abuse: If all tags were permitted, hostile webmasters could vandalize your site by including malicious code in their sites' news feeds. The default tags are safe and allow for basic formatting.
   - Change how many items show up in the source and category pages; additional items appear below a "more" link, as **H** shows.

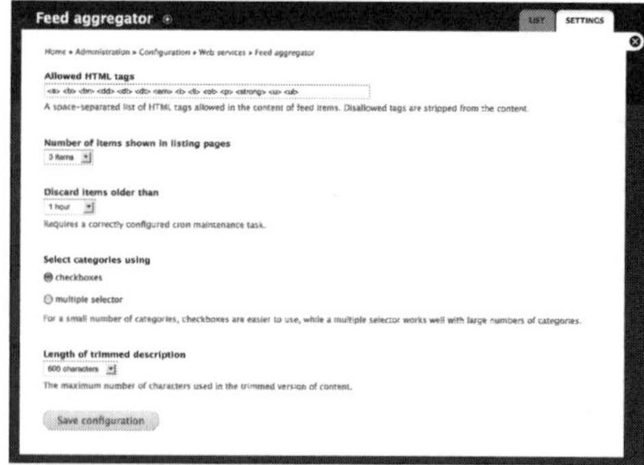

G The Aggregator settings page

Sources
News from RVBusiness.com
Dealer Open Houses: A Good Week in Elkhart 2 days 1 hour old
Upscale RVC Outdoor Destinations Expands 2 days 3 hours old
Michigan Tourism Up; Better Times Ahead? 2 days 3 hours old
More
RV News Service
Sex in RV leads to arrest 4 days 4 hours old
50-state cell phone driving ban? Not quite yet, says Governors Association 6 days 3 hours old
Battle over RVs heats up with music video 1 week 1 day old
More

H The default appearance of the Sources page, showing three items per feed

How Do I Find News Feeds to Feature on My Site?

News feeds are great because they automatically provide your site with content that's both free and fresh. In fact, some popular (and profitable) sites are nothing but collections of news feeds! Practically no maintenance is needed for such sites, except to check back once in a while to make sure the feed source is still working. That's all I do on my **`savemyhomebook.com`** site these days. The book it advertises is nearly out of print, so it's not worth my time to write original content for it. News feeds let me continue to provide value to visitors interested in the subject of foreclosure.

But you have to find news sources provided in a format Drupal's aggregator understands, namely RSS (Really Simple Syndication), RDF (Resource Description Framework), or Atom. First, try entering a typical search term (such as *RV news*) in a search engine such as **`google.com`**. Then look through the sites it finds for pages with lists of relevant news items. When you find one you like, check the web browser's location bar. Does it have the little radio-like RSS symbol ? If not, the content can't be (easily) syndicated.

But if it does, click that icon. If your browser presents you with a choice of formats, select one of the three that Drupal understands. The resulting page is the one you want; copy its URL from your web browser's location bar and paste it into the URL field of a new feed page, as described above.

- Specify how long news feed items appear on the site before being removed. (Remember, no actual nodes are created or destroyed on your site when you set Drupal to aggregate a news feed.)
- Determine whether to use check boxes or a multiple-select list to categorize news feeds, as was shown in step 4.
- Set how many characters of each news feed item will appear on your site. You could set this to Unlimited to show news feed items in their entirety, so that visitors don't have to click the "more" link (and leave your site). However, news feed publishers often limit the length of feed items on their sites, so your settings might not affect the information that comes through.

To create books of linked content:

1. Enable the Book module.
2. Click "Add content" in the Shortcut bar and then click the newly added option, "Book page."
3. Fill out the node entry form as outlined in the section "To create a new node" earlier in this chapter. (Like articles, book pages by default permit visitor comments. However, book pages aren't promoted to the front page.)

   The book concept is that each node can be the parent and/or child of another node, much like a real-world book contains chapters, which contain sections, which contain subsections, and so on. Drupal book "pages" automatically gain links at the bottom leading to the previous and next pages, and going up to the level above. It's not a perfect analogy, but it does give you a way to create structured texts within Drupal. In fact, the book structure comprises much of the instructional material on the **drupal.org** web site.

   One thing that's somewhat confusing is that you can't create an empty book, then later add pages to it. Rather, the title of the first page that you create becomes that book's title. But don't worry: You can change it around later if you want, as you'll see in the section "To change a book's structure."

4. Because you turned on the book module, there's now a new "Book outline" tab at the bottom of the screen **I**. For the superuser, this tab actually appears in the edit form for nodes of *every* content type—articles, basic pages, blog entries, and anything you add later. You can control which types other site members can add to books by clicking

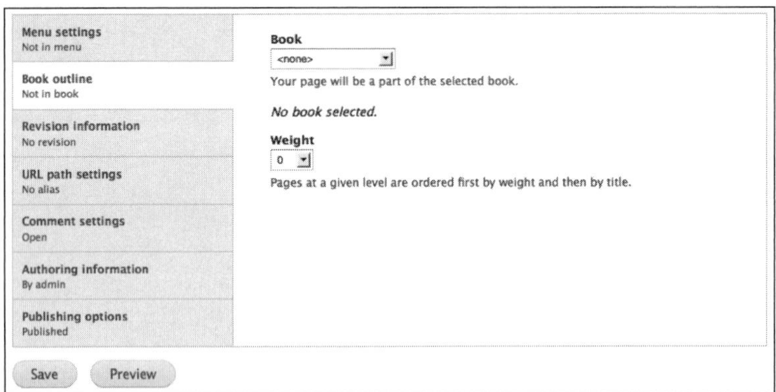

I The "Book outline" tab at the bottom of a node's edit form

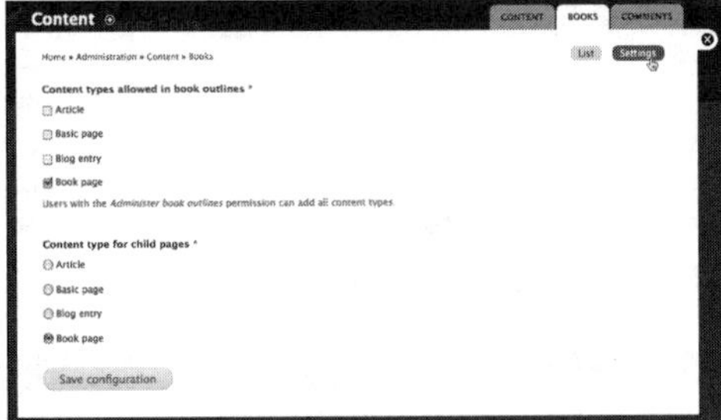

J The Books settings page

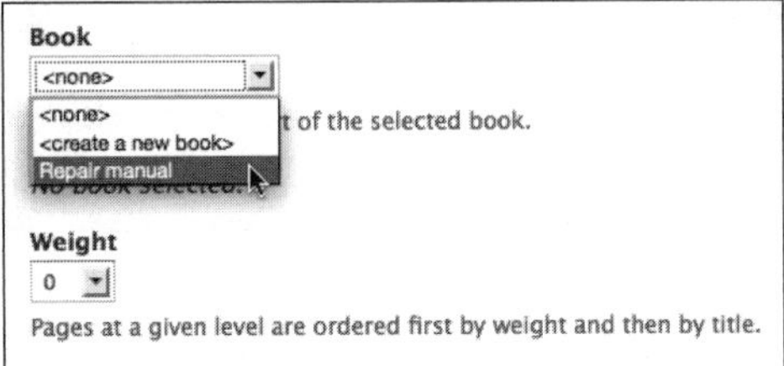

K Deciding in which book a node should go

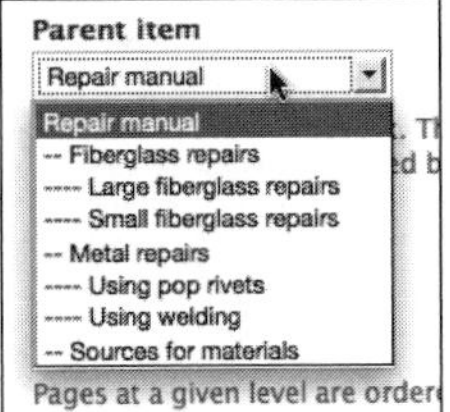

L Putting a node into a specific place within a book

Content in the Toolbar and then clicking Books > Settings J. You can define which content type new book pages will be when you add them through the "Add child page" link, as you'll see later.

But back to our node. The Book pop-up menu lets you define whether this node is part of an existing book, the first page created of a new book, or in no book at all. K shows what the menu would look like if you'd already created a book called "Repair manual."

5. If you select an existing book from the Book pop-up menu, a "Parent item" pop-up menu appears beneath it, listing all the pages currently in that book. Choose the page you'd like to be the parent of the page you're editing L.

   The Weight pop-up menu lets you order book pages that have the same parent, much like reordering subsections within a chapter. You'll learn a much easier way to order book pages in the section "To change a book's structure."

6. Click Save.

   M shows a book page in a book that has several levels of content.

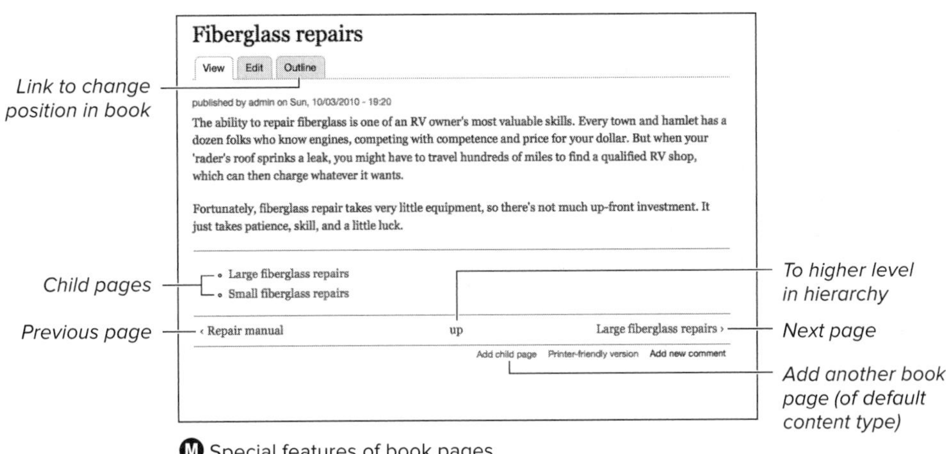

M Special features of book pages

To change a book's structure:

1. Click Content in the Toolbar, then click the Books tab to see a list of books on your site **N**.

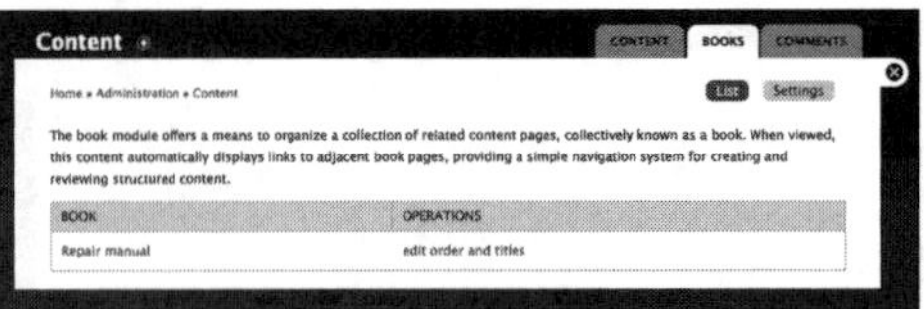

N The Books administration page

2. Click "edit order and titles" next to the book you want to edit.

   O shows the resulting book editing screen.

   Each row represents one page in a book, regardless of its content type. In the Operations column are quick links to view, edit, and delete the page's content.

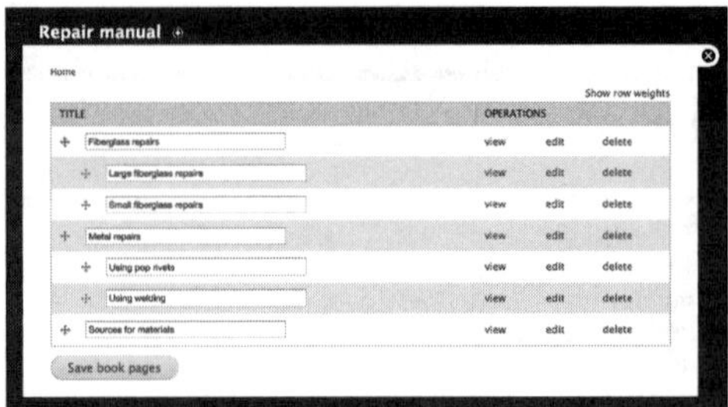

O The book editing screen

3. Under the Title column, you can quickly change the titles of any pages in this book by typing them in and clicking "Save book pages."

4. To move pages within a Book, grab the compass-like icon ✥ and drag the page to its desired location. Drag a page up or down to change how early it appears in the book. You can also drag an item to be a "child" of another page by dragging it to the position directly beneath the parent and then dragging to the right. (Don't worry if this seems confusing from the description—it immediately becomes clear when you start doing it.)

   A small orange asterisk appears on the right next to pages whose locations have changed **P**. When you're finished moving pages around, click "Save book pages." If you want to erase your changes anywhere during the process, simply close the window or go elsewhere in your Drupal site without clicking "Save book pages."

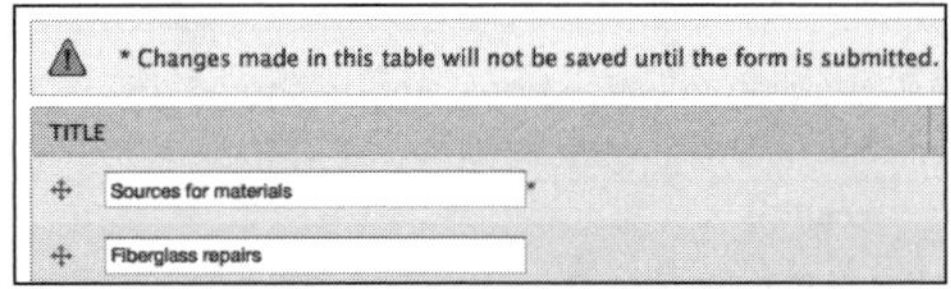

P The warning that shows the "Sources for materials" page has moved

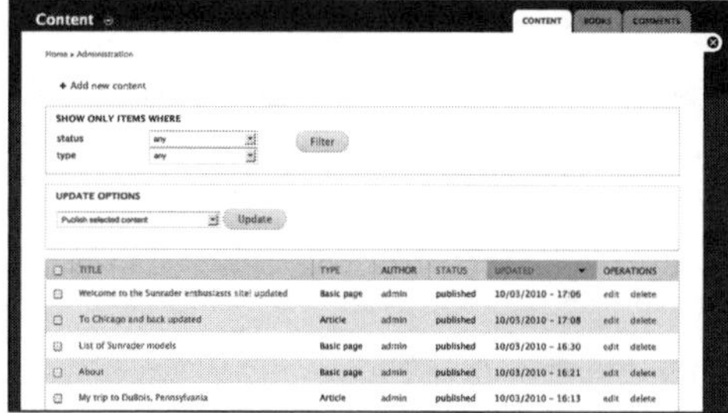

A The Content administration page, showing nodes

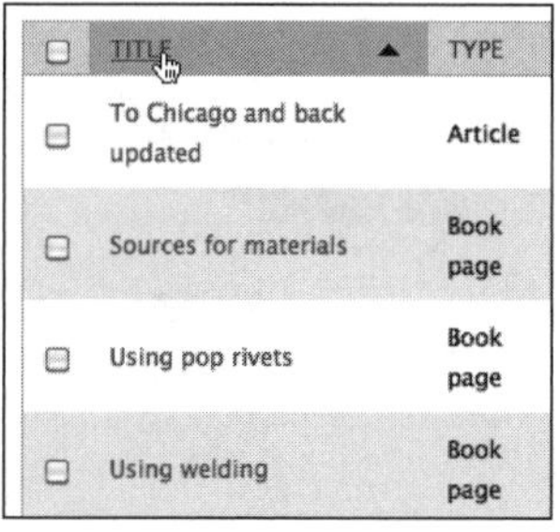

B Sorting nodes alphabetically by title

Finding, Editing, and Deleting Content

Once you start creating articles, basic pages, blog entries, and book pages with wild abandon, you quickly realize how easy it is to lose track of what's on your site.

Fortunately, Drupal includes an administration page that shows all your site's content in an easy-to-manipulate form, and lets you filter it by criteria such as content type to find the nodes you want. Through that page, you can jump straight to editing individual pages or change certain characteristics of multiple nodes at once.

To see a list of content on your site:

1. Click Content in the Toolbar **A**.
2. Each row represents one node and has several links to manage that node directly:
   - View it by clicking its title.
   - Edit it by clicking its "edit" link.
   - Delete it by clicking its "delete" link.
   - View the user page for the node's author by clicking the name in the Author column.
3. By default, the page lists nodes with the newest at the top. But you can sort by any other criteria by clicking the title at the head of any column. In **B**, for example, clicking the Title header sorted the list alphabetically by node title. If you were to click the Title header again, the list would appear in reverse alphabetical order by title.

continues on next page

4. You can filter the list so that only (for example) nodes of the "book page" content type appear. To do so:
   - Choose whether you want to filter the list by content type or status. (Other options might be available as you add or enable other modules.) If you want to filter on multiple criteria, select any criterion to filter on first. You'll have an opportunity to filter further on other criteria after you've set the first filter.
   - Click Filter. The screen now shows only those nodes that meet your stated criterion. Once you've selected your first filter term, the options will change to Refine, Undo, and Reset.
   - Continue adding criteria, clicking Refine after each one **C**. To go backward one step in the filtering process, click Undo. To return to seeing the full list of nodes, click Reset.

To perform bulk changes on multiple nodes at once:

1. Select the check boxes of those nodes you want to affect. To select all nodes showing on the screen, select the check box at the top of the column, next to the Title header.
2. Under "Update options," click the pop-up menu and choose the operation you want to perform **D**. (The list of available options may grow as you install and enable modules.)
3. Click Update and Drupal will change the selected nodes.

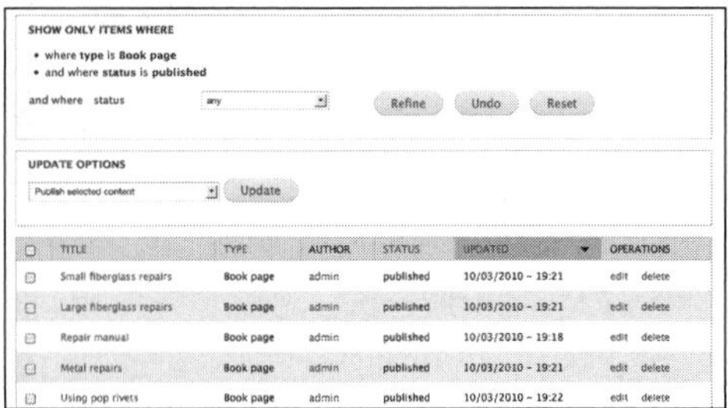

C Filtering to show only book page nodes that have been published

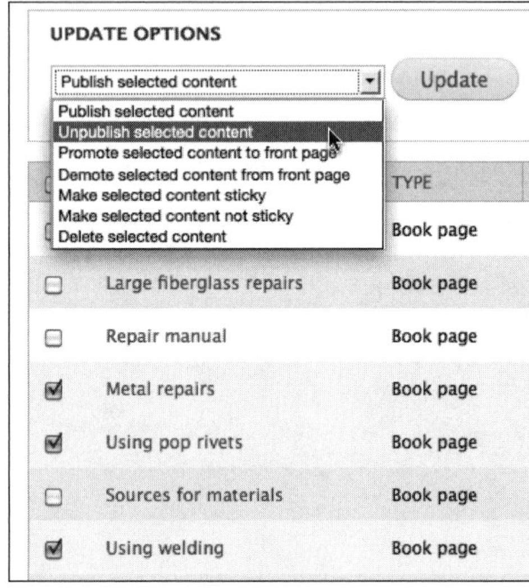

D Unpublishing three nodes

Customizing Content

Drupal suffers from the "blind men describing an elephant" syndrome. In that Indian fable, one man touches the trunk and declares that an elephant is like a tree branch; another touches the tail and says an elephant is like a rope; a third touches an ear and says the elephant is like a great leaf; and so forth. The thing observed is seen by its parts, according to the needs of the individual.

Since Drupal's audience has historically been software developers, that's translated into strong support for text and add-on programming. Two areas where it's not been as capable are in creating content types with custom fields, and in supporting graphics and text styling within nodes.

Fortunately, both areas are getting better. This chapter tells you how to create more flexible content using tools that are available today. However, a constant stream of new solutions passes through the library of contributed modules at **drupal.org/project/modules**. For details on how to find and use them, see Chapter 9, "Extending Drupal with Modules."

In This Chapter

Defining Custom Types of Content

Now we come to one of Drupal's most useful features: custom *content types.* Through them you can move far beyond built-in types and into a world bound only by your imagination. For example, an "employee" content type could include fields for position and salary, and a "catalog page" content type would have fields for prices, colors, and sizes.

Nearly all Drupal sites today have custom content types. But amazingly, Drupal succeeded for years without this feature. It was first available in 2005 through a contributed (non-core) module called Flexinode, which was replaced by Content Construction Kit (CCK) in 2006. Now, Drupal 7 incorporates most of CCK in its core.

Although this section teaches how to create new content types, the instructions are essentially the same if you want to edit an existing content type, such as an article or basic page. If you do so, be aware that changes to an existing content type will primarily affect only *newly created nodes* of that content type. If you add an age field to an existing content type, for example, and require that the age field contain a value, then existing nodes without a value in that field will be unaffected—at least until you go to edit the node. At that point, you'd be prompted to fill in the required field.

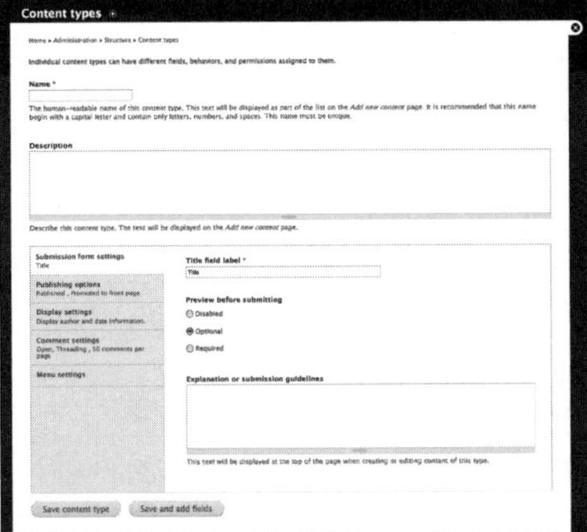

Ⓐ The form for editing a content type

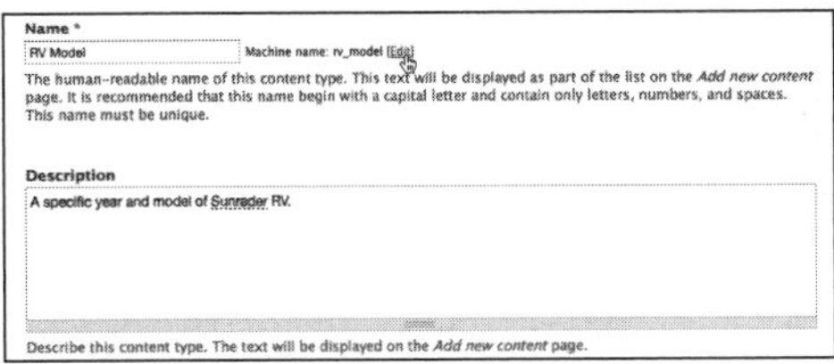

Ⓑ Naming and describing a new content type, with the pointer indicating how to change its machine name

To create a new content type:

1. Click Structure in the Toolbar and then click "Content types."
2. Click "Add content type" to go to the content type edit form Ⓐ.

   Most of this form is familiar to you, because it looks somewhat like the one you use to create and edit nodes, which you learned about in Chapter 2, "Establishing Your Drupal Site."

   But there's an important difference. Changes you make on a *node* edit form affect only a single node; changes you make on the *content type* edit form affect every node of that content type. You're creating a *template* for future nodes.
3. Complete the two fields that give the content type its identity:
   - The Name field is where you type the "human-readable" name of the content type. Drupal automatically creates a "machine name" that converts spaces to underscores, and uppercase characters to lowercase characters. (Drupal uses this machine name internally.) However, you can choose to change the machine name by clicking the Edit link in this area Ⓑ.
   - The optional Description field is where you add explanatory text that appears on the "Add new content" page to help content editors select the right content type.

continues on next page

4. Complete the “Submission form settings” section, which controls the appearance of several parts of the node edit form for this content type:

   - The “Title field label” field comes with the default value of *Title*. I like to change it to something more descriptive, such as *Model name* **C**. You can’t leave this field blank.
   - The “Preview before submitting” setting determines whether node creators see a Preview button at the bottom of the node edit form. If Disabled is selected, they see only the Save button; if Optional is selected, they see both the Save and Preview buttons; and if Required is selected, they see only the Preview button and are allowed to save a node only after previewing it.
   - The “Explanation or submission guidelines” field lets you add a note that appears at the top of the node edit form for the benefit of node creators and editors **D**.

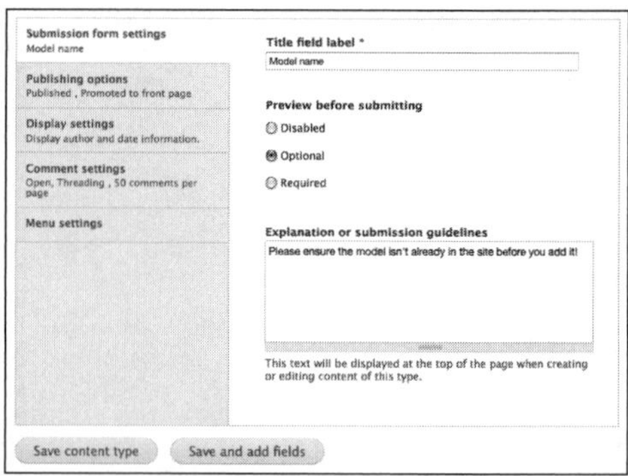

C Settings that affect the node edit form, with some options changed for our “Sunader Fans” site

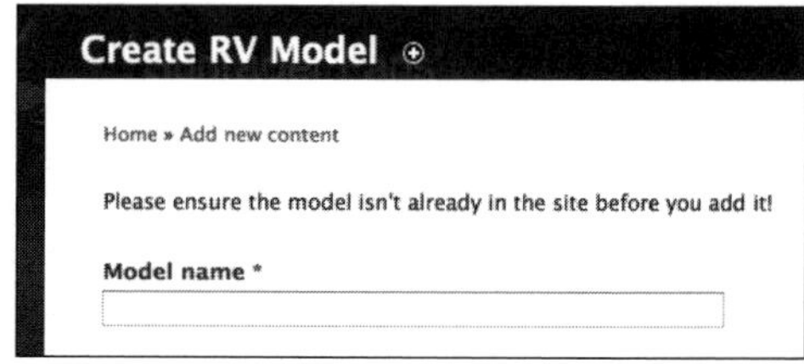

D A portion of the node edit form, reflecting changes we made

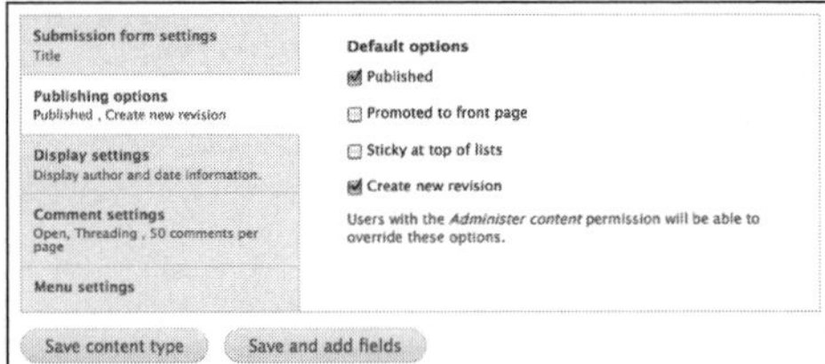

E Publishing options settings on the content type edit form

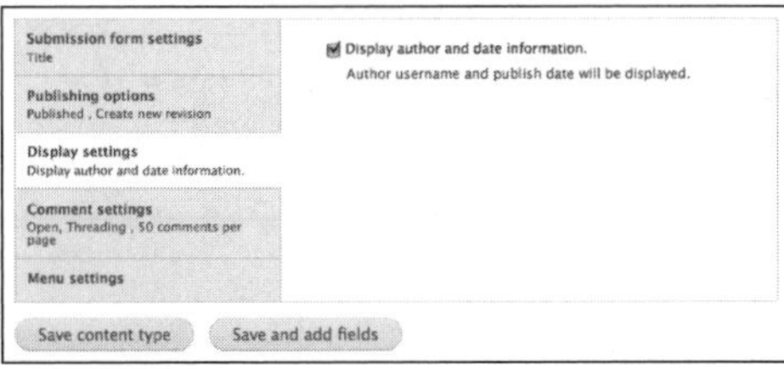

F The display settings options for a content type

1986 Adventure-II
View
Edit
published by admin on Tue, 10/05/2010 - 12:48
The 19-foot Adventure-II holds a special place in the hearts of collectors.

G The title and beginning of a node as it appears when the "Display author and date information" check box is selected

5. Click the "Publishing options" tab **E** to set default values for that part of the node edit form. To learn about these settings, see Chapter 3, "Creating and Managing Content."

6. Click the "Display settings" tab **F** to choose whether a node shows its author and date of creation **G**, taken from the "Authoring information" section of the node edit form. Exactly *how* this information displays is defined by programming in the active theme.

continues on next page

7. Click the "Comment settings" tab **H** to control how visitors can "talk back" in response to nodes:

- The "Default comment setting for new content" pop-up menu lets you set whether comments will be allowed at all on nodes of this content type. (You can change this setting on individual nodes, however.)

  Open means comments are allowed.

  Closed prevents further comments from being added, but displays any that were already there.

  Hidden means all existing comments will be hidden, and no more will be allowed.

- Threading affects whether text is indented so that conversations are easier to follow **I**. When not selected, all comments appear at the same indentation level. This "flat" format is graphically clean but (sometimes) makes it hard to follow individual conversations, which are known as "threads" **J**.

- The "Comments per page" setting defines how many comments appear before the reader has to click links at the bottom of the page to see more. A low value makes comment pages display more quickly, because there's less information for Drupal to put together and for the server to push through the Internet. I generally don't find the delay too onerous, so I usually change it to the maximum value (300).

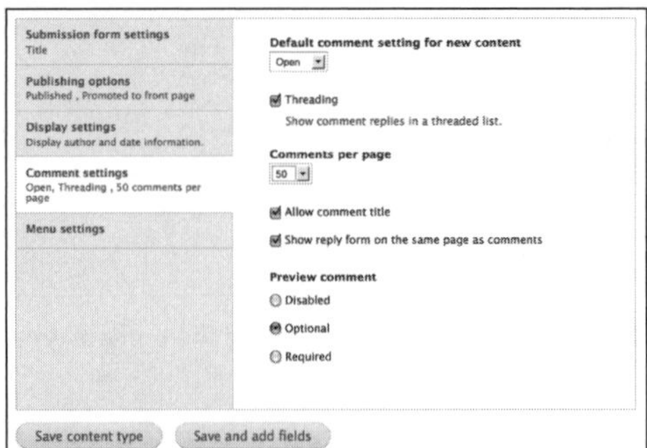

H Changing the comment settings to affect visitors' interaction with a content type

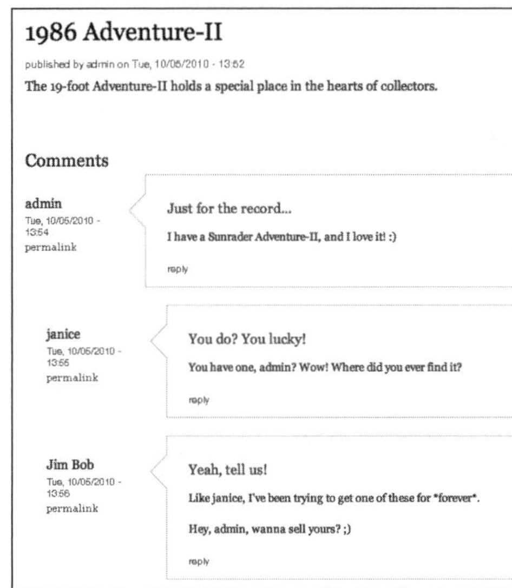

1986 Adventure-II
published by admin on Tue, 10/05/2010 - 13:52
The 19-foot Adventure-II holds a special place in the hearts of collectors.
Comments
admin
Tue, 10/05/2010 - 13:54
permalink
Just for the record...
I have a Sunrader Adventure-II, and I love it! :)
reply
janice
Tue, 10/05/2010 - 13:55
permalink
You do? You lucky!
You have one, admin? Wow! Where did you ever find it?
reply
Jim Bob
Tue, 10/05/2010 - 13:56
permalink
Yeah, tell us!
Like janice, I've been trying to get one of these for *forever*.
Hey, admin, wanna sell yours? ;)
reply

I Comments displayed as a threaded list, making it clear that the third comment is in response to the first

1986 Adventure-II
published by admin on Tue, 10/06/2010 - 13:52
The 19-foot Adventure-II holds a special place in the hearts of collectors.
Comments
admin
Tue, 10/05/2010 - 13:54
permalink
Just for the record...
I have a Sunrader Adventure-II, and I love it! :)
reply
janice
Tue, 10/05/2010 - 13:55
permalink
You do? You lucky!
You have one, admin? Wow! Where did you ever find it?
reply
Jim Bob
Tue, 10/05/2010 - 13:56
permalink
Yeah, tell us!
Like janice, I've been trying to get one of these for *forever*.
Hey, admin, wanna sell yours? ;)
reply

J Comments displayed as a flat (unthreaded) list, which is prettier but harder to follow

- The "Allow comment title" check box determines whether commenters can write their own subject lines. When unselected, or if a commenter fails to provide a title, Drupal automatically creates one using the first few words of the comment. For example, for a comment that reads "I agree very strongly with your post," Drupal will generate the (somewhat awkward) subject line "I agree very strongly with."
- The "Show reply form on the same page as comments" check box determines whether visitors see a comment form directly below the node's content or have to click an "Add new comment" link to see it. Your choice makes a difference in how many comments you get; it's surprising how many people won't bother to click! To encourage *more* comments, leave this check box selected.
- "Preview comment" options work very much like those for a node's "Preview post" options. When you select Required, commenters are forced to read through what they wrote before being allowed to post. In practice, selecting Required means that some commenters will fail to realize that they have to preview their posts before saving them and will simply lose their comments by going to another screen. On the other hand, some administrators believe the Required selection cuts down on frivolous, misformatted, and hotheaded comments.

continues on next page

8. Click the "Menu settings" tab **K** to control where you can put menu links to nodes of this content type when you create or edit nodes. See the section "To create a menu item that links to a node" in Chapter 3 to understand how your choice here affects users. You can always add links from any menu by directly editing it: For details, see Chapter 6, "Improving Access to Content."
9. When you've made all necessary changes, click "Save content type."

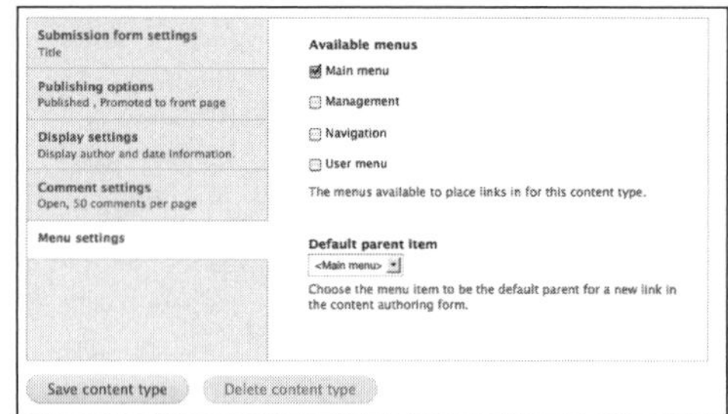

K Controlling where nodes of this content type can get automatic menu links

Deleting Content Types: Harder Than It Sounds

By now you might have noticed that it seems as easy to delete a content type as it is to create one. Easier, in fact. You can delete them on both the content type edit form and the page that lists content types.

But beware: Nodes of a content type become "orphans" when you delete that content type, available for view but not editing. Only sophisticated monkeying around in the database will make them work again.

Also note that content types that are created by modules, such as "blog entry," don't have "delete" links in the usual places. Instead, you get rid of them by turning off the relevant module. Nodes of such content types also become orphaned when you do this, so be sure to delete them as you learned in the section "Finding, Editing, and Deleting Content" in Chapter 3. You can then re-create those nodes as a different content type. (Unfortunately, Drupal doesn't currently offer any way to change a node's content type.)

To change a field's display and input options:

1. In the Toolbar, click Structure and then click "Content types."

2. Click the "manage fields" link next to the content type you want to affect. Besides being a place to add fields, on this screen Ⓛ you can also:

   - Delete a field by clicking its "delete" link, if it's a type of field that can be deleted. However, you can't delete fields that modules create or the node's title field (shown in Ⓛ by the name we gave it earlier, "Model name").

   - Edit the field's basic criteria by clicking the "edit" link. We discuss the many options on the resulting page in the next step.

   - Change the order of fields by clicking and dragging their ✣ icons. Note that you have to click Save after reordering fields: You'll lose all reordering changes if you click other links on this page before clicking Save.

   - Change a field's type, for example from List to Long text, by clicking the link that shows the current type. For the Body field in Ⓛ, that's "Long text and summary." (It's rare that you'll want to do this.)

   - Change a field's "widget"—that is, the selection tool for entering data in the field. Examples of widgets included in Drupal include check boxes, radio buttons, pop-up menus, and text fields; contributed modules may add other widgets (such as a date selection calendar). In Ⓛ, the widget is currently "Text area with a summary."

continues on next page

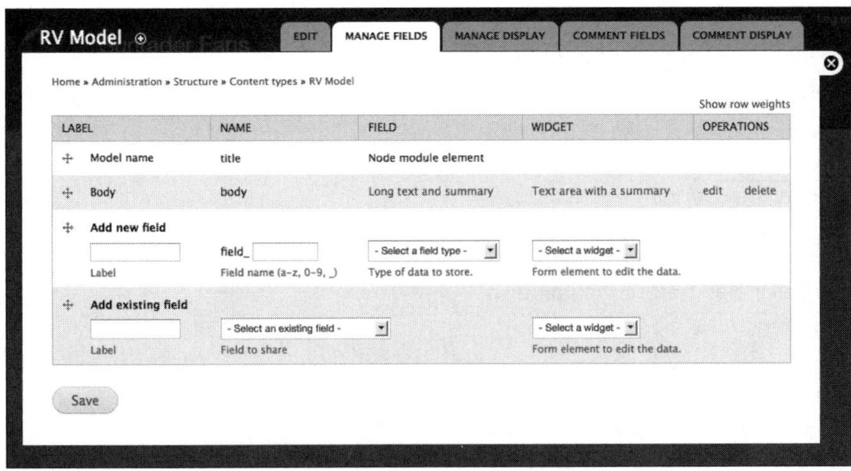

Ⓛ The screen where you manage a content type's fields

3. Click the "edit" link to go to the field settings form.

   Options on this form vary considerably, depending on the field's type and widget. (Our example is of the Integer field type.) In fact, some field types and widgets break these options into more than one screen, in which case you'll simply have to fill out the first screen, then click "Save field settings" before moving on to the second.

   The screen shown in **M** is for a newly created field that's intended to hold an integer. (You'll learn how to add fields in the next section, "To add fields to a custom content type.") The form's top part is for changing the field's basic information, including:

   - The Label, which you entered when you first created the field.
   - The "Required field" check box, which determines whether to force node editors to enter a value in this field.
   - The "Help text," which will appear near the field as a guide for node editors.
   - The Minimum, Maximum, Prefix, and Suffix allow you to limit the range of values the user can enter, or to change how the field appears when displayed. For example, you could put a dollar sign before the value so a "5" appears as "$5."

   There are many other options, depending on the field type and widget selected. For example, the "Long text and summary" field type includes a "Summary input" check box that lets you permit (or forbid) entry of a summary section. For more about summaries, see the "Gaining More Control of Individual Nodes" section in Chapter 3.

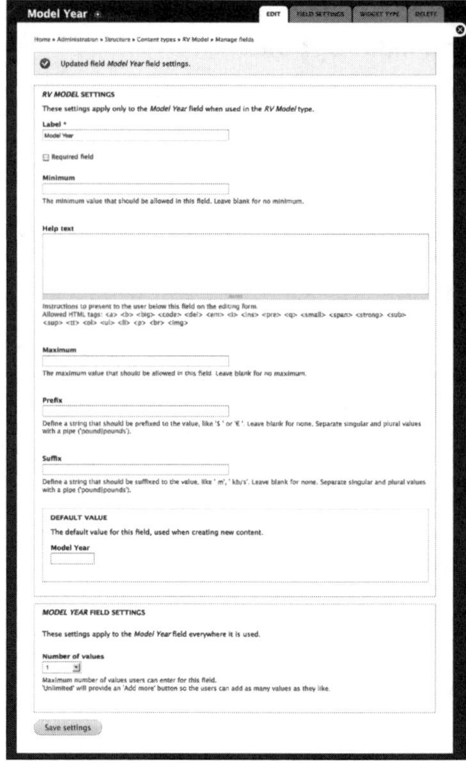

M The field edit form, where you change a field's basic information

4. Fill out the “Default value” parts of the field edit form. Whatever data you enter here will appear prefilled in the field when someone later creates a node that contains it.
5. Complete the “Number of values” pop-up menu that allows you to decide how many values you can have in a multiple value field.

   Multi-value fields can be a hard concept to grasp, and it’s best explained with a few examples. Such a field might be used to show:

   - The names of gold, silver, and bronze medalists in a content type for Olympic sports events. (In that case, you’d set the “Number of values” pop-up menu to 3.)
   - The instruments that a musician plays in an “orchestra member” content type (with the pop-up value set to Unlimited).
6. When you’ve finished modifying the field’s settings, click “Save settings.”

To add fields to a custom content type:

1. Click Structure in the Toolbar and then click "Content types."
2. Click the "manage fields" link next to the content type you want to change.
3. Put the human-readable name in the Label area and the machine-readable name in the "Field name" area. Select a field type, which determines the kind of data this field can contain.

   Generally speaking, Drupal's field types **N** fall into five categories:

   - Text, including Text, Long text, and Long text and summary
   - Numbers, including Integer, Float, Decimal, and Boolean
   - Selection lists
   - Files
   - References, for example Term reference. (Downloadable modules permit references to other entities, such as nodes and users.)

   Other field types may become available as you add modules, as Chapter 9 describes.
4. Once you've indicated the type of data this field will contain, the widget pop-up menu becomes available and reflects the widgets for the selected field type. Choose the one you want and then click Save.
5. The "Field settings" screen displays, where you specify details that are specific to the field type you chose. This section is broken into two screens: The first affects this field in every content type where it appears, while the second is specific to this content type. Complete the field settings form as was described in the section, "To change a field's display and input options" earlier in this chapter. When you've provided all required details, click "Save field settings." You will return to the list of fields for this content type.
6. Put fields in the order you want by clicking and dragging their ✥ icons. Click Save when finished.

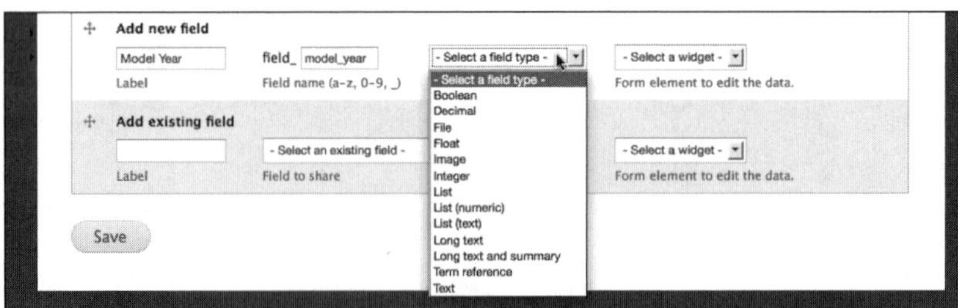

N Types available for custom fields in a content type

Putting Images and Styled Text in Content

Drupal creator Dries Buytaert gives a "State of Drupal" keynote presentation at every semi-annual DrupalCon conference (**drupalcon.org**) to talk about progress during the last six months and plans for the next six. At that talk he also presents the results from his web poll on **buytaert.net** that asks, "What improvements does Drupal need most?" Lately, the same item has been at the top of Drupal developers' wish list: better media handling.

With Drupal 7, that wish finally came true—at least, for graphics. In previous versions, you had two options. You could upload the graphic to the server, figure out where it was being stored, and write some HTML to put the graphic where you wanted; *or* you could find, download, and figure out a half-dozen modules to speed the process.

Under the guidance of Dries and long-time developer Angela Byron (known on the Drupal.org site as "webchick"), Drupal 7's developers made a special effort to incorporate those modules into Drupal itself. The results aren't perfect, but they're definitely encouraging. As you learned in Chapter 3, you can now attach graphics to articles with the click of a button; this chapter tells you how to attach graphics to nodes of *any* content type and how to place graphics with greater precision than Drupal naturally allows. Finally, you'll learn how to add text styles such as bold and italics without needing to resort to HTML code.

To add an image to article nodes:

1. To add an image to an existing article node, go to the node and click the Edit tab. Otherwise, create the article node as you learned to do in Chapters 2 and 3.
2. Complete the Title and Body fields as usual and make all desired changes to the settings tabs at the bottom of the page.
3. Click the Browse button next to the Image field to get a file-selection dialog box. Navigate to the graphics file you want to add and select it.
4. Click the Upload button. Depending on your connection speed, you might have to wait a while until the file uploads to your server. When it's finished, you'll see a small (thumbnail) version of the image, and the Upload button will become labeled Remove.
5. **Optional:** Add a description of the photo in the "Alternate text" field. This text will be useful to those visitors, such as blind people, who use non-graphical web browsers **A**.
6. At the bottom of the node-creation form, click Save to save the node. You'll view the newly changed article, with your full-size graphic at the top **B**.

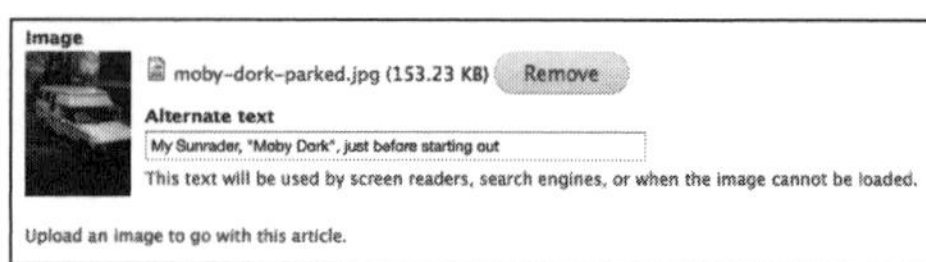

A The node-creation form after adding an image and some alternate text

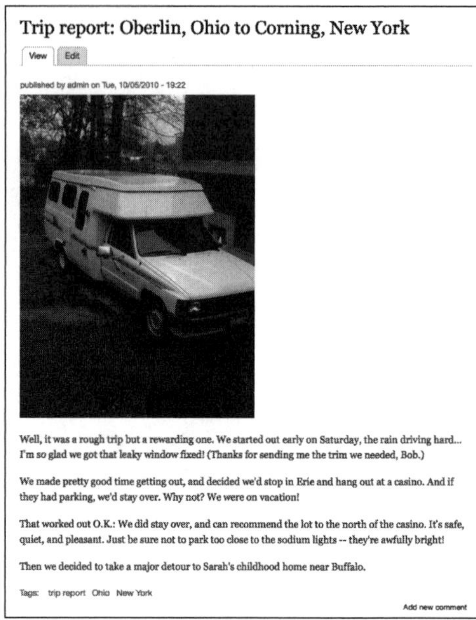

B An article with an added image

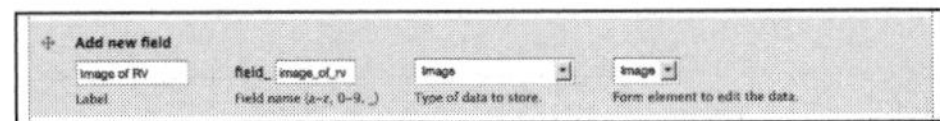

C Adding an image field to a content type

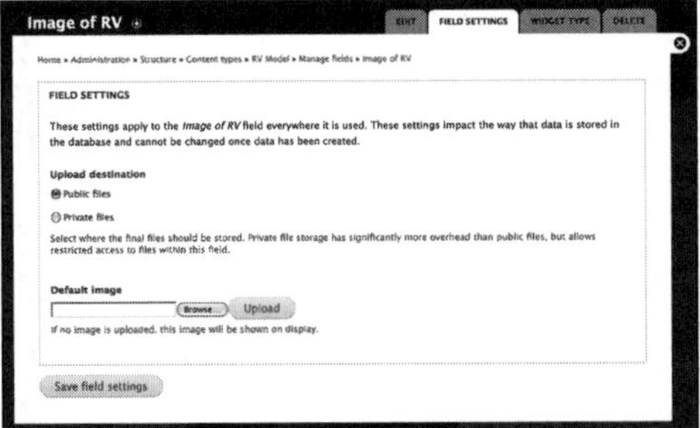

D The "field settings" screen

To enable images in nodes of any content type:

1. Go to the list of content types by clicking Structure in the Toolbar and then clicking "Content types."
2. Click the "manage fields" link next to the content type you want to affect.
3. In the "Add new field" area, enter the human-readable and machine-readable names for the image field you're going to add, as was decribed in the section "To add fields to a custom content type."
4. In the area labeled "Type of data to store," change the pop-up menu to Image. The widget pop-up menu to its right should also change to Image automatically **C**.
5. Click Save. You now see the "Field settings" screen **D**, which offers two choices:
   - "Upload destination" allows you to choose whether to make the images accessible to everybody who can find the URL (Public files) or only to those people who have special permission (Private files). It's an advanced subject, and rare that you would want to specify the latter. Suffice it to say that if you don't have a specific reason to select "Private files," leave this selection on its default, which is "Public files." (On some Drupal installations, "Public files" is the only option.)
   - "Default image" lets you select an image that will appear in this field for every node of this content type that doesn't have its own image.
6. Click "Save field settings" to arrive at the settings page for this field, which we'll discuss in the next section, "To control image criteria."

To control image criteria:

1. When you create an image field, you eventually come to a second screen full of settings for that field.

   To change these settings *after* a field has been created, you need to return to that second field settings screen. To do so, first go to the "Content types" list screen by clicking Structure in the Toolbar and then clicking "Content types." Click "manage fields" next to the content type that contains the field you want to affect. Then click the "edit" link next to the relevant field **E**.

   In either case, you'll see the settings page for this image field **F**.

2. We described what many of these fields are in the section "To change a field's display and input options." Some of the options that are especially relevant to images include:

   - "Allowed file extensions" lets you specify which file types are permissible in this field. The defaults (**png, gif, jpg, jpeg**) cover most graphic types that can be displayed in web browsers, but you might want to add other types (such as **svg**) for special applications.

   - "Maximum image resolution" and "Minimum image resolution" let you ensure that graphics aren't too big or small. People will still be able to upload larger graphics—Drupal will simply resize them down to fit these values. However, your site will reject attempts to upload graphics that are smaller than the minimum size. (If Drupal attempted to resize too-small graphics, the result would be an ugly, low-quality image.)

E Reaching the second field settings page from the list of fields

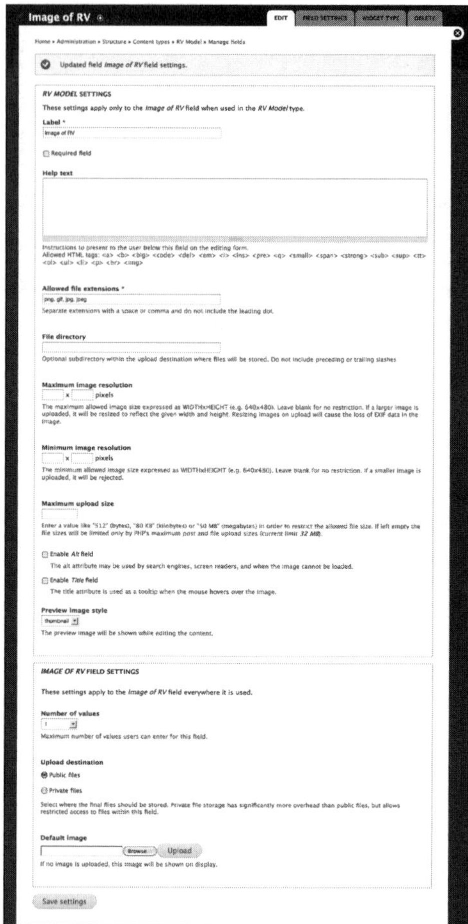

F The second field settings screen for images

- "Maximum upload size" lets you limit how much disk space each image may occupy. If you don't enter anything, the limit will be defined by settings in the **php.ini** file in your AMP stack. For more about this, see Chapter 1, "Getting Drupal Up and Running."
- "Enable *Alt* field" and "Enable *Title* field" check boxes allow anyone who adds an image to also include text that appears in the HTML code that surrounds that image. As the help text explains, the *alt* field appears in places where the image itself can't be loaded, such as in non-graphical web browsers; the *title* field determines what appears when a visitor hovers the cursor over the image.

3. Click "Save settings" to return to the list of fields for this content type. The changes you made will affect all nodes of this content type that you edit or create, but they won't affect existing nodes.

TIP It's a good idea to set the first value (which defines the width) in the "Maximum image resolution" field to 800 or less. If you don't, people will upload graphics that are wider than visitors' screens. When visitors look at the node, that graphic will force them to scroll horizontally to see the whole thing, and it could make your site's design ugly and hard to read.

TIP If you leave the "Maximum upload size" setting blank, you'll probably allow people to upload *very* big files, which could quickly fill your hard drive and will probably appear inconveniently large in your site. A value of 2 MB or 4 MB should be sufficient for most purposes.

TIP Enabling the Alt and Title fields is good practice, because it improves your site's accessibility for people with limited vision and those browsing the web with unusual devices.

To include images in content using HTML:

1. Find and copy the URL of the image you want to use. One way of doing this is to go to the web page that contains it, put your pointer over the image, right-click (or Control-click if you have a one-button mouse), and select Copy Image Location.
2. Edit the node where you want to place an image by going to it and clicking the Edit tab.
3. In the node's Body field, type the HTML code **<img src="*URL*" alt="*description*" />**, replacing ***URL*** with the web address you copied. You can style the image further using additional HTML, if you like.
4. Choose Full HTML from the "Text format" pop-up menu **G**.

   Warning: Switching to the Full HTML text format opens a security hole if anyone else has permission to edit this node. For more information about text formats, see Chapter 5, "Making Content Interactive."

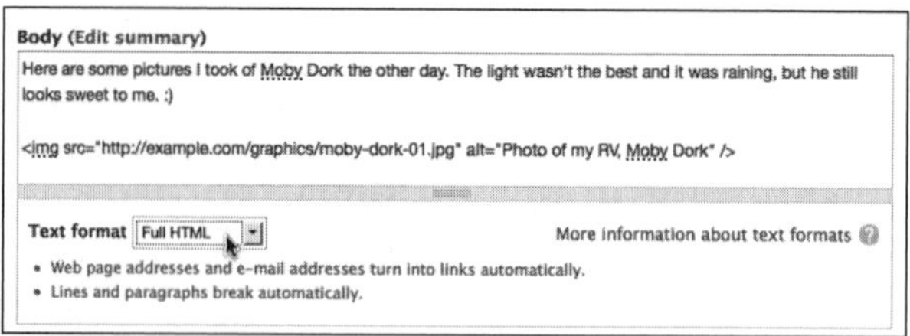

G Displaying a remotely hosted image in the body of a node

What About Other HTML Tags?

The act of changing the text format from Filtered HTML to Full HTML opens the door to any and all HTML stylings, including text styles such as `<b>` (bold) and `<font>`.

However, your HTML might not appear as you expect. Drupal themes format pages using an extensive set of CSS directives, which can substantially change the appearance of even the most basic HTML tags.

5. Scroll to the bottom of the screen and click Save. The image now appears in the body of the node.

TIP To link to files that exist elsewhere on your Drupal site, you don't need the `http://` *`domain-name`* part of the URL. In fact, including that part slows down image retrieval, since your Drupal site is forced to look up its own address! A typical code in that case would be `<img src="/sites/default/files/moby-dork-01.jpg">`.

TIP I recommend that you reference only graphics that are hosted on your own server. For one thing, you have more control over the images and know they won't suddenly change or disappear; for another, it's considered impolite (and possibly illegal) to "hotlink" graphics that are hosted elsewhere, unless you have explicit permission from their owners, because the remote server pays the bandwidth charges for the image to appear on your web site.

By the same token: Once a file is on your server, you can display it in any node, not just the one to which it's attached.

To style text using a rich-text editor:

1. In a web browser, go to the Wysiwyg *project* page at **`drupal.org/project/wysiwyg`**.
2. Download and install the latest Drupal 7 version of the Wysiwyg module, using the techniques described in the "To install, enable, and configure modules" section of Chapter 9.
3. Click Modules in the Toolbar.
4. Scroll to the bottom of the page. Select the Wysiwyg check box and then click "Save configuration" **H**.
5. This module doesn't actually add rich-text tools to your site. Instead, it connects your Drupal site to many rich-text editors that are available in the wider web-development world. You now need to download and install one of those packages.

   Click Configuration in the Toolbar and then click "Wysiwyg profiles."
6. On the resulting page you'll see a list of rich-text editors that work with the Wysiwyg module. You'll need to download and install one of them: I'll demonstrate using the first one on the list, the popular CKEditor.

   Click the Download link **I** to go to the CKEditor site **J**. (You'll need to return to this page for the instructions it contains, so I recommend that you open the CKEditor site in a new browser window or tab.)

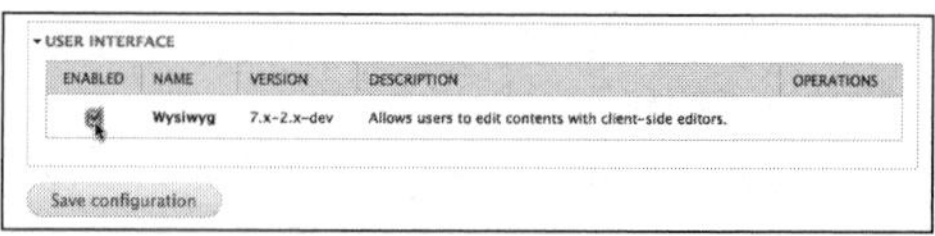

H Enabling the Wysiwyg module

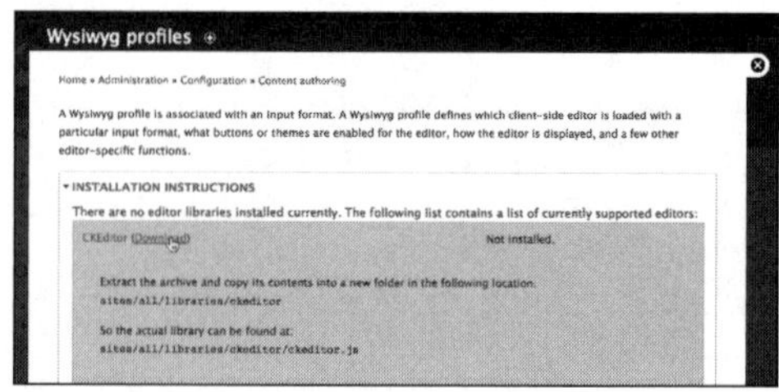

I The link to download the CKEditor package

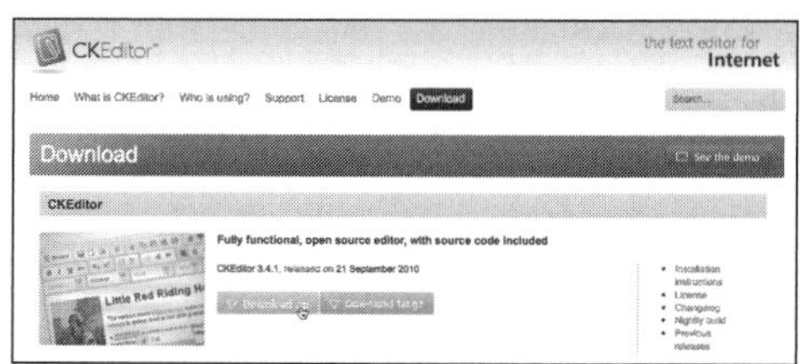

J The CKEditor home page with the pointer indicating the package's download link

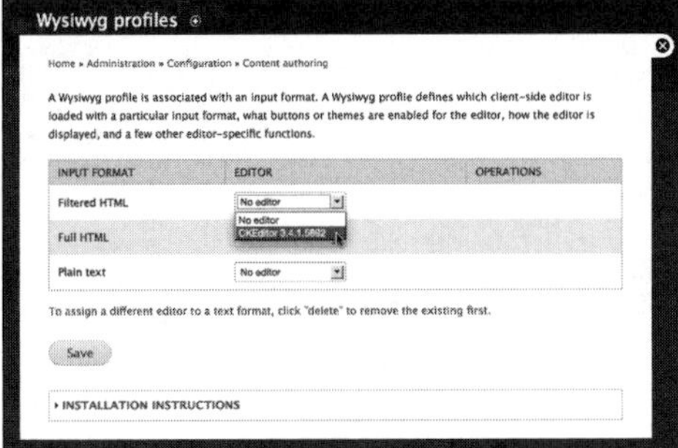

K Selecting CKEditor for all times when users enter text in the Filtered HTML format

7. You'll now download and unpack CKEditor.

   - On Mac or Windows: Click the "Download zip" button. Find the downloaded package on your computer and double-click it to uncompress it. (If you have problems doing so on a Windows computer, see the sidebar "Help! I Can't Uncompress the File!" in Chapter 1.)

   - On *nix using the command-line interface: Copy the URL linked from the "Download tar.gz" button. In a terminal program, type **`wget`** ***`URL`***. When the package has finished downloading, type **`tar -xzvf`** ***`downloaded-package-name`***.

8. Return to the Wysiwyg profiles page to determine where you'll need to put the files you just downloaded and uncompressed. Move the files as directed.

   Since we're using CKEditor, we'll need to create a new "libraries" directory inside **`/sites/all/modules`**.

9. Reload the Wysiwyg profiles page, either using your browser's Reload function or by clicking Configure in the Toolbar and then clicking "Wysiwyg profiles."

   The page has changed to now allow you to select which editor to use for each text format that's active on your site. (For more information about text formats, see Chapter 5.) You could also load other rich-text editors by clicking the "Installation instructions" link to expose the instructions you saw on this page earlier.

10. In the pop-up menu next to "Filtered HTML," select CKEditor **K** and then click Save.

continues on next page

11. The rich-text editor now appears whenever you have an opportunity to enter Filtered HTML text, for example when creating a basic page **L**.

TIP As you might guess from the long list of rich-text editors on the Wysiwyg configuration page, there are lots of debates in the web-development community about the advantages and disadvantages of each. Links from the Wysiwyg project page at `drupal.org/project/wysiwyg` lead you to those discussions and additional resources for understanding this complex topic.

TIP You can direct your site to use the rich-text editor when entering text in any text format, but I generally use it only for Filtered HTML. When I enter something in Plain Text format I usually don't want any rich-text formatting at all, while I reserve Full HTML format for times when I want to explicitly provide formatting in code.

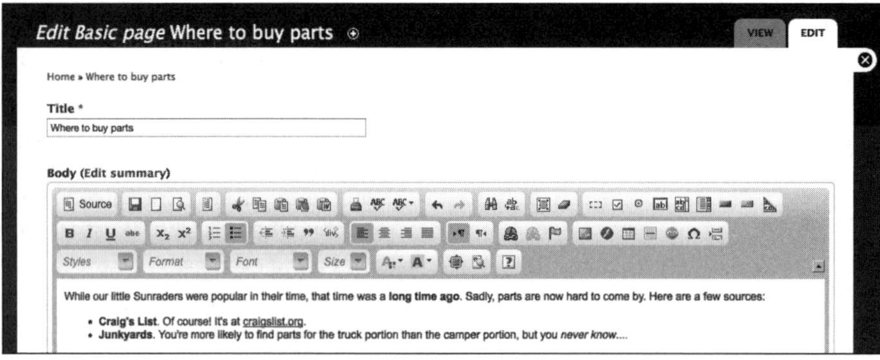

L Editing a node with CKEditor's controls active

Making Content Interactive

In the first four chapters of this book you learned how to create a solid, information-filled site. But you've only scratched the surface of what Drupal can do. Now we're going to start working with features to:

- Let users have a more active role in the site by taking part in polls and discussion forums.
- Group nodes into categories.
- Define and select allowed input formats for content.
- Change how uploaded images appear in varying contexts.

In short, you'll learn features that add depth to nodes, letting them interact more with each other—and your users.

Any time we mention users, we have to talk about user security. Drupal allows you to make features available to all users, to a subset, to administrators, or to just the superuser. This chapter includes brief instructions for granting those permissions; for complete control, see Chapter 7, "Wrangling Users."

In This Chapter

Enabling Interactive Content Types

In Chapter 3, "Creating and Managing Content," you learned how to extend your Drupal site beyond articles and basic pages, first by enabling the Book and Blog modules, and then by adding news feeds via the Aggregator module. Now we continue in that vein by enabling and configuring modules that let you:

- Create polls, in which each user is permitted only one vote, with the totals automatically tallied.
- Establish forums where your users can talk amongst themselves in a convenient and familiar "bulletin board" environment.

Both of these features work especially well when limited to authenticated users—that is, those who have created and logged in to an account on your site. In fact, these features are unavailable to anonymous (non-member) users unless you specifically let them in.

To create polls:

1. Click Modules in the Toolbar. Enable the Poll module, then scroll down and click "Save configuration."
2. You now have access to a new content type called "poll." To create a poll node, click Add content > Poll. The poll edit form appears.
3. Type a name for the poll in the Question field, which is like the Title field in other content types.

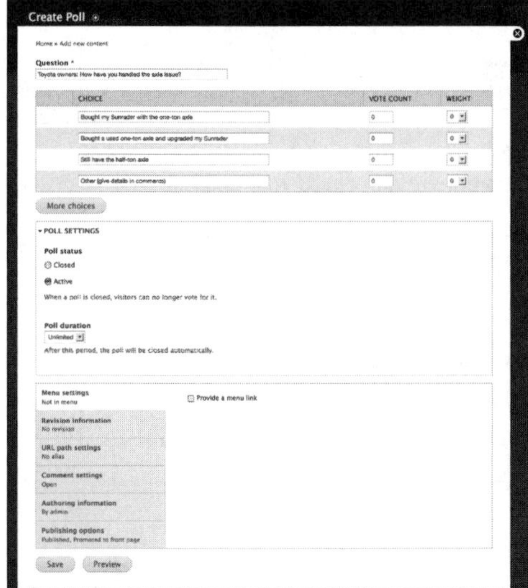

A The poll edit form partially filled out

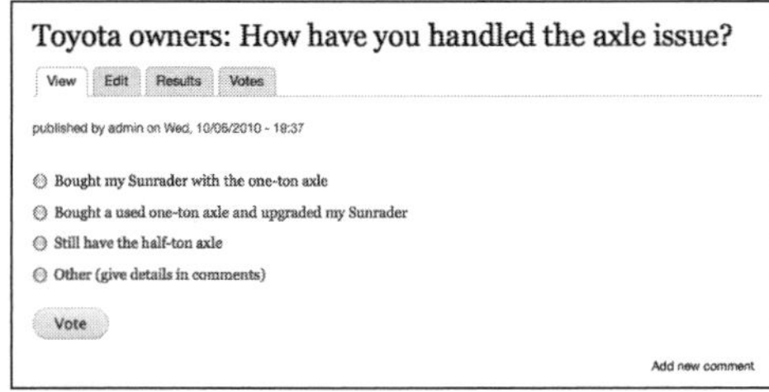

B The poll from **A** as visitors with voting permission see it

4. Enter options in the Choice fields **A**.
   - You can "fake" votes by typing a number in the "Vote Count" column. At first glance this feature seems devious, because it allows you to stack the deck for options that you want to win. But it also has honest applications, for example if you wanted to preserve the vote count from a survey that you started offline or on another web site.
   - Initially, the form presents only two spaces for choices. To add another, click "More choices." Repeat as necessary.
5. In the "Poll Settings" option, the Active selection indicates that you're still soliciting votes; you can turn off voting at any time by changing the radio button to Closed. Doing so doesn't unpublish the poll. Rather, users who visit a Closed poll see the poll's results instead of a list of choices.

   By default, the poll will continue until you click the Closed radio button. But you can make Drupal close the poll at a future point in time by selecting an option (other than Unlimited) from the "Poll duration" pop-up menu.
6. Make any desired changes to the tabbed section of the edit form. (For help, see Chapter 3, "Creating and Managing Content.") By default, polls are promoted to the front page, with open commenting.
7. Click Save. You now see your poll as visitors with voting permission see it **B**.

To manage polls:

1. By default, only users with the administrator role may vote in polls. To allow others to vote, click People in the Toolbar **C**. Then click the Permissions tab and scroll down to the Poll section to select the check boxes next to "Vote on polls." Scroll to the bottom and click "Save permissions."

   For more details about permissions and roles, see Chapter 7.

   Visitors vote by clicking the radio button of choice, then clicking Vote. Anyone who has voted already, or who doesn't have permission to vote, sees a bar-graph representation of the results instead of the poll questions **D**.

2. To see how people voted, click the Votes tab. You'll see only votes cast by individuals, not those faked by the administrator **E**. Votes from anonymous users (if permitted) appear with the user's Internet Protocol (IP) address in the Visitor column, or **::1** if the vote is from the machine on which the site is hosted.

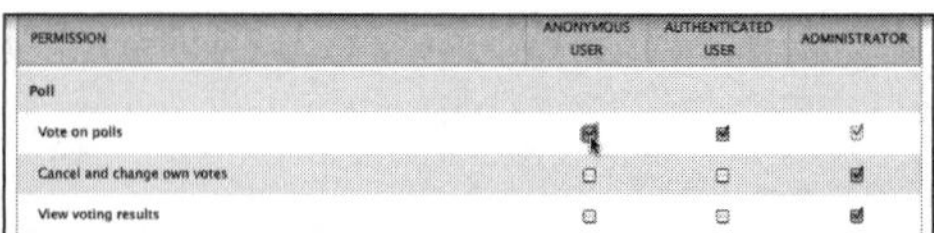

C Setting permissions to allow anonymous and authenticated users to vote on polls

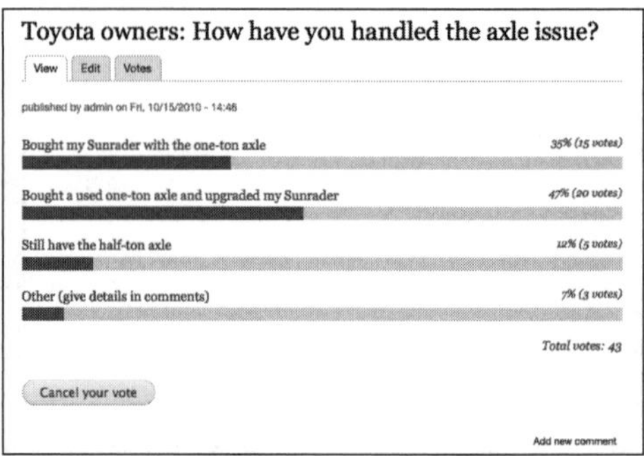

D Poll results with a count of 43 votes, whether by individual voters or faked by the administrator

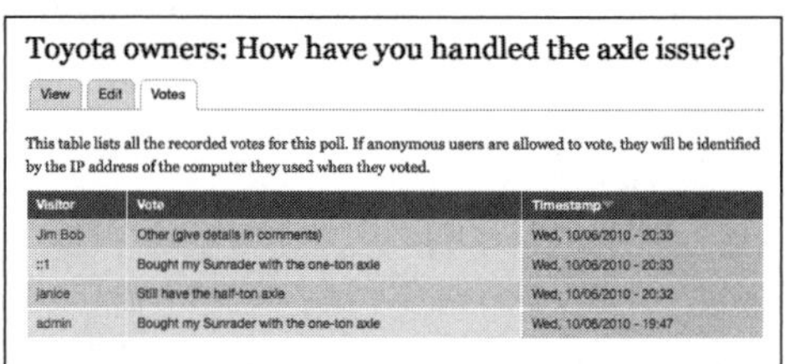

Toyota owners: How have you handled the axle issue?

View | Edit | Votes

This table lists all the recorded votes for this poll. If anonymous users are allowed to vote, they will be identified by the IP address of the computer they used when they voted.

Visitor	Vote	Timestamp
Jim Bob	Other (give details in comments)	Wed, 10/06/2010 - 20:33
::1	Bought my Sunrader with the one-ton axle	Wed, 10/06/2010 - 20:33
janice	Still have the half-ton axle	Wed, 10/06/2010 - 20:32
admin	Bought my Sunrader with the one-ton axle	Wed, 10/06/2010 - 19:47

E Vote records showing how authenticated and anonymous users voted

To set up discussion boards (forums):

1. Click Modules in the Toolbar. Enable the Forum module, then scroll down and click "Save configuration."

   The Forum module requires that the Comment and Taxonomy modules also be enabled (they are by default). If they've become disabled for any reason, Drupal will display a screen offering to enable them when you click Continue.

2. A new Forums link appears in the Navigation menu in the left column. Clicking that link leads to the forums themselves. To reach the Forums administration page, click Structure in the Toolbar and then click Forums.

   This page shows a list of forums and containers you created, which at first contains only one forum, "General discussion" **F**. It also has links to add forums and containers, which we'll discuss in the section "To create forums and containers."

continues on next page

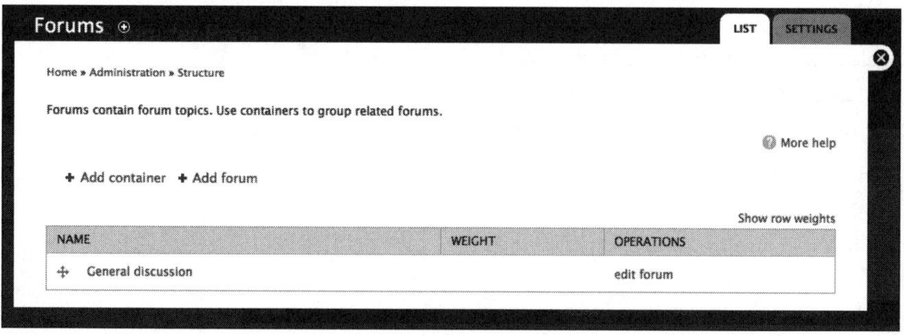

F The Forums administration page as it appears before you make any changes

3. The Settings tab leads to a screen where you can change three facets of your forums' appearance **G**.

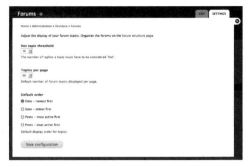

   ▸ Hot topic threshold: Determines how many comments a topic needs to receive before its icon changes to show that it's unusually active, or "hot" **H**.

   ▸ Topics per page: Says how many topics appear without the visitor having to click a "next" link at the bottom of the screen. Smaller numbers allow the page to load faster but could be inconvenient to visitors in busy forums.

   ▸ Default order: Lets you change how a forum's page of topics initially appears to visitors. (Once there, they can change the order of topics on the page by clicking headers at the top of each column, as you saw in the section "To see a list of content on your site" in Chapter 3.)

4. By default, only users with the administrator role may create, edit, or delete forum topics. To grant these permissions to other roles, click People in the Toolbar and then click the Permissions tab. Select the appropriate check boxes to grant permissions, then scroll to the bottom and click "Save permissions" **I**.

   For more details about permissions and roles, see Chapter 7.

G The forum settings screen

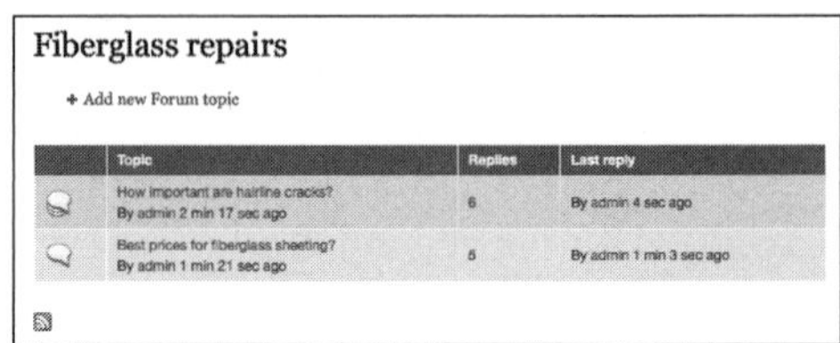

H Icon difference between topics with five and six comments when the "Hot topic threshold" is set to five

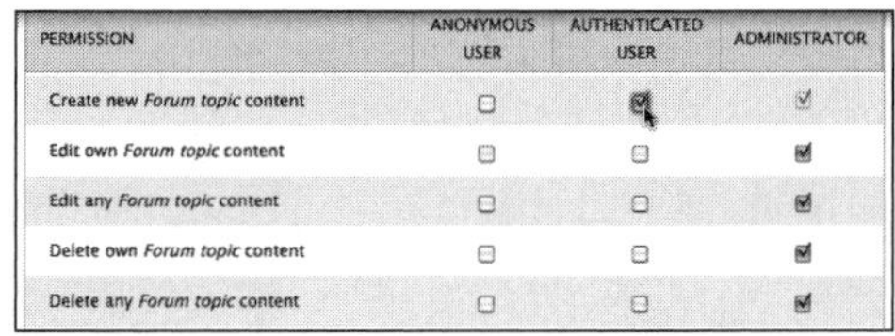

PERMISSION	ANONYMOUS USER	AUTHENTICATED USER	ADMINISTRATOR
Create new *Forum topic* content	☐	☑	☑
Edit own *Forum topic* content	☐	☐	☑
Edit any *Forum topic* content	☐	☐	☑
Delete own *Forum topic* content	☐	☐	☑
Delete any *Forum topic* content	☐	☐	☑

I Allowing authenticated users to start forum discussions

The Strange Language of Forums

Containers, forums, topics... Drupal's forum system introduces a new set of *terms,* some of which seem redundant. Here's what they all mean, going from the largest unit (the forum system as a whole) to the smallest (comments).

The page at **`http://domain-name/forum`** lists all forums and containers that you created. Containers, as the name implies, can contain either forums or other containers. You might, for example, have a container named "Car manufacturers" inside of which are the forums Toyota, Chevrolet, and Kia.

But forums can also contain other forums, so the Toyota forum might have Prius, Yaris, and Corolla forums inside it **J**. Someone could post a message inside any of those subforums (Prius), but also post directly to the top-level forum (Toyota).

However, nobody can post a message inside the container that encompasses them all ("Car manufacturers"): Containers can't directly hold messages.

Oh, and those messages? They're simply nodes of the content type "forum topic," and show up alongside articles and basic pages in the list of content you see when you click Content in the Toolbar. Comments made in response to forum topics are treated like any other comments within Drupal and appear in the Comment administration list.

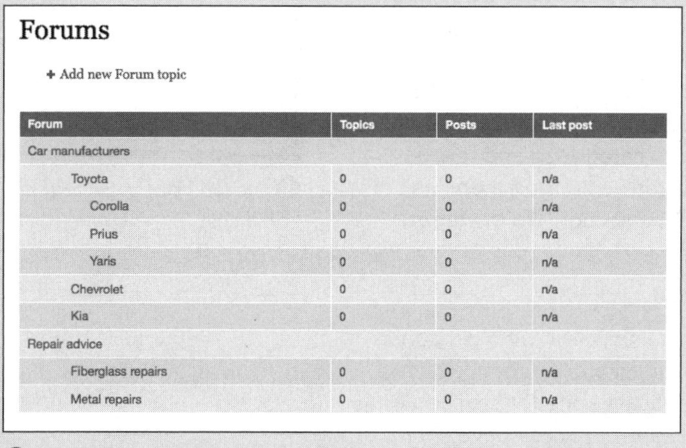

Forums

+ Add new Forum topic

Forum	Topics	Posts	Last post
Car manufacturers			
Toyota	0	0	n/a
Corolla	0	0	n/a
Prius	0	0	n/a
Yaris	0	0	n/a
Chevrolet	0	0	n/a
Kia	0	0	n/a
Repair advice			
Fiberglass repairs	0	0	n/a
Metal repairs	0	0	n/a

J A forum structure with containers and forums in a multi-level structure

To create forums and containers:

1. Click Structure in the Toolbar and then click Forums.

   Here you can create forums (where discussions take place) and containers (which group forums together). We'll first create a forum and then create a container for it. But Drupal's system for forums is flexible: You can create forums and containers at will and then reorganize them later if you prefer, as you'll see in the section "To manage forums."

2. Click the "Add forum" link and complete the form on the resulting page **K**.

   The Parent and Weight pop-up menus are handy for categorizing and reordering forums as you create them. These are very similar to the Book and Weight pop-up menus you see when you create book pages, as the section "To create books of linked content" in Chapter 3 described. As with books, it's often easier to categorize and reorder forums after you've created them, as you'll see in the section "To manage forums."

   When finished, click Save.

3. To add a container, click the "Add container" link and fill out the form, which is nearly identical to one for creating a forum. When finished, click Save.

   After you've created a forum or container, you return to the list of forums, with your new item in it **L**. To make any changes to an item, click the "edit forum" or "edit container" link to its right.

K Creating a forum

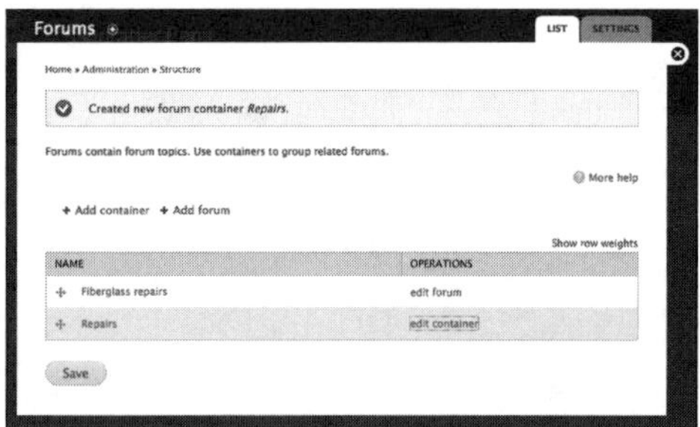

L The forum list page, after creating a forum and a container

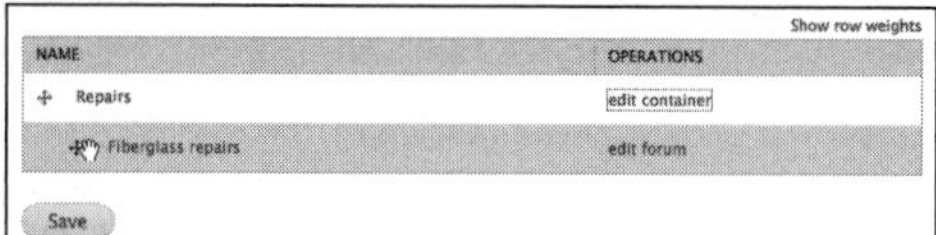

Ⓜ Moving the "Fiberglass repairs" forum so it's inside the Repairs container

To manage forums:

1. Click Structure in the Toolbar and then click Forums.
2. To rearrange items in the list, or to make one item contain another, grab the compass-like icon ✥ and drag it to the desired location Ⓜ. The process is similar to the one demonstrated in the section "To change a book's structure" in Chapter 3. After making changes, click Save.
3. Visitors with appropriate permissions can visit your forums by clicking the Forums link in the Navigation menu, or by going directly to **`http://`*`domain-name`*`/forum`**.
4. There are two ways to post a forum topic:
   - Click "Add new Forum topic" on any forum page, then select the desired forum from the Forum pop-up menu on the resulting page. If you clicked that link while viewing a specific forum, the Forum pop-up menu will already contain its name. Fill out the node edit form as usual and then click Save.

   or

   - Create a new node of the content type "Forum topic" by clicking Add content > Forum topic. Once on the "Create Forum topic" page, select the desired forum from the Forum pop-up menu, fill out the node edit form as usual, and then click Save.

Categorizing Content with Taxonomies

Many Drupal beginners overlook a powerful feature of Drupal: its system of labeling content with categories, known as *taxonomy*. That's because Drupal taxonomy is difficult to understand in the abstract and its terminology can be confusing at first. But a hypothetical example clarifies both its use and its value.

Let's say your site sells T-shirts, and you've set up a node for each T-shirt design. You have two taxonomy *vocabularies* set up: Color (with the terms Black, Gray, and White) and Size (with the terms Small, Medium, and Large). You "tag" each T-shirt node with terms from those vocabularies, according to the shirt's availability. A visitor to your site can then click a Medium link and see a page of all your shirts of that size, or click Gray to see all shirts of that color.

You've already used taxonomies in this chapter without realizing it: When you create a forum or forum container, Drupal actually adds its name as a term in the Forum *vocabulary*. Further, Drupal comes with a vocabulary called *Tags* to hold terms you enter when creating or editing a node of the article content type.

Now you're going to learn how to create your own vocabularies and fill them with terms that will make your site easier to navigate and more useful to visitors.

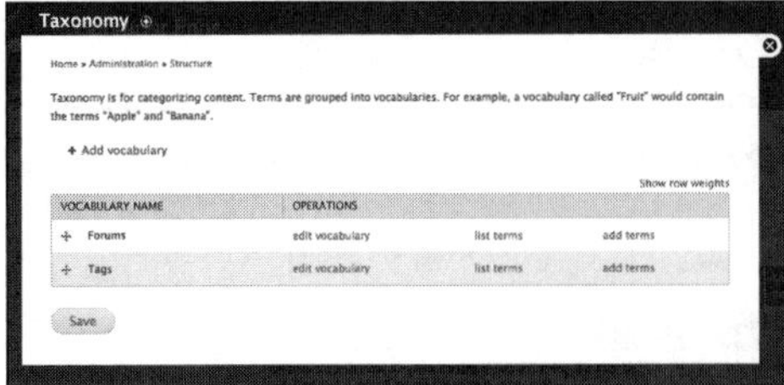

A The Taxonomy settings page, showing both the Forums vocabulary (enabled by the Forum module) and the default Tags vocabulary

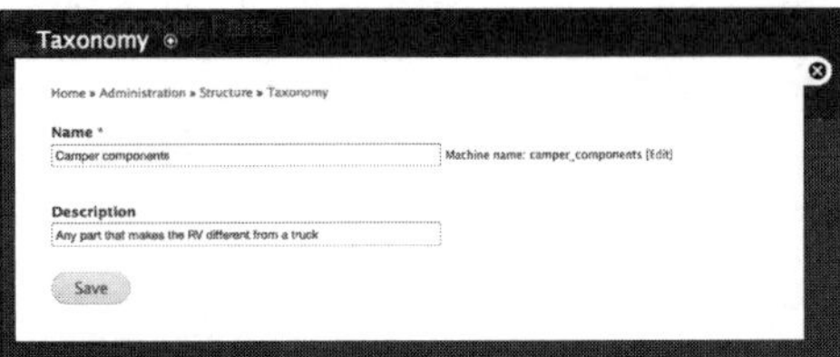

B A completed vocabulary edit form

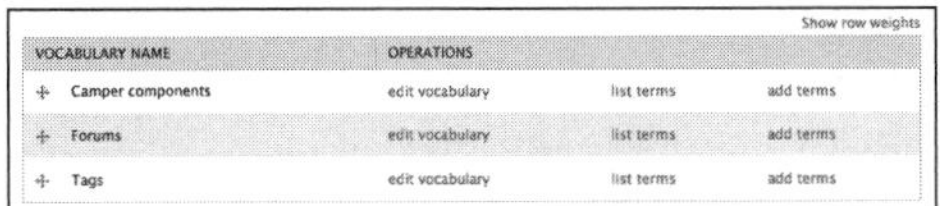

C The Taxonomy page, with the new vocabulary in place

To set up a taxonomy's vocabulary:

1. To see a list of active vocabularies, go to the Taxonomy administration page by clicking Structure in the Toolbar and then clicking Taxonomy **A**.
2. Click "Add vocabulary" to go to the vocabulary edit form **B**. The Description is not displayed directly by Drupal at all. But it's available to developers, so it might show up when you install modules or add custom programming. (For information about installing modules, see Chapter 9, "Extending Drupal with Modules.")
3. When finished, click Save. You now see your new vocabulary in alphabetical order on the Taxonomy page **C**. You can move it to another place by dragging the compass-like icon ✣.

To use a vocabulary in content:

1. Click Structure in the Toolbar and then click "Content types." Click "manage fields" next to the content type whose nodes you'd like to categorize.

   If you need help with creation or management of content types, see the "Defining Custom Types of Content" section in Chapter 4, "Customizing Content."

2. Add a new field, as you learned to do in the "To add fields to a custom content type" section in Chapter 4. Select "Term reference" as the field type **D**.

   You have three options for the widget:

   - Select list: Presents terms as either a multiple-select list, or as a pop-up menu if you've specified that users can select only one option **E** **F**. (You can control how many options a user may select on the field settings page.) When presented as a multiple-select list, users can choose multiple options by pressing Command (Mac), Control (Windows), or Shift (both) while clicking.

     In either case, you'll need to manually add terms to the vocabulary to provide the options from which users will select. (You'll learn how to do that in the section "To add terms to a vocabulary.")

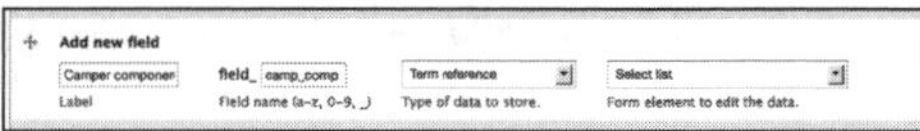

D Adding a vocabulary field to a content type

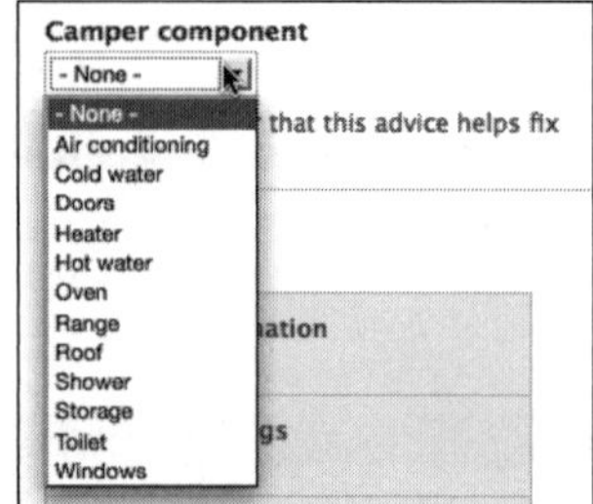

E Appearance of the term entry field when you select "Select list" and allow users to enter only one term

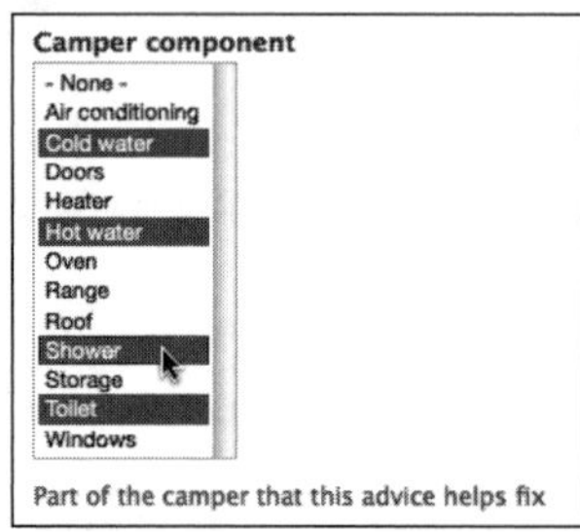

F Appearance of the term entry field when you select "Select list" and allow users to enter more than one term

- Check boxes/radio buttons: Presents terms as check boxes, or as radio buttons if you've specified that users can select only one option **G** **H**.
- Autocomplete term widget (tagging): Lets users add terms to a vocabulary by typing them in when editing a node with that vocabulary available **I**. As they type, Drupal suggests existing terms by presenting a list of terms that begin with the letters entered.

3. When you've finished configuring the vocabulary, click Save.

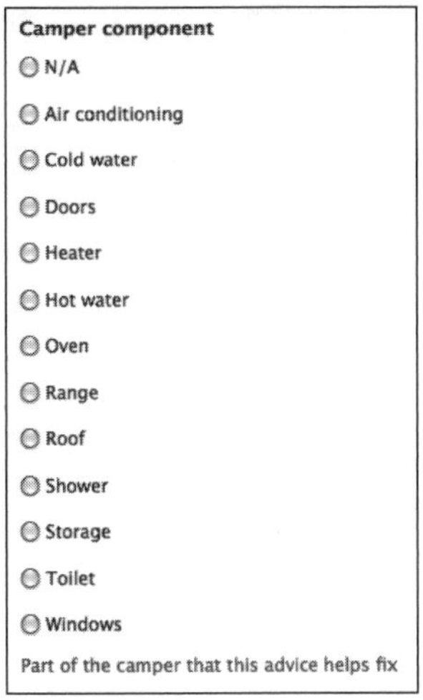

Camper component

- N/A
- Air conditioning
- Cold water
- Doors
- Heater
- Hot water
- Oven
- Range
- Roof
- Shower
- Storage
- Toilet
- Windows

Part of the camper that this advice helps fix

G Appearance of the term entry field when you select "Check boxes/radio buttons" and allow users to enter only one term

Camper component

- Air conditioning
- Cold water
- Doors
- Heater
- Hot water
- Oven
- Range
- Roof
- Shower
- Storage
- Toilet
- Windows

Part of the camper that this advice helps fix

H Appearance of the term entry field when you select "Check boxes/radio buttons" and allow users to enter more than one term

Camper component

Part of the camper that this advice helps fix

I Appearance of the term entry field when you select "Autocomplete term widget (tagging)"

To add terms to a vocabulary:

1. Go to the Taxonomy administration page by clicking Structure in the Toolbar and then clicking Taxonomy.
2. There are two ways to add terms to a vocabulary. Next to the vocabulary you want to augment, *either*:
   - Click "add terms."

   or

   - Click "list terms" and then click the "Add term" link.
3. On the resulting term edit form, the only field you're obliged to fill in is Name **J**.

   The text in the Description field appears both in news feeds that your site publishes automatically, and at the top of the page that Drupal presents when someone clicks the term. The URL alias lets you define an alternative way to get to that page, in the form of **`http://domain/`*`url-alias`***. Whether you indicate a URL alias or not, the page URL will be in the form of **`http://`*`domain`*`/taxonomy/term/`*`number`***.
4. Click the Relations link for greater control over this taxonomy term **K**.

   The "Parent terms" field lets you set up taxonomy terms as a complex hierarchy. For example, let's say we wanted to group our terms into larger categories, so that Toilet and Shower would both be under a Water category. If we'd planned that from the beginning, we would create the Water category first, then select it as the parent when creating the Toilet and Shower categories.

   One advantage to this system is that you can set multiple parents for a term. For example, a "Hot water" entry could have both Water and Heating as parents.

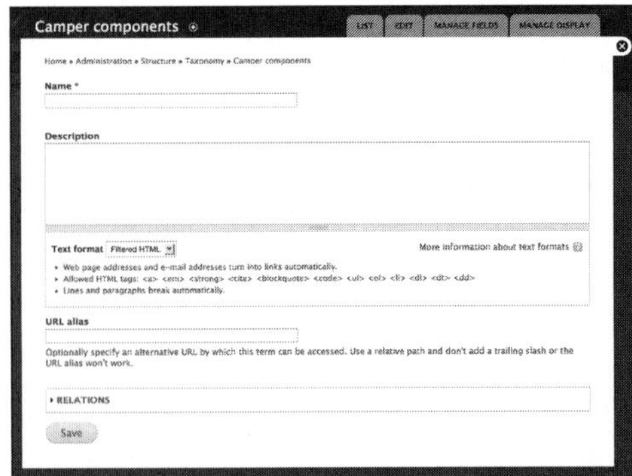

J Adding a term to the "Camper components" vocabulary

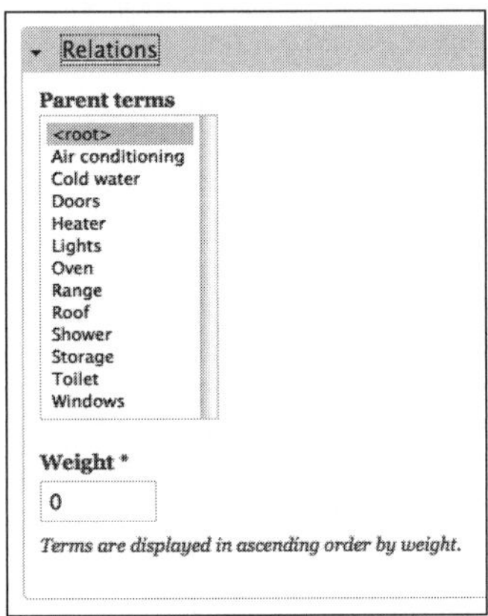

K Controls to change term relationships and positioning in a vocabulary's list of terms

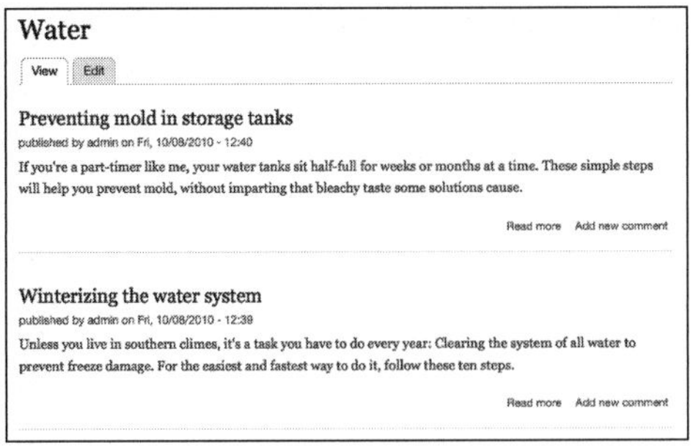

Water

View Edit

Preventing mold in storage tanks

published by admin on Fri, 10/08/2010 - 12:40

If you're a part-timer like me, your water tanks sit half-full for weeks or months at a time. These simple steps will help you prevent mold, without imparting that bleachy taste some solutions cause.

Read more Add new comment

Winterizing the water system

published by admin on Fri, 10/08/2010 - 12:39

Unless you live in southern climes, it's a task you have to do every year: Clearing the system of all water to prevent freeze damage. For the easiest and fastest way to do it, follow these ten steps.

Read more Add new comment

L The page that appears when a user clicks the Water link, showing all nodes tagged with that taxonomy term

Keeping Tags on Taxonomies

Even people who are completely comfortable with taxonomy concepts can get bogged down on the details of their implementation. Often it's a matter of choice whether to divide information by content type or taxonomy term, and the Parent feature complicates the matter further.

If your site requires complicated taxonomy, I recommend that you plan it first on paper—but expect to change it as you go. Start with a fairly simple, non-hierarchical system: You can always change its organization later. If you intend to allow visitors to tag nodes freely, keep an eye on what terms they're adding by occasionally clicking the "list terms" link next to the relevant vocabulary on the Taxonomy administration page.

The Weight pop-up lets you rearrange terms so they appear in your chosen order rather than alphabetical order.

TIP Although Drupal permits multi-word terms (for example, "Trip reports"), it's a good idea to limit yourself to single-word terms when you have the choice. There are some situations where terms appear right next to each other, and it can be hard to tell the difference between a two-word term and two one-word terms.

TIP As with forums, it's much easier to set "Parent terms" and Weight *after* you've created your terms, because Drupal provides a graphical interface to do so on the "List terms" page. To use it, click the "List terms" tab and drag terms around as the section "To manage forums" described. However, you can't set up multiple parentage (as in our "Hot water" example) using this graphical system.

To view taxonomy terms in content:

1. When you create or edit a node that allows entry of taxonomy terms, you'll have the option to choose terms that relate to the node's content. The interface varies depending on settings for the taxonomy's vocabulary. For clarification, see the section "To set up a taxonomy's vocabulary" earlier in this chapter.
2. When visitors view nodes that have been tagged, its terms generally appear near the node's main content. (Exactly where they appear depends on your site's active theme.) Clicking a term leads to a page that shows the Summary section of all nodes tagged with that term **L**.

Mastering Text Formats

A lot of Drupal's genius is hidden from view, for example in its security safeguards. One such safeguard is its handling of user input, which counteracts attacks made on a site through "tricky" input such as PHP code or malformed HTML. By default, Drupal blocks such input by throwing away any part that seems unusual, allowing only a few tried-and-true HTML tags via its "Filtered HTML" format. A second format, "Full HTML," allows all HTML tags. That's potentially more dangerous because it could (for example) allow an attacker to redirect visitors to another site, but it's often useful when you've allowed input only from trusted sources. A third option allows entry of code in the programming language PHP, providing unbridled flexibility at an even greater cost of security.

You can also add your own text formats for special purposes—if, for example, you'd like to allow only the HTML tags for bold and italic styles. Further, Drupal's core (and some contributed modules) extends text formats with additional filters that format input automatically. For example, the htmLawed module (**`drupal.org/project/htmLawed`**) adds filters to make users' HTML entry more secure and "correct."

To select a text format for an individual node:

1. Go to the node's edit form, either by creating a new node or by editing an existing one.
2. Below the area where you enter the node's "Full text" content is the "Text format" pop-up menu **A**. Three are available by default: Filtered HTML (which limits available tags to a small handful), Full HTML, and Plain text (which strips all HTML content while converting web and email addresses into clickable links).

   Just below the pop-up menu is text that briefly clarifies features of the currently selected text format. For a considerably longer description, click the "More information about text formats" link to the right of the pop-up menu.
3. When you've finished editing the node, click Save. Drupal applies your text format choice to both the Summary and Full text of the node when it is displayed.

To change the default text format selection:

1. Click Configuration in the Toolbar and then click "Text formats" to reach the Text Formats administration page.
2. Click the compass-like icon next to the text format you'd like to be the default selection and drag it to the top of the list, then click "Save changes" **B**.

   All new nodes from now on will show this selection by default in the node edit form. (Text formats of existing nodes remain the same.)

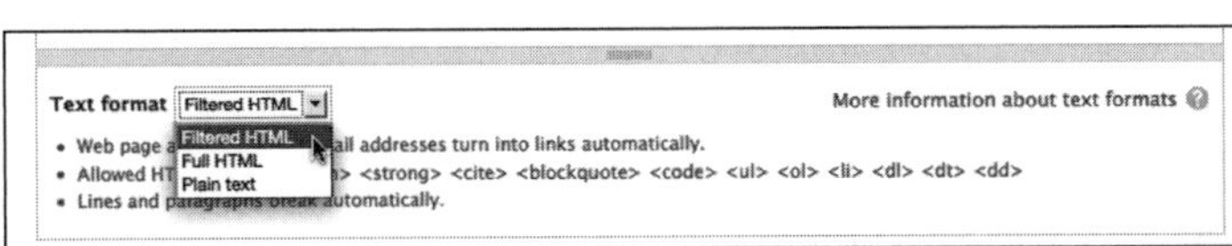

A Selecting a text format from the three default choices

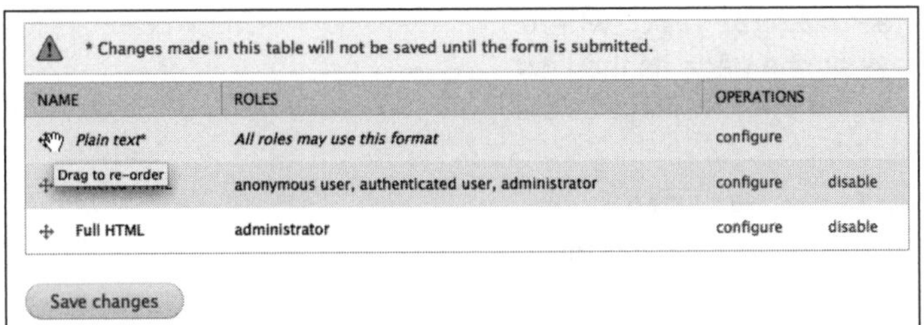

B Changing the default text format to Plain text

To add a new text format:

1. Click Configuration in the Toolbar and then click “Text formats.” Click “Add text format” **C**.

2. Enter a name for the text format in the Name field. This will appear alongside Filtered HTML and Full HTML in the list of text formats on the Text Format administration page and in the “Text format” pop-up menu when you edit a node.

3. Select which user roles have access to this text format. The options are discrete. That is, even though authenticated users usually have more access to your Drupal site than anonymous users, here you can grant text-format access to anonymous users without automatically granting it to authenticated users. For more information about user permissions, see Chapter 7.

4. Select desired options in the Filters section. They are:

   - Limit allowed HTML tags: Lets you permit only tags that you specify. Selecting this check box reveals controls at the bottom of the screen where you can specify permitted tags.

   - Display any HTML as plain text: Shows HTML exactly as it’s entered, without applying it to the text. For example, a tag such as `<br />` would be converted to `<br />`, where `<` displays on the page as the less-than bracket and `>` displays as the greater-than bracket.

   - Convert line breaks into HTML (i.e., `<br>` and `<p>`): Prevents paragraphs from running together.

   - Convert URLs into links: Allows content contributors to simply

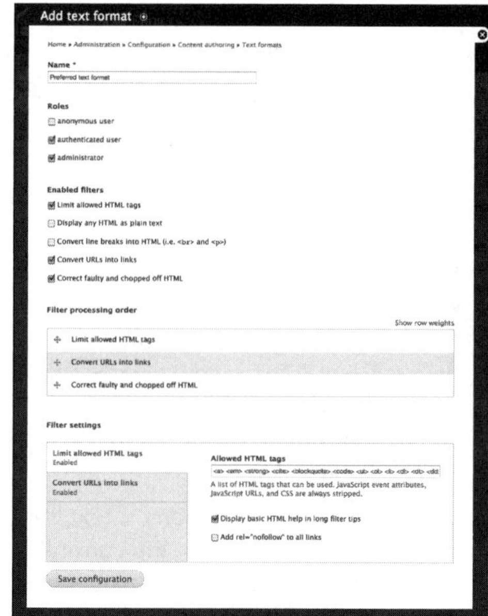

C Creating a custom text format

type web and email addresses that become clickable without the addition of any HTML code. As a result, the typed text **http://www.example.com** effectively becomes **<a href="http://www.example.com" title="http://www.example.com"> http://www.example.com</a>**, and **user@example.com** becomes **<a href="mailto:user@example.com">user@example.com</a>**.

- Correct faulty and chopped off HTML: Redeems a number of sins, for example by closing improperly entered tags. Without this filter enabled, an errant tag could affect all content that follows it on the page.

Both the "PHP filter" in Drupal's core and some downloadable modules add other filters. (The "Filters/editors" category at **drupal.org/project/modules** contains most of the downloadable modules that add text format filters.) For information about the PHP filter module, see the section "To permit PHP in content" later in this chapter.

5. If you have multiple filters enabled, you might find that they're not acting as you expect because they're processing text in the wrong order.

   For example, let's say you wanted to teach someone HTML by letting them enter a simple URL like **http://www.example.com** and receive the HTML code **<a href="http://www.example.com" title="http://www.example.com">http://www.example.com</a>**. To do so, you'd want the text to first go through the "Convert URLs into links" filter, and then the "Display any HTML as plain text" filter. But if they go in

continues on next page

the reverse order, the results are quite different!

In such instances, you can change the order in which text format filters are applied by grabbing the compass-like icons and dragging the text formats to their desired locations **D**.

6. If you selected the "Limit allowed HTML tags" check box, you'll see a vertical tab at the bottom of the page where you can change that option's settings **E**. The settings are:

   ▸ Allowed HTML tags: This is where you list all tags that you want to permit content contributors to use.

   ▸ Display basic HTML help in long filter tips: Provides substantial help text if a content contributor clicks the "More information about text formats" link when editing a node, as the section "To select a text format for an individual node" described.

   ▸ Add rel="nofollow" to all links: Adds a small amount of text to link HTML in order to reduce the effectiveness of spam activity on your site.

   Spammers often attempt to post garbage content that contains a popular search phrase linked to the URL for a site they're advertising. Their goal is to make search engines (such as Google and Yahoo) relate their sites to those popular search phrases, so that when people search for those phrases, the spammers' sites will show up near the top of the list.

   But most popular search engines discard links that have the **`rel="nofollow"`** tag, so such trickery on your Drupal site won't work when you've selected this check box.

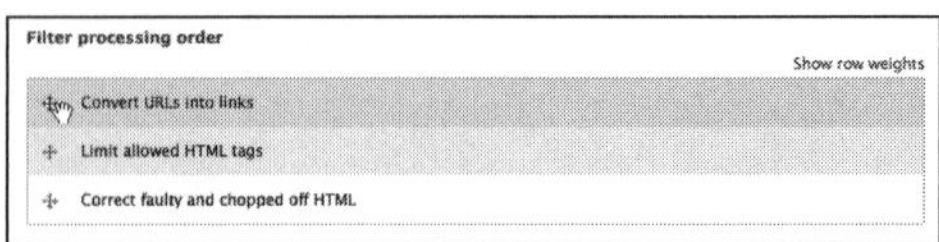

D Changing the order of filters on a text format

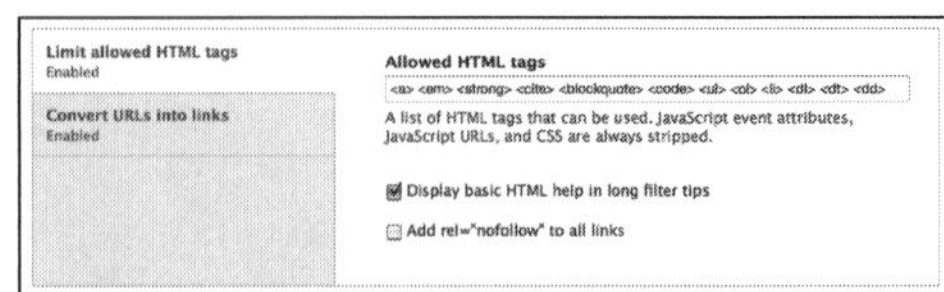

E Options available when you select the "Limit allowed HTML tags" check box

7. If you selected the "Convert URLs into links" check box, you'll see a vertical tab at the bottom of the page where you can specify how long URLs may appear.

   The link works the same regardless of this setting: Only the text *displayed* changes. For example, if you set the "Maximum link text length" value to 15 and then type in the URL **`http://www.example.com/path/index.html`**, Drupal will display the link as **`http://www.exam...`**. (The **`http://`** is considered part of the URL's character count.)

8. When you've set up the text format as you wish, click "Save configuration."

To permit PHP in content:

1. Go to the Modules page by clicking Modules in the Toolbar.
2. Select the check box to enable the "PHP filter" module, then scroll to the bottom of the screen and click "Save configuration."
3. Click Configuration in the Toolbar and then click "Text formats." Along with Filtered HTML, Full HTML, and any text formats you created, there is now a text format "PHP code"; however, nobody (except the site's superuser) has permission to use it when posting content.
4. To make the PHP code text format available to other users, click the "configure" link. The resulting page is similar to the one you see when creating a new text format, as was demonstrated in the section "To add a new text format." Select check boxes to allow users of specific roles to use the PHP code text format. (For more information about user roles and permissions, see Chapter 7.)

continues on next page

5. Permitted users may now enter PHP code in a node by choosing "PHP code" from the "Text format" pop-up menu **F**.

   There are subtleties in Drupal's PHP handling, and errors can damage or even break your site. Therefore, it's imperative that everyone with PHP posting access read the information available by clicking the "More information about text formats" link.

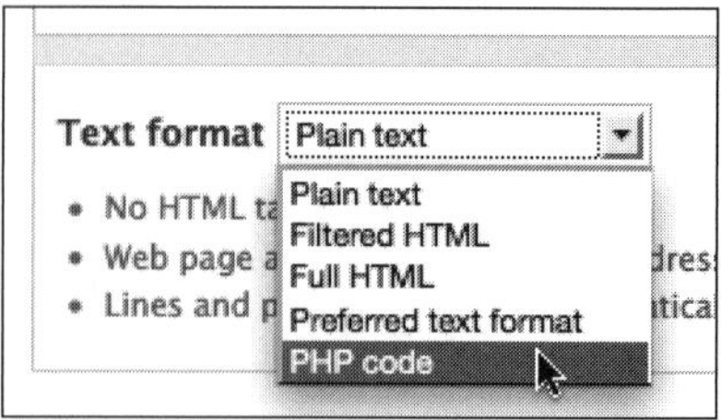

F Applying the PHP code text format via a menu that also includes a custom text format and the three default text formats

Danger Zone: "Full HTML" and "PHP code" Text Formats

You can't permit PHP input without talking about security, because PHP is the very rock on which Drupal is built. Exposing it is like exposing the thoracic cavity for open-heart surgery: necessary and useful, perhaps, but not for beginners.

How dangerous is it? At the very least, someone could learn the details of your server's configuration with the simple line `<?php phpinfo(); ?>`, and then take advantage of any weaknesses found within. Worse, someone could do all sorts of tricks using something called code injection, essentially bypassing Drupal's security measures and giving orders directly to your MySQL database. An attacker could delete all your site's content, take it offline, and change the superuser's password with just a few lines of code.

Even if there's no malice intended, a small PHP error could crash your site or destroy its data. So you have to be sure that your code is correct in a general sense *and* that it conforms to what Drupal expects. Some guidelines are in the "More information about text formats" link next to the "Text format" pop-up menu; further details are at **drupal.org/handbook/customization/php-snippets**.

Less risky—but still unsafe—is the Full HTML text format. Although someone can't reach into Drupal's innards with the same recklessness, it still exposes your site to such exploits as cross-site scripting (XSS), which could be used to (for example) steal private data from your site's users.

The twin solutions? First, enable the PHP filter module only if absolutely necessary. (You could also delete the Full HTML text format, although its lower risk makes that less crucial.) Second, check the text formats' permissions to ensure that they're available only to those user roles that need them—and can use them responsibly.

Mastering Image Styles

When you create an article-type node, you have the option to upload an image. While you're editing the node, it appears in a small "thumbnail" format; when visitors see it on the page, it's been resized to be no larger than 480 pixels square.

You can change both of those settings and even add your own. You could do this in Drupal 6, but only if you uploaded and configured the ImageAPI, ImageField, ImageCache, and FileField modules. Drupal 7 incorporates the important parts of those modules into its core and simplifies their interfaces.

Drupal's system of image styles makes graphic fields consistent throughout the site: If you change the size of the "large" image style, then the appearance of every image with that style will change automatically. (It doesn't change images that you've embedded using HTML, however.) Drupal holds onto the original image, so you don't need to worry about upsampling if you first shrink an image and then later enlarge it.

To change image styles in content:

1. Edit the display settings for an image field. For our example, we'll change the settings of the Image field in the article content type. To do so, click Structure in the Toolbar and then click "Content types." Then click "manage display" in the Article row **A**. You now see the page where you can change the appearance of fields in the article content type **B**.

   For further help editing a field's settings, see the section "Defining Custom Types of Content" in Chapter 4.

2. Click the small gear icon in the Image field's row. A set of controls appears **C**.

3 Click the "Image style" pop-up menu to change how images in this field will appear. (You can also affect what will happen when visitors click the image by changing the "Link image to" pop-up menu.) Click Update.

4. Click Save. All images in that field will be resized to reflect your changes the next time a visitor views them.

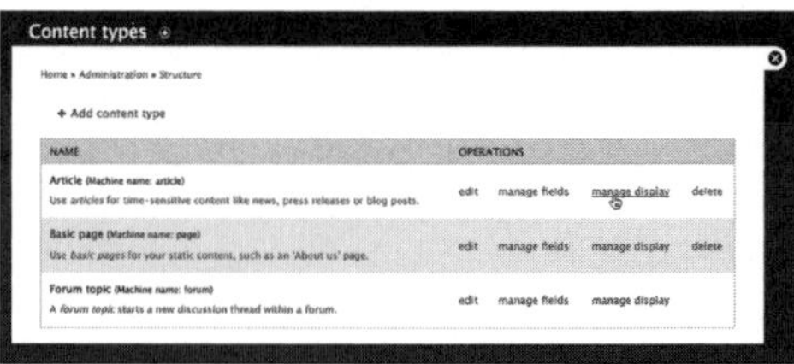

A The link to manage field display for the article content type

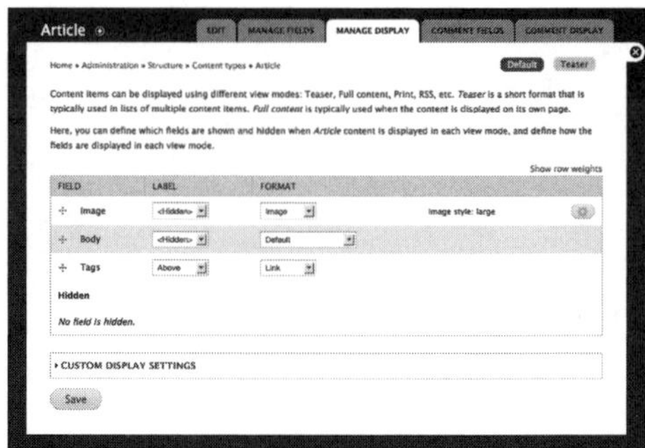

B The Manage Display screen for the article content type

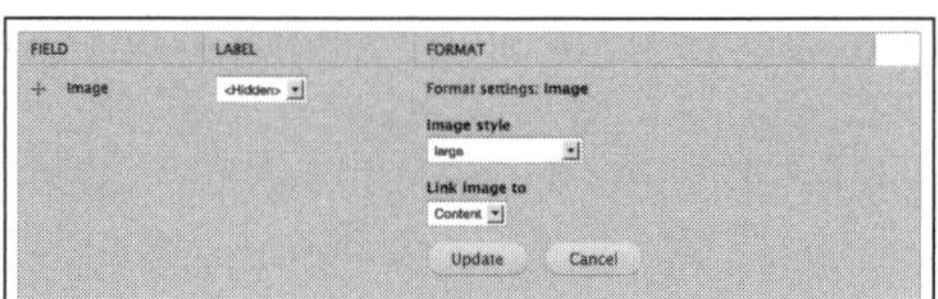

C Controls to change the appearance of the Image field

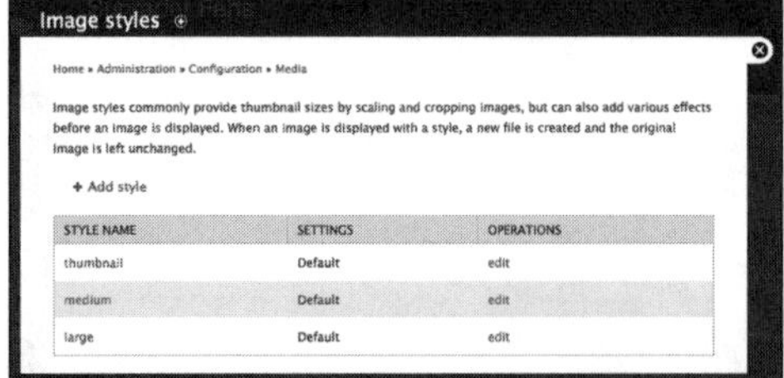

D The image styles management page

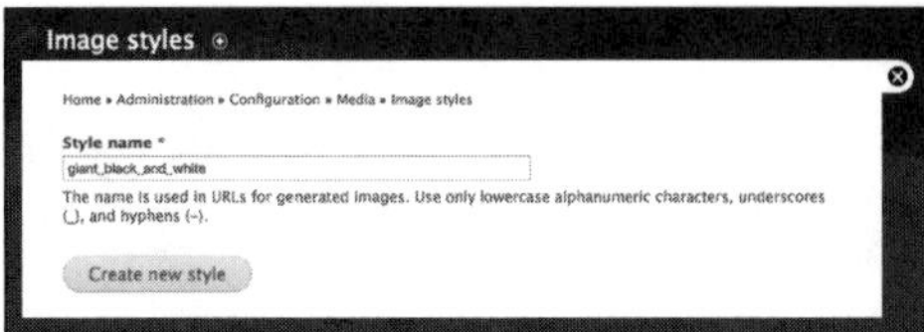

E Creating a new image style

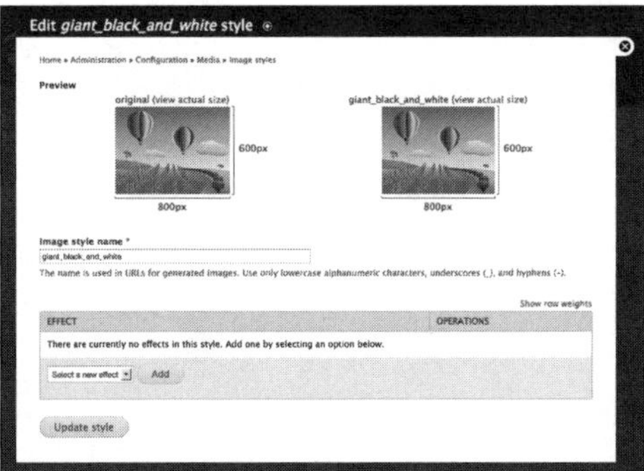

F The page where you change the image style's effects

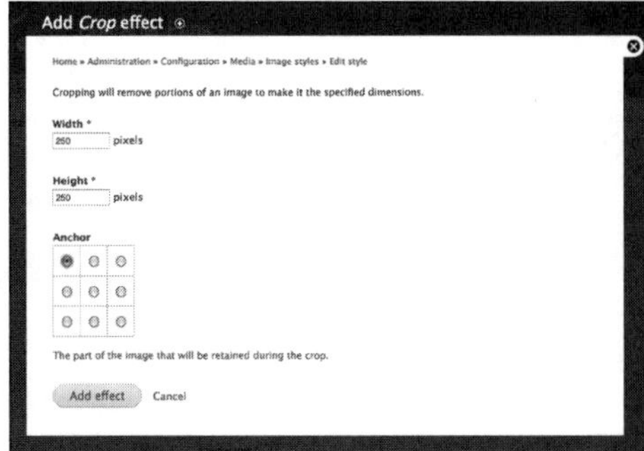

G Setting criteria for the Crop effect

To create or edit image styles:

1 Click Configuration in the Toolbar and then click "Image styles" to go to the image styles management page **D**.

2. To add a new style, click the "Add style" link.

3. On the resulting page, enter the name for your new style and click the "Create new style" button **E**.

   The next page provides a preview of your changes, an opportunity to change the image style's name, and a place to apply effects to your image style **F**. We'll focus only on this last section.

4. Click the "Select a new effect" pop-up menu. The options are:

   - Crop: Cuts off portions of the image that are larger than the size you specify. When you select this option and click Add, a screen of settings appears where you can decide which of nine regions is most important to keep; the image will be trimmed from the edge that is farthest from that "anchor" **G**.
   - Desaturate: Removes color information from the image—in other words, makes it a black-and-white graphic.
   - Resize: Forces the image to be the width and height you specify on its settings screen. This option may "stretch" the image so it appears taller or flatter than before.
   - Rotate: Spins the image from its center point. This effect's settings screen lets you specify the degree of rotation and the color that will appear in areas vacated by the corners of the images. There's also a Randomize check box, which applies a random rotation

continues on next page

angle and makes the "Rotation angle" setting meaningless **H**.

- Scale: Shrinks the image to fit in the dimensions you specify, while maintaining its proportions. Selecting the "Allow upscaling" check box tells Drupal to enlarge smaller images to the specified size.
- Scale and crop: Forces the image to fit into your specified dimensions by shrinking to the point that one dimension fits, then trimming off the other dimension from the center as needed.

For all effects except Desaturate (which has no settings screen), click the "Add effect" button when you're finished providing the effect's settings.

5. The Effects list now shows which effects will be applied to images of this style and in what order **I**. The order could make a difference, particularly if your list of effects includes cropping; to change it, grab the compass-like icon ✣ and drag the effects into your preferred order.
6. When you've made all the changes you want, click "Update style."

   To edit an existing image style, return to the image styles management page and click "edit" next to the style you want to change.

TIP **Use the Scale option when you want to resize a graphic but retain the entire image in its original proportions. Crop and "Scale and crop" may remove portions of the image, while Resize may change its proportions.**

TIP **Selecting the "Allow upscaling" option when scaling an image will give images a consistent size, but will also make most smaller images look worse.**

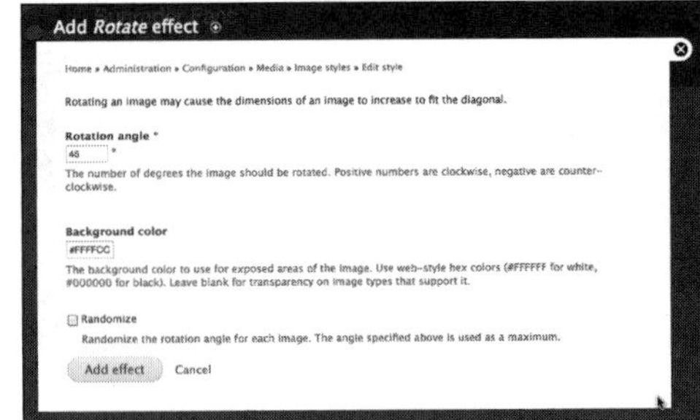

H Setting criteria for the Rotate effect

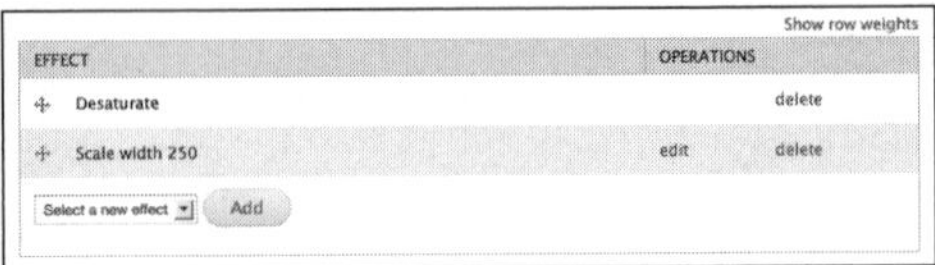

I A list of effects to apply to an image style

6

Improving Access to Content

Librarians have a saying: "You don't need to know everything. You just need to know how to *find out about* everything." As the administrator for your Drupal site, you're the librarian, with power to make information easy to find and understand... or not.

Drupal gives you tools to organize your content, most importantly:

- Search
- Menus
- Blocks

The first two are fairly easy to explain, and in fact you already learned a little about menus in the section "To create a menu item that links to a node" in Chapter 3, "Creating and Managing Content."

Blocks, on the other hand, have far more options. They are in essence a layout system, albeit one that's corralled into specified *block regions*, defined by the theme. Despite their limitations, blocks give you a lot of opportunities to turn a generic theme into a presentation of content that's distinctly yours.

In This Chapter

Making Content Searchable

Google shocked the Internet in 1998 by proposing a minimalist search interface as an alternative to Yahoo's sprawling home page. Rather than categorizing content into numerous squirrel-holes, as Yahoo did, Google presented visitors with a simple search box—and changed the direction of the web for the better.

The simple search box continues to dominate how people find content, and your Drupal site comes with one already installed. Drupal shields you from most of the complicated inner workings of its search engine, but it does give you a few points of control, should you decide to take advantage of them.

Specifically, you can change how the site prepares content for searching; the minimum length of search terms; and how important various aspects of content are in deciding which to list first.

PERMISSION	ANONYMOUS USER	AUTHENTICATED USER	ADMINISTRATOR
Search			
Administer search	☐	☐	☑
Use search	☑	☑	☑
Use advanced search	☐	☑	☑

A Setting search permissions to allow anonymous users to search the site, and authenticated users to perform both simple and advanced searches

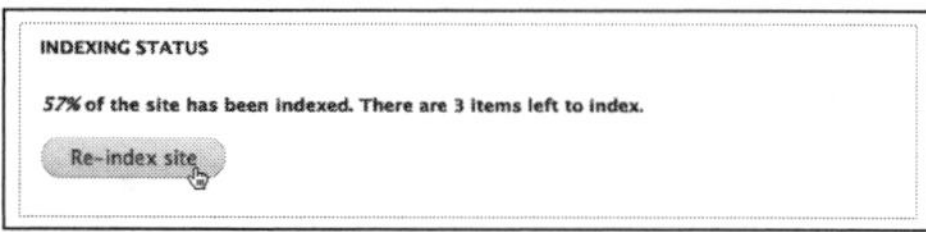

INDEXING STATUS
57% of the site has been indexed. There are 3 items left to index.
Re-index site

B Forcing Drupal to review all nodes on the site to make their contents available for searching the next time cron runs

To make your site searchable:

1. Drupal comes with its Search module enabled by default, but only allows the superuser and those users with the administrator role to search the site.

   To grant that permission to others, click People in the Toolbar and then click Permissions. Scroll down to the Search section and select the appropriate check boxes **A**. When finished, scroll to the bottom and click "Save permissions."

   For further information about user roles and permissions, see Chapter 7, "Wrangling Users."

2. Although the site appears to be searchable, searches find only text that Drupal has processed, or *indexed*. That indexing occurs every time Drupal's periodic housekeeping processes run—which, by default, is once every three hours.

   However, you can force Drupal to index content immediately by running cron, a program that performs periodic maintenance tasks on your site. To do so:

   - Click Reports in the Toolbar and then click "Status report."
   - Click the link under "Cron maintenance tasks" labeled "You can run cron manually."

   If you want to force Drupal to delete the old index and re-index the entire site:

   - Go to the Search settings page by clicking Configuration in the Toolbar and then clicking "Search settings."
   - Click the "Re-index site" button **B**. Drupal will re-index your site the next time that cron runs, whether that happens manually or at the end of cron's three-hour period.

To perform simple and advanced searches:

1. In Drupal's default configuration, a search box is in the left column for all users with search access **C**. A search page that includes advanced search options is available at **`http://`** ***`domain-name`*****`/search`**.

   To perform a search, simply enter the desired text and click the magnifying-glass icon or press Return. Drupal will look for nodes that contain *all* the words you specify, in any order **D**. The resulting page shows:

   - The search box, containing the text you searched for. (You can perform another search here as well.)
   - A link that reveals controls for advanced searches.
   - A short snippet from each search result (*hit*), with the sought-after term highlighted.
   - Other information about the node that contains the hit.

   To see the full node, click the hit's title—in this case, "Welcome to the Sunrader enthusiasts site!"

C Drupal's search box

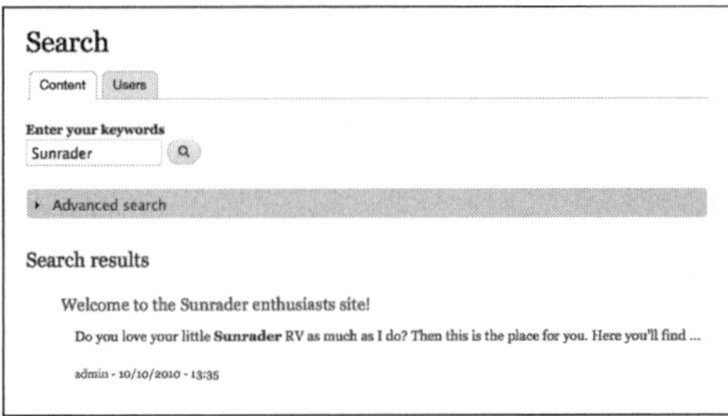

D The resulting page from a search with one "hit"

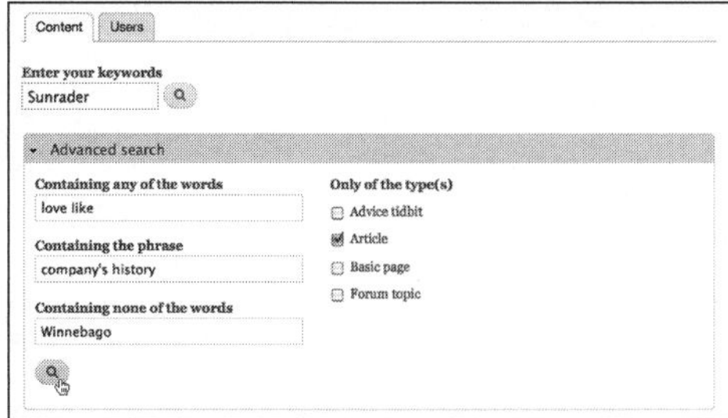

E The "Advanced search" form

2. From here, users with "Use advanced search" permission can perform complex searches by clicking the "Advanced search" link **E**. Newly revealed options let them:
   - Search for words logically separated by *or*, so a search with **`Sunrader parts`** in this field will search for **`Sunrader`** *or* **`parts`**.
   - Search for phrases.
   - Search for pages that contain a certain term, but that *don't* contain another term.
   - Search only within nodes of certain content types.

TIP Searches find full words only: A search for `under` or `stand` won't find a node containing the word "understand."

TIP Case doesn't matter, so a search for `pizza` returns the same results as one for `Pizza`.

TIP Searches must contain at least one "positive" search term. That is, you can't find all pages that *lack* a certain term. (Drupal displays an error if you fill out only the "Containing none of the words" field.)

TIP All the features of the "Advanced search" form are actually available within the simple search form as well: You just have to know how to construct advanced search queries manually. For example, the search in E would be `http://`*`domain-name`*`/search/node/Sunrader%20type%3Aarticle%20love%20OR%20like%20-Winnebago%20%22company%27s%20history%22`. However, such searches are still only available to those users with permission to access Advanced search.

TIP If you want to perform the same search on user profiles rather than nodes, click the Users tab above the search results. From there you can change the search to continue to search for users.

To further control search results and indexing:

1. Click Configuration in the Toolbar and then click "Search settings" to see the Search settings page **F**.
2. The previous section "To make your site searchable" tells how to use the "Re-index site" button to force Drupal to re-catalog the contents of all nodes in your site for searching.
3. The "Number of items to index per cron run" setting determines how many nodes and comments Drupal will index *automatically* the next time that cron runs. You generally won't need to change this setting unless either:
   - You run a site that averages over 100 posts or comments per cron run (in which case you should increase the value).

   or

   - Your server has difficulty indexing as many items as you indicated (in which case you should decrease the value).
4. The field "Minimum word length to index" dictates how short search terms may be: Users who enter a shorter search term get an error; if they enter a combination of valid and too-short words, Drupal ignores the too-short ones. It's rare that you would have a reason to change the default value of 3, unless you have a lot of two-letter abbreviations on your site that you'd like to make searchable (in which case you should set the value to 2).

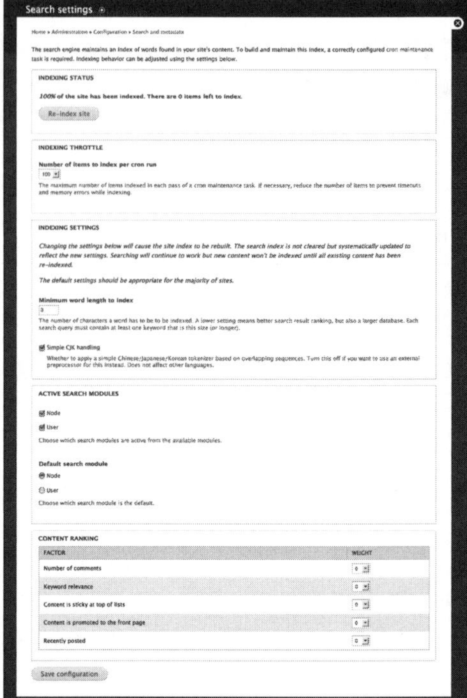

F The Search settings page

5. Leave the "Simple CJK handling" check box selected unless you're incorporating a non-Drupal search solution for Chinese, Japanese, or Korean text.

6. The "Active search modules" section lets you decide whether visitors can search for users, nodes, or both, and also lets you determine which one the search results page returns by default.

7. The "Content ranking" section lets you control factors that put nodes near the top of the search results page. You have control over five criteria:

   - Number of comments: Considers the number of comments attached to a node, where a larger number makes the node seem more important and therefore more worthy of appearing near the top.
   - Keyword relevance: Considers the number of times a keyword occurs in a node and *where* in the node it occurs. (A keyword in the title scores higher than one in the body, for example.)
   - Content is sticky at top of lists: Simply checks whether you've selected the "Sticky at top of lists" check box in the "Publishing options" of that node. (See the section "To make a node appear at the top of the page when grouped with other nodes" in Chapter 3 for details about this option.)
   - Content is promoted to the front page: Changes a hit's ranking based on whether that node's "Promoted to front page" check box is selected.
   - Recently posted: Compares posting dates, with the most recent nodes floating to the top.

   To increase a criterion's importance, increase its Weight by clicking its pop-up menu. The Weight interface here is counter to how it appears elsewhere in Drupal, for example when changing the menu settings on a node (as was demonstrated in the section "To create a menu item that links to a node" in Chapter 3). In other places, items with *smaller* numbers float to the top of the screen. But here, *larger* numbers result in items floating to the top of the screen.

TIP Robert Douglass's article "Drupal's search module and scoring factors" at `lullabot.com/articles/drupals_search_module_and_scoring_factors` examines search settings in great depth (albeit with an old version of Drupal).

Directing Traffic with Menus

Menus are like those slushy winter puddles that look shallow but swallow your leg up to the calf when you step off the curb. Behind a small set of links is a lot of intelligence that determines where, when, and how menus appear.

Drupal's way of building menus is one of the oldest parts of the software, going back (in one form or another) to Version 1.0. It has some surprisingly intuitive features—for example, menu links remain valid even after you change the paths they lead to. But with maturity has come complexity, so some explanation is necessary to understand them.

In Drupal's default configuration, two menus are always on your screen: The Main menu shows up as tabs near the screen's upper left, while the User menu is in the upper right. These two menus also appear as *blocks*, which you can place in various regions around the page.

The Navigation menu shows up as a block in the "Sidebar first" region by default **A**. A fourth menu ("Management") exists only as a hidden block. You can learn how to control the appearance of this or any other menu in block regions by reading the "Laying Out Your Site with Blocks" section in this chapter.

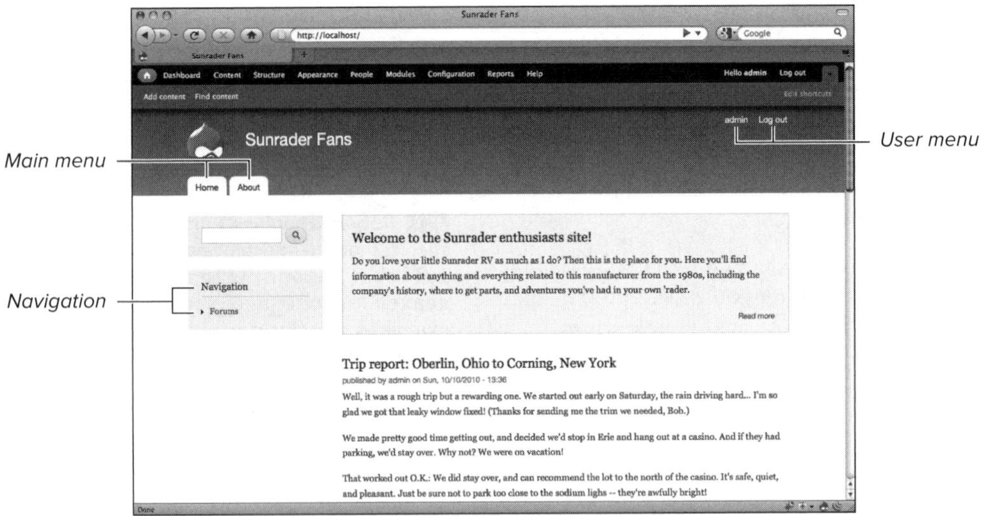

A Default menu locations in the Bartik theme

To create a menu:

1. Click Structure in the Toolbar and then click Menus to reach the Menus administration page **B**.

   The four rows on this page are the menus that come installed with Drupal. They are:

   - Main menu: Whose links appear by default as tabs in the upper-left corner of the screen. (You can change which menu appears in that area. See "To change which menus appear in the Main and User links locations.")
   - Management: By default it contains only one top-level link and Administration. The Administration section has many sublinks, leading to all of Drupal's administrative controls. Its contents are echoed in the Toolbar: Changing this menu changes the appearance of the Toolbar as well.
   - Navigation: Has only the "Add content" link enabled by default, although others appear there automatically as you enable modules. For example, enabling the Forum module puts a Forums link there.
   - User menu: Appears, by default, in the upper-right corner of the Bartik theme. Like the Main menu, you can change whether this menu appears in that area: See "To change which menus appear in the Main and User links locations."

   The User menu is also echoed in the Toolbar for those users with permission to see the Toolbar.

continues on next page

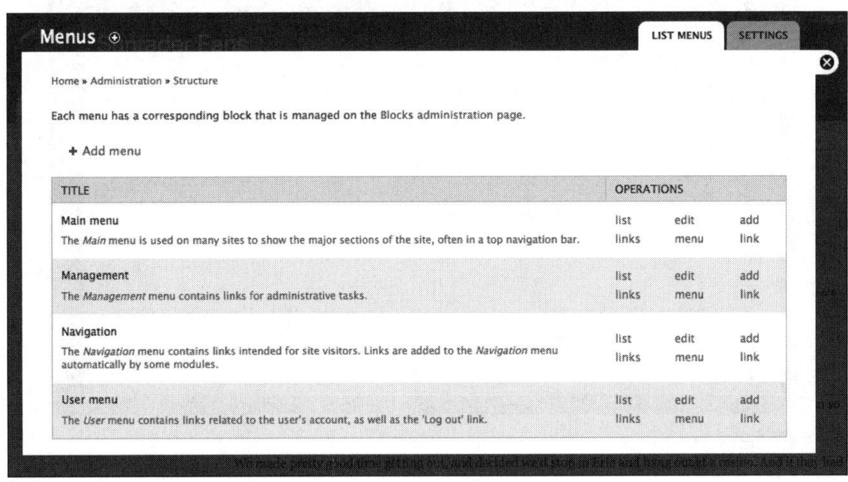

B The Menus administration page

2. To add a menu, click the "Add menu" link. Fill out the form and click Save when finished **C**. Drupal automatically creates the URL path for accessing this administration page, but you can change it by clicking its Edit link. It can contain only numbers, lowercase letters, and hyphens. (This is in contrast to many internal names you set up in Drupal, which can contain underscores but not hyphens.) The Title appears near menu links (for example, "Management"); the Description appears only in administrative contexts and isn't visible to non-privileged visitors.

3. You've now created the menu, but it's not terribly useful yet because it has no links. The next section shows you how to add them.

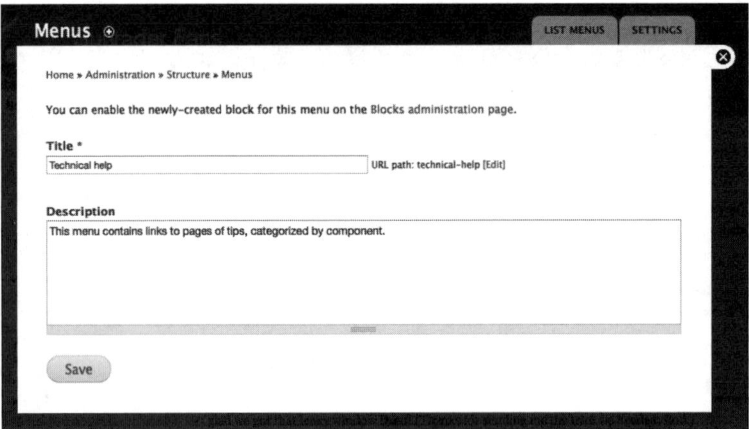

C Setting up a menu

To add menu links to a menu:

1. There are two main places in Drupal where you can add links to menus:
   - When you create or edit a node. However, you can link only to menus specified by the node's content type. To learn how to specify those menus, see "To create a new content type" in Chapter 4, particularly the section about menu settings.
   - In several places in and around the Menus administration page, which you reach by clicking Structure in the Toolbar and then clicking Menus.
2. To add menu links when editing a node, click the "Menu settings" tab at the bottom of the screen and fill out the form. This was described more fully in the "To create a menu item that links to a node" section in Chapter 3.
3. There are several ways to add menu links from the menu administration pages:
   - On the page Drupal displays when you've created a menu, click either of the "Add link" links **D**. You can also reach this page by clicking the "List links" page next to a menu's name on the Menus administration page.
   - Click "add link" next to the menu's name on the Menus administration page shown in **B**.

   Some downloadable modules, including the popular *Views* module (**`drupal.org/project/views`**), provide other ways to add menu links.

continues on next page

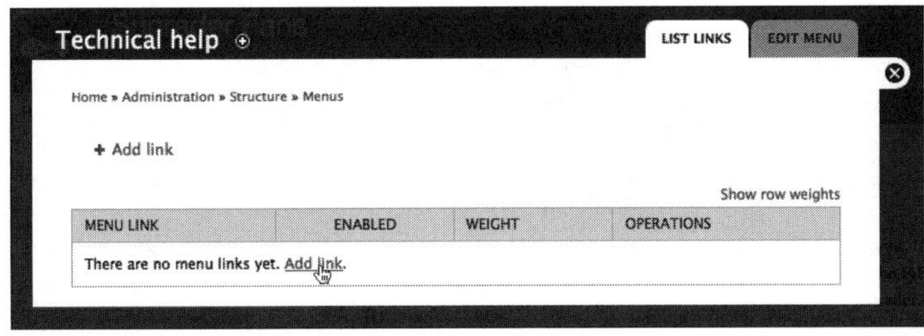

D Creating a menu link from the "List links" page

4. Drupal delivers you to the menu link edit form **E**. Enter a Menu link title, which becomes clickable text leading to the location you choose.

5. Enter a Path, which can be a valid URL in any of the following forms:

   - An external link (for example, **`http://www.example.com/page.html`**).
   - A node on the site, referred by node ID number (for example, **`node/1`**).
   - A node on the site, referred by URL path (for example, **`rv-parts/page-of-information`**).
   - A non-node part of your Drupal site that is accessible via a static (non-changing) URL path, for example the path to a downloadable file such as **`http://`*`domain-name`*`/sites/default/files/spec-sheet.pdf`**.
   - A location created by Drupal itself or by a downloaded module, for example **`user/register`** (which leads to the user registration page).
   - The front page, given simply as **`<front>`**.

   Don't add a leading slash when indicating URLs on your Drupal site. So if the URL to which you want to link a menu is **`http://`*`domain-name`*`/node/1`**, you would enter **`node/1`**, not **`/node/1`**.

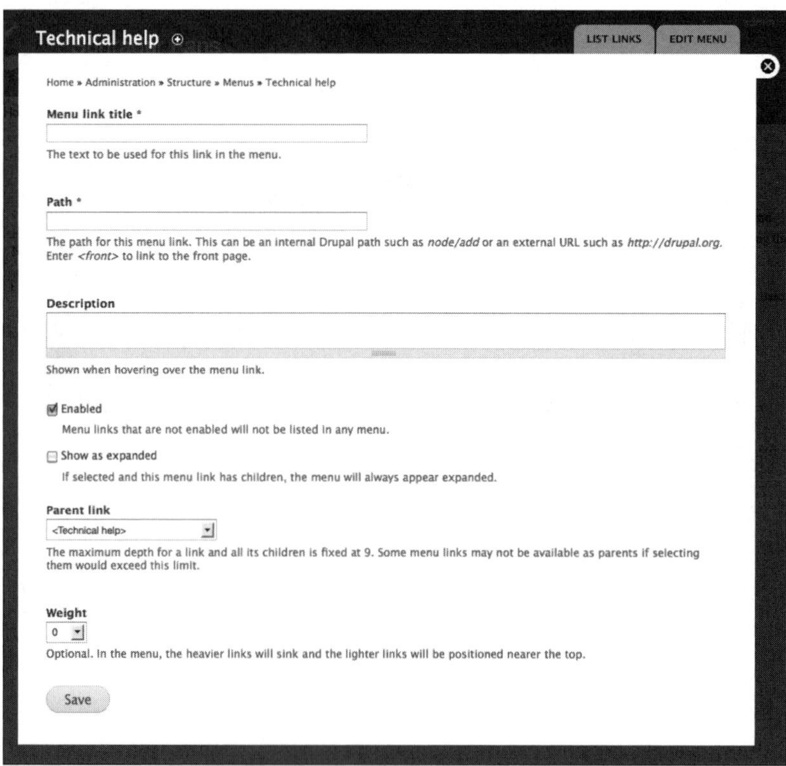

E The form to add a menu link

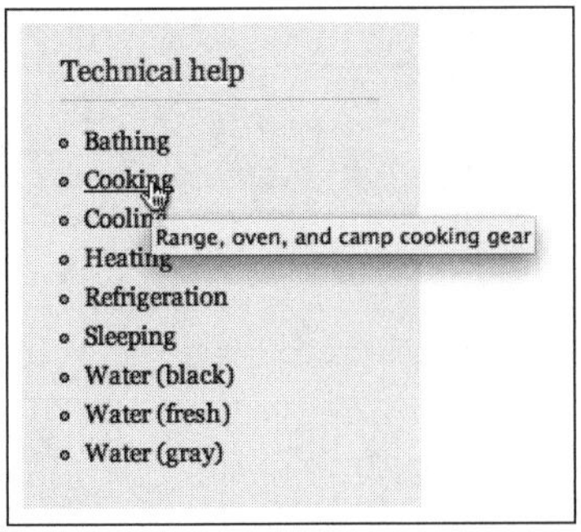

Technical help

- Bathing
- Cooking
- Cooling
- Heating
- Refrigeration
- Sleeping
- Water (black)
- Water (fresh)
- Water (gray)

Range, oven, and camp cooking gear

F A menu link's Description text as it appears to visitors

6. Enter optional Description text, which shows up in a floating box when visitors hover their pointers over the link **F**.
7. The Enabled check box lets you quickly turn off a menu link so it doesn't appear to any visitors. Deselecting the Enabled box doesn't delete the menu link. You can turn it on again at any time by editing the menu link and reselecting this check box.
8. The "Show as expanded" check box comes into play when you create multi-level ("hierarchical") menus, as you'll learn about in the section "To rearrange menu links."
9. The "Parent link" pop-up menu gives you a quick way to change which menu a menu link is in, or to set up multi-level menus. You'll see how to do that in the section "To rearrange menu links."
10. The Weight pop-up menu lets you re-order this menu link among the others by making it "lighter" (with a lower value) or "heavier" (with a higher value) than other menu links in the same menu. However, you'll see a much easier way to do so in the section "To rearrange menu links."
11. When you've finished creating the menu link, click Save.

TIP When you create a menu link to a node, that link shows up in the node's edit form in the "Menu settings" tab. Multiple menu links can lead to the same node, but that tab shows only the first link created. If you delete that link, the second one created appears in that tab. You can always edit all menu links through the Menus administration interface.

To delete a menu link:

There are several ways to delete a menu link. Do any of the following:

- Go to the Menus administration page by clicking Structure in the Toolbar and then clicking Menus. Click "list links." On the resulting page, click "delete" next to the appropriate link.
- While on a menu link's edit page, click the Delete button at the bottom of the form.
- While on a node's edit page, deselect the "Provide a menu link" check box, then click Save at the bottom of the form. If multiple menu links lead to this node, only the first one will be deleted.

These techniques work only on menu links you explicitly created, not on those created by a module or Drupal itself.

To delete a menu:

1. Go to the Menus administration page by clicking Structure in the Toolbar and then clicking Menus.
2. Click the "edit menu" link next to the menu you want to delete.
3. On the resulting page, click the Delete button. You'll see a warning screen that informs you of how many menu links you'll destroy by deleting this menu. To confirm your choice, click Delete.

   Deleting a menu removes all menu links it contains, but it does *not* affect the locations those links led to. Don't worry: You're not deleting any nodes, only the links that lead to them.

TIP You can't delete any of Drupal's core menus: Main menu, Management, Navigation, and User menu. (These menus don't have a Delete button on their "edit menu" pages.)

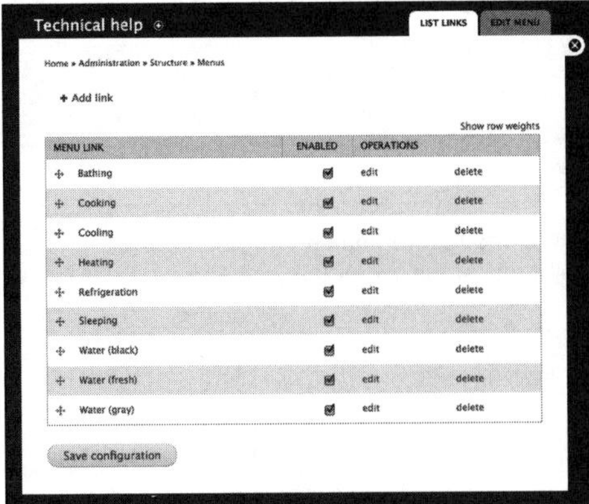

G The "List links" page for a menu named "Technical help"

To rearrange menu links:

1. Click Structure in the Toolbar and then click Menus to go to the Menus administration page.
2. Click "list links" next to the menu whose links you want to rearrange.
3. On the resulting page, you can perform several tasks in addition to rearranging menu links **G**.
   - Clicking the link in the "Menu link" column takes you to the linked-to page.
   - The check box in the Enabled column determines whether a menu link is visible to visitors.
   - The Operations column contains links to edit or delete the specified menu link.
4. To change the position of a menu item, click and drag its ✥ icon, much as you saw in the section "To change a book's structure" in Chapter 3.

   Click "Save configuration" after reordering menu items. If you navigate away from the page before saving your changes, Drupal will discard the new menu link order.

To rearrange menu links into a hierarchy:

1. You can also make some menu items "parents" of others, creating a *hierarchical menu*. There's one good opportunity in G: The three menu links that start with "Water" would do well grouped under a parent link. Here's how we'll do that.
2. Create a new menu item by clicking "Add link" and filling out the link creation form. In our example, we'll give it the title "Water."
3. Drag each of the three targeted links so they're subordinate to the one we just created H. (It might take some mousing practice to drag them into the right place.) Click "Save configuration."
4. Click "edit" next to the newly created Water link. On the resulting page, enable the "Show as expanded" check box. (We could also have enabled this check box on the link's edit form when we created it.)
5. Click Save. The "Technical help" menu now has the structure you see in I. Note, however, that you haven't actually made it visible to visitors yet: You'll learn how to do that in the section "Laying Out Your Site with Blocks."

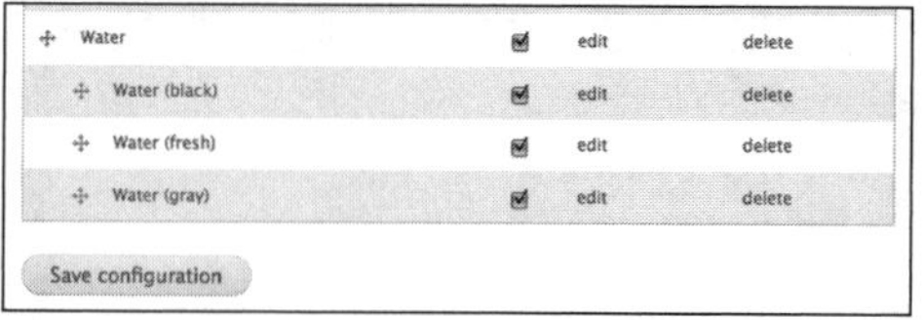

H Our menu after making three links the "children" of the Water link

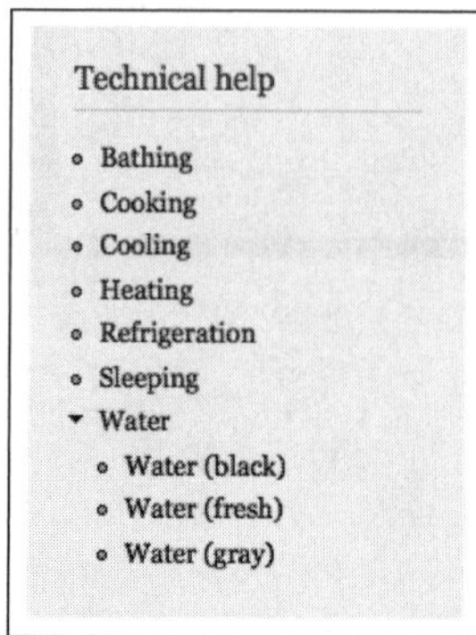

I The menu after selecting "Show as expanded" next to the Water link and making three links subordinate to it

TIP **Drupal requires every item in a menu to link to a URL. That's unfortunate, for a reason that's obvious in I: Where should the Water link go to? You could link it to a simple page that lists its children's menu links, for example, or have it go to the same page as the first child link. Neither solution is very good; better ones are possible through custom PHP programming.**

TIP **Menu appearances vary widely depending on your theme and the block region in which you've placed the menu. For example, hierarchical links placed in the Main menu of the Acquia Marina theme (`drupal.org/project/acquia_marina`) automatically expand as a pop-up menu. That is, hovering your mouse over our Water menu would reveal the other three choices.**

TIP **Menu hierarchies can be up to nine levels deep, but I recommend you make them no more than three levels deep.**

TIP **An alternative way to make one menu link the child of another is to click its "edit" link and then select the desired parent item in the "Parent link" pop-up menu. Then click Save as usual.**

To change menu titles:

1. Visit the Menus administration page by clicking Structure in the Toolbar and then clicking Menus.
2. Except for four menus that are part of Drupal's core—Main menu, Management, Navigation, User menu—you can change the title of any menu. To do so, click the "edit menu" link that corresponds to the menu you want to change.
3. On the resulting page, type the menu's new name into the Title field.
4. Click Save at the bottom of the form.

To change which menus appear in the Main and User links locations:

1. You can place any menu into any block region on the page, as you'll learn in the section "Laying Out Your Site with Blocks." But many Drupal themes also have two special areas called "Main links" and "Secondary links."

   By default, Drupal puts the Main menu in the Main links area and puts the User menu in the Secondary links area. But you can change which menus appear in those areas. To do so, go to the menu settings page by clicking Structure in the Toolbar and then clicking Menus. Then click the Settings tab **J**.

2. On the resulting page, select your preferred menus on the "Source for the Main links" and "Source for the Secondary links" pop-up menus. Then click "Save configuration."

TIP In some themes, if you set the "Source for the Main links" and "Source for the Secondary links" pop-up menus to refer to the same Drupal menu, the Secondary links area will change depending on what's selected in the Main links area. To take our example: If both pop-up menus were set to "Technical help," and you clicked Water in the Main links area, the Secondary links area would list Water (black), Water (fresh), and Water (gray). (Unfortunately, this feature doesn't work with the default Bartik theme.)

TIP You might remember that each menu comes with a block that you can place in block regions. Putting a menu into the Main links or Secondary links area doesn't use up its block: You can make that menu appear in another part of the page by moving its block there. (See "Laying Out Your Site with Blocks" to learn how.)

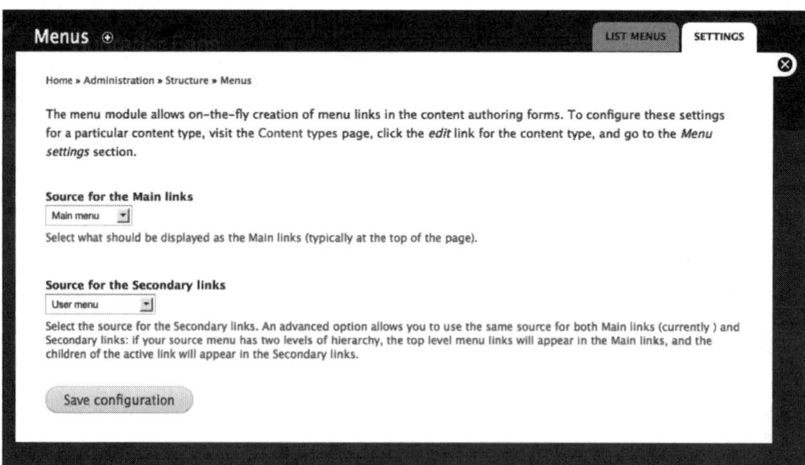

J The menu settings page, where you can determine which menus appear in the Main and Secondary link areas

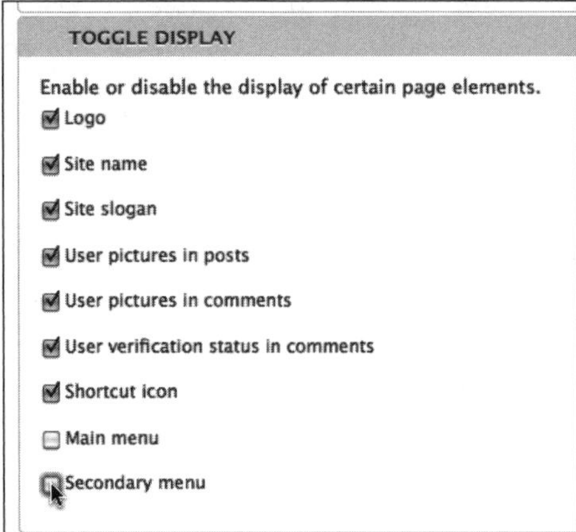

K Turning off the Main and Secondary menus by deselecting their check boxes on the theme settings page

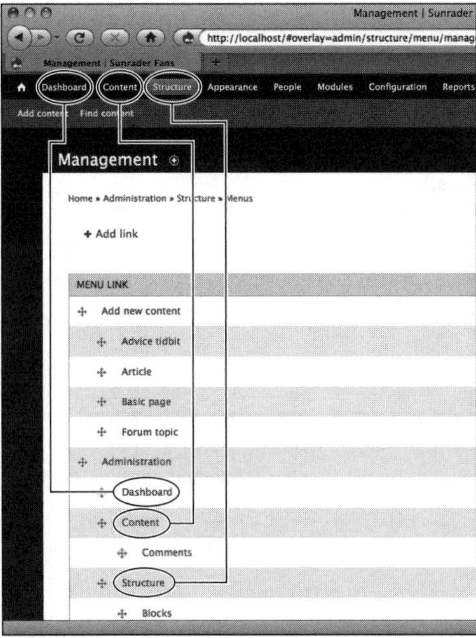

L The Toolbar echoes the Administration section of the Management menu

To disable the Main, Secondary, and Toolbar menu areas:

1. There are two ways to hide the Main and Secondary links areas. *Either*:

   - Go to the menu settings page as described in the section "To change which menus appear in the Main and User links locations." Select "No main links" from the "Source for the Main links" pop-up menu, or "No secondary links" from the "Source for the Secondary links" pop-up menu, or both. Click "Save configuration."

   or

   - Go to the theme's settings page by clicking Appearance in the Toolbar and then clicking Settings next to the current theme. In the "Toggle display" section, deselect the "Main menu" or "Secondary menu" check boxes, or both **K**. Click "Save configuration."

2. The Toolbar is the black area at the top of every screen that, by default, displays top-level links from the Administration part of the Management menu to everyone with permission to see it **L**.

   To turn it off, go to the Modules administration page by clicking Modules in the Toolbar. Then, deselect the check box for the Toolbar module and click "Save configuration."

TIP You can change what appears in the Toolbar by monkeying with the Administration section of the Management menu, it's true. But I prefer to leave that as it is and customize the Shortcut bar instead; that's what it's designed for, so changes are much easier to make. To learn how, see "To change which items appear in the Shortcut bar" in Chapter 2.

Laying Out Your Site with Blocks

Drupal's restrictions frustrate many traditional web designers who are used to working in pure HTML, which lets them put whatever they want anywhere on the page. Why can't Drupal do that?

The fact is, Drupal *can* do that—if managed by someone with enough knowledge of PHP and CSS. But that's a feature, not a bug. By forcing designers to work within a well-defined structure, Drupal (usually) prevents bad design decisions from obscuring content and navigation. As Marge Simpson said, "One person can change the world, but most of the time you probably shouldn't."

Somewhere between fill-in-the-blank inflexibility and HTML's Wild West approach to page structure, Drupal offers a compromise in a system of content containers called *blocks*. Drupal includes some blocks to start with, automatically makes others when you do certain actions (such as creating menus), and lets you create further blocks explicitly. You place blocks in *block regions* that are defined by the theme. (Drupal's default theme—Bartik—has 15 block regions.)

This section will show you how to create blocks, move them around, restrict their visibility to specified groups of users, and make them show up only on certain pages. Blocks might not offer HTML's flexible layout options, but they do provide features that ultimately enhance content access in ways that aren't possible with plain HTML.

A The Blocks administration page, which lists blocks and the block regions that contain them

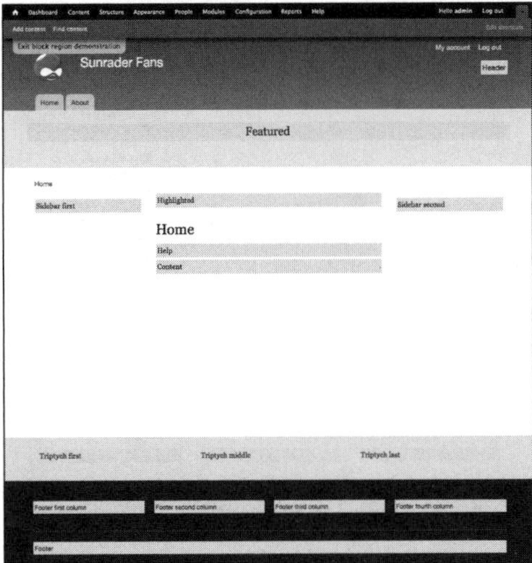

B The block region demonstration page, which graphically shows where block regions appear on the page for a specific theme

To move blocks among and within regions:

1. Click Structure in the Toolbar and then click Blocks to reach the Blocks administration page, which lists available blocks and the block regions into which you can place them **A**.

   Here we see the Bartik theme's Blocks administration page with one small addition to its default state. When we built the "Technical help" menu earlier in this chapter (in the "Directing Traffic with Menus" section), Drupal automatically created a block for it, but put that block in the "Disabled" group so it doesn't show up anywhere on the page. We're going to move that block into the"Sidebar first" area, which in this theme is the left column.

   To get a visual representation of where block regions are on a page, click the "Demonstrate block regions" link **B**. To return to the Blocks administration page, click "Exit block region demonstration."

continues on next page

2. There are two ways to move a block into a block region. *Either*:

   ▸ Click and drag its ✥ icon, as you saw in the section "To change a book's structure" in Chapter 3.

   or

   ▸ Select a block region from the pop-up menu next to the block's name **C**.

   In either case, the block will move to its new region and an orange asterisk will appear next to the menu, showing that you've changed its location.

3. After moving a block into its region, you might want to change its position within that region. To do so, click and drag its ✥ icon.

4. Click "Save blocks." If you click another link on this page before doing so, you'll lose all the block positioning changes you just made.

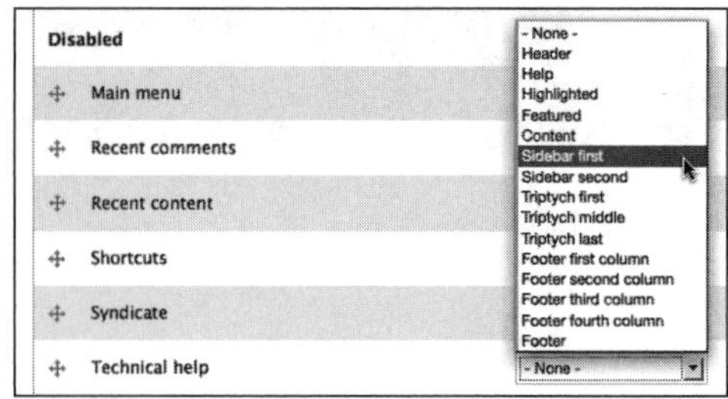

C Moving the "Technical help" block to the "Sidebar first" region

TIP Some block regions grow and shrink depending on whether there's content in the block regions adjoining them. The shape-shifting behavior of such "flexible" blocks usually makes your site look better, but it can be a surprise if you're not expecting it. As with most interface changes, the solution is to browse the site thoroughly before publishing to ensure that it looks the way you want—or, at least, that the shifting of flexible block regions doesn't destroy your design.

TIP Block styles often vary depending on which region the block is in, especially in the Header and Footer regions. (Yet another reason to double-check your design before publishing!)

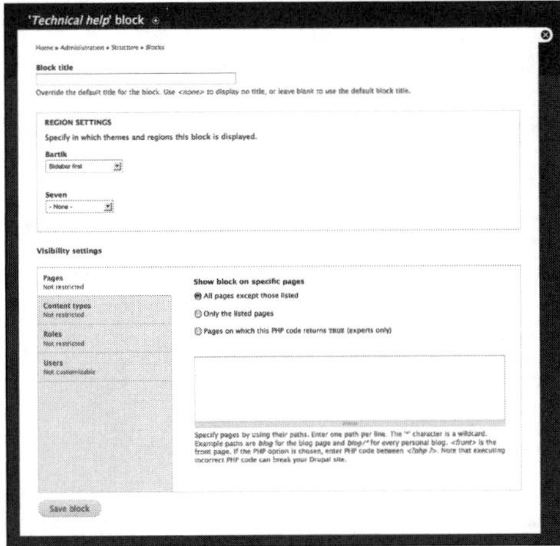

D The configuration page for a specific block

To configure where and how a block appears:

1. Go to the Blocks administration page by clicking Structure in the Toolbar and then clicking Blocks. Click the "configure" link next to the block you want to change.

   The resulting configuration page may vary somewhat, depending on the type of block you're configuring. Those created by Drupal modules may have additional (or fewer) controls. We'll look at the configuration page for the block that appeared when we created the "Technical help" menu, which is fairly typical **D**.

2. This block configuration page is broken up into six sets of controls, the first one being "Block title." If you leave this field empty, the block will usually display with the block name as its title—in this case, "Technical help." (Whether the block title appears at all depends on the theme and the region in which you place the block.) To change the block title that visitors see, enter it in this field, or hide the title entirely by entering **<none>**. Note that this doesn't change the *name* of the block, which you see in the administrative interface.

3. The next section lets you specify where this block should appear in enabled themes. (To learn how to enable a theme, see the section "Selecting a Visual Theme" in Chapter 2.) These pop-up menus serve the same function as those on the Blocks administration page you saw in the section "To move blocks among and within regions."

continues on next page

4. At the bottom of the page are four tabs for Visibility settings. The one shown by default, Pages, lets you determine on which page (or pages) this block displays. You have a choice of listing pages where the block *should* or *shouldn't* display. If you've enabled the PHP text format (as described in Chapter 5, "Making Content Interactive"), you can also specify pages for block display with a PHP program.
5. Clicking the "Content types" tab presents controls that let you show the block only on pages containing nodes of specific content types. (For more information about content types, see Chapter 4, "Customizing Content.") Drupal automatically displays one check box for each content type in your site, and leaving them all unselected means that the block will appear with nodes of all content types **E**.
6. Clicking the Roles tab lets you define which groups of users can see the block. Each role in your Drupal site has its own check box. Select the users that you want to be able to see the block **F**. (For more information about user roles, see Chapter 7.)

   If you leave all check boxes unselected, the block will be visible to all users. Further, these selections have no inheritance. That is, making the block visible to anonymous users doesn't automatically make it visible to administrators, even though administrators usually have more permissions than anonymous users.

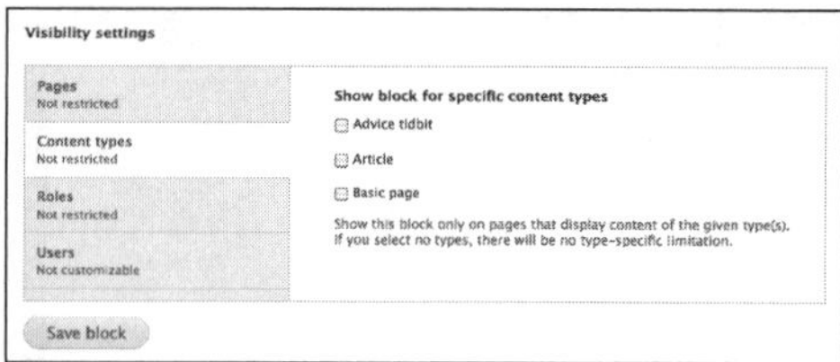

E Options for displaying the block on pages containing nodes of specific content types

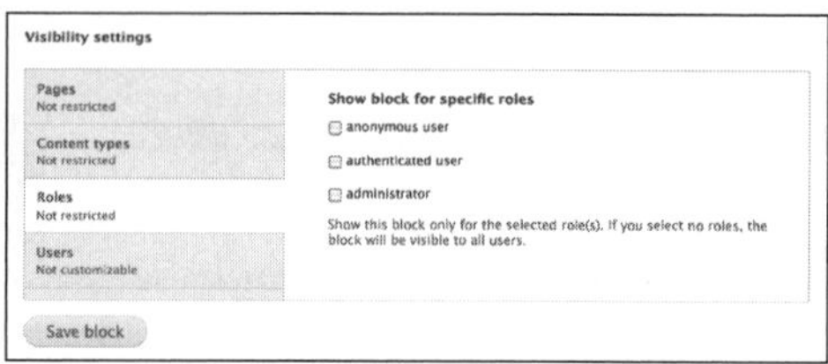

F Options for displaying the block to selected roles

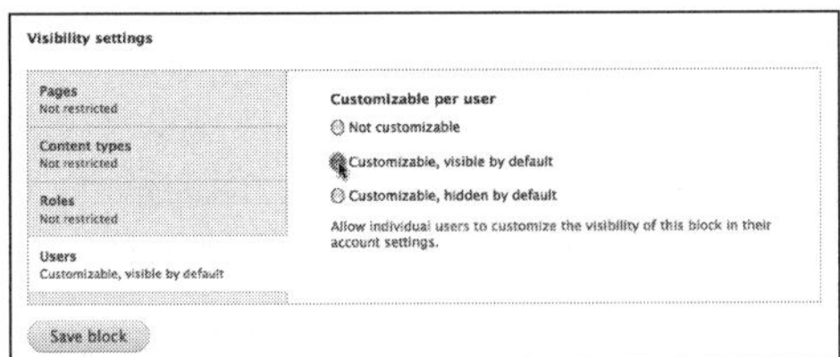

G Changing a block's settings so that authenticated users can choose to turn it off

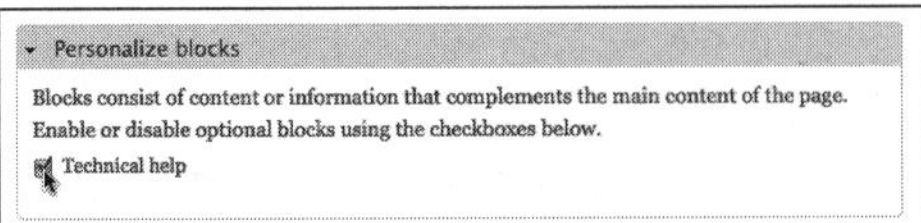

H The control on an individual user's page to hide or display the "Technical help" block

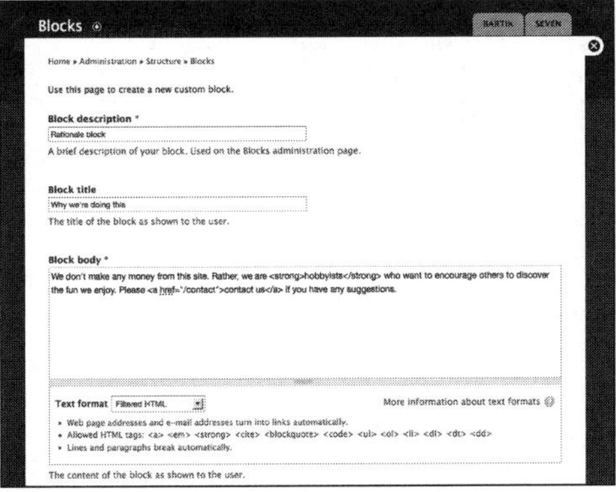

I Creating a new block with simple HTML tags in the body

7. Finally, the Users tab lets you give users the option of displaying or hiding this block wherever it appears **G**. This choice is only available to registered ("authenticated") users: They make that selection by going to their user page at **`http://`*`domain-name`*`/user`** and clicking the Edit link, then selecting (or deselecting) the block's check box **H**.

8. When you've made all the desired configuration changes to a block, click "Save block."

To add a block:

1. Go to the Blocks administration page by clicking Structure in the Toolbar and then clicking Blocks. Click the "Add block" link.

2. The resulting page looks almost exactly like the one you saw in the section "To configure where and how a block appears," except the top area provides you two additional fields: "Block description" (which appears on the Blocks administration page) and "Block body" **I**.

   The "Block body" field actually holds the contents of the block. Earlier in this chapter, we were working with a block that contained a menu's links; but blocks that you create using the "Add block" tab can contain anything you want. The "Block body" field is just like a node's Body field, where you can enter plain text, HTML, or any other text format available on your Drupal site. (See Chapter 5 for more information about text formats.)

3. When you're finished, click "Save block."

The Future of Drupal Layout

While Drupal's block system has served well for many years and continues to be the chief lightweight method to define layout, alternatives (in the form of contributed modules) are starting to emerge.

One of the most promising is Panels (**drupal.org/project/panels**), which essentially lets you create block-like layout sections and place them in juxtaposition anywhere on the page. Besides being more flexible graphically, Panels can also handle a much wider range of content than blocks can, including various kinds of changing (dynamic) content. Its complex abilities come with a complex interface, though, so you need a fairly good grasp of Drupal concepts to use it.

Another module that's attracted attention recently is Skinr, available at **drupal.org/project/skinr**. It lets Drupal themers expose controls for their Cascading Style Sheets (CSS) through Drupal's interface so that administrators can apply them much more easily and flexibly. The module's gotten a big boost from the popular theming company TopNotchThemes (**topnotchthemes.com**), which has made Skinr an essential part of its new Fusion theming system (**fusiondrupalthemes.com**).

As this book goes to press, neither of these modules has been released yet in final form for Drupal 7. But we believe (and hope!) that both will be soon.

7

Wrangling Users

The Internet's history proves the old adage "Anything that can be used will be abused." Post an email address online and spam attempts begin within hours; launch a web site that permits user comments and every manner of stupidity will find you.

Fortunately, Drupal has included anti-abuse technologies since its beginnings. Chief among them is its system of user *roles* and *permissions*, which gives you broad power to regulate who can perform specific actions on your site while keeping those rules manageable, even as the site grows to thousands of members.

But user management is as much about enabling communication as preventing abuse. In this regard, Drupal has ways to let users define their online personalities (through profiles) and talk directly to one another (through contact forms). Further, you have a lot of ways to control and guide the user registration process, to both encourage participation and guard against unwanted behavior.

In This Chapter

Managing User Accounts

As your site's administrator, you can add users, change their personal information, and prevent them from accessing the site. You can also display a list of all users who have certain permissions or roles, and perform certain actions on the found set.

In a perfect world, you'd never have to deal with user accounts: Users would fill out their registration forms correctly, manage their own accounts, and never attempt to do anything they shouldn't. But the real world doesn't work like that, of course. You might meet someone in the street who wants to join your site, for example: Drupal lets you create the account yourself, then sends the new member a user name and password. In addition, you can decide what happens to user accounts when someone decides to leave your site, and you can choose to keep or delete the content they created.

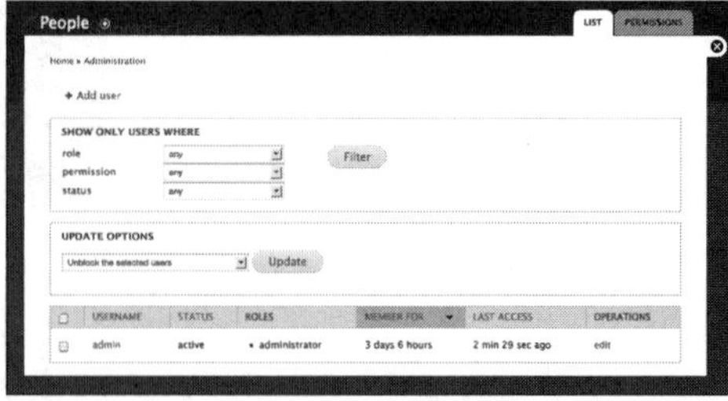

Ⓐ The People administration page

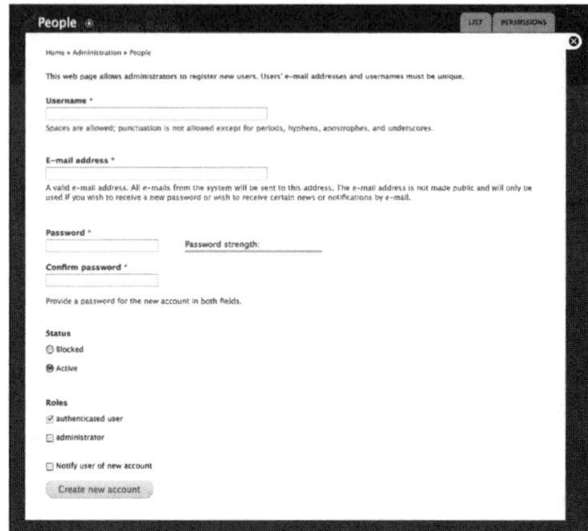

Ⓑ The form for adding a user to your Drupal site

To create a user account:

1. Click People in the Toolbar to go to the People administration page Ⓐ.
2. Click the "Add user" link to go to the new user creation form Ⓑ.
3. Complete the "Add user" form.
   - Username: Required, must be unique, and may contain only letters, numbers, and those characters specified in the help text below the field. (The ability to include apostrophes in user names is new in Drupal 7.) User names are *not* case sensitive: If there's a user named **`Joseph`**, Drupal won't let you create another user named **`joseph`**. (That user will be able to log in as either **`Joseph`** or **`joseph`**.)

- E-Mail address: Also required and must be unique. Drupal uses this email address in several ways, so an invalid or incorrect address can cause quite a few problems, especially if the user is also an administrator. Further, Drupal doesn't include any features to manage bouncing email, so you might never find out that an email address is wrong. Double-check that address!
- Password: Required. You can use any password that contains letters, numbers, or punctuation; spaces are also fine, but the password can't be composed of *only* spaces! As you enter the password, Drupal provides suggestions for making the password *stronger*—that is, harder to guess. As you follow its suggestions, the bar next to *Password strength* grows longer, as encouragement to create a more secure password.

  The "Confirm password" field helps prevent password typos by forcing you to type the same password again. As long as the second password field differs from the first, the word next to "Passwords match" shows as "no." When the two fields match, the word changes to "yes" **C**.
- Status: Radio buttons indicating whether the user will be able to log in and use the account. Leave the Active button selected unless you want to create the account now but make it unavailable until later.
- Roles section: Contains check boxes for each role available for registered users on your Drupal site. By default, there are only two: "authenticated user," which is always true for registered users, and "administrator." (There is technically one other role on your Drupal site, "anonymous user," but by definition nobody with a user name can have that role, so it's not an option here.)

  If you've added any other roles (as you'll learn how to do in the "Defining User Roles and Permissions" section), they'll also appear as options here.
- The last field is the "Notify user of new account" check box. If selected, an email will go to the address provided earlier in the "E-mail address" field on the form. You'll learn how to change the contents of this email in the section "To modify automated administration emails and determine when to send them."

continues on next page

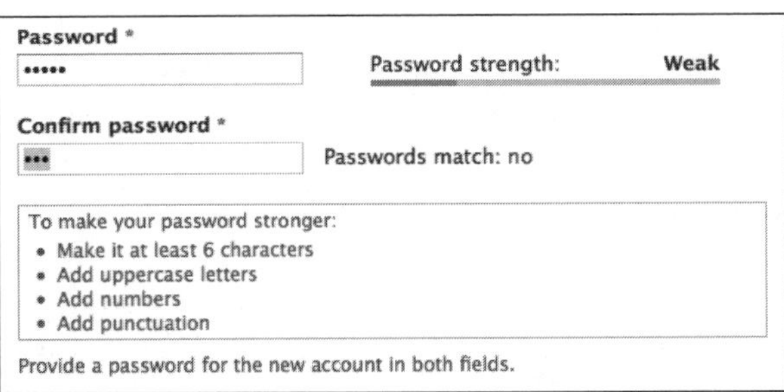

C Drupal's feedback to improve a password's strength and ensure it's been entered correctly

4. When you've completed the form, click "Create new account." Drupal creates the account and sends the user-notification message (if you selected the "Notify user of new account" box in step 3), and you're taken back to a blank user-creation form so you can create multiple new users in quick succession.

You don't need to create any other users unless you want to, of course. To escape the process at any time, close or navigate away from the "Add user" window.

I'm a Person, Not a User!

You might have noticed the words *users* and *people* used interchangeably in this chapter. The traditional term is *user*—that's what you'll find in Drupal 6, in all previous versions, and in the computer industry in general. But discussions within the Drupal community led to the use of *people* for two main reasons:

- Not everybody who interacts with a Drupal-based site is, strictly speaking, a *user* of it. For example, a site could contain a list of people who plan to attend a real-world event, although those people might never visit the web site themselves.
- Some commentators felt that *people* would help make Drupal 7 seem friendlier, particularly to inexperienced administrators.

But the transition to *people* isn't absolutely clear in Drupal 7. The URL for the administration page is **http://*domain-name*/admin/people** and the text at the top is "People," yet there's a link that reads "Add user," and the URL for your own membership page is **http://*domain-name*/user**. That's technically consistent with the idea that a *user* is someone with an account on a site, while a *person* might not have such an account. But that's a quibble: For our purposes, the two words have an identical meaning in Drupal.

In this book, I use the following terms:

- User or authenticated user: Someone with an account on your site.
- Visitor: Someone who is visiting your site but doesn't have administrative privileges. Visitors can be anonymous users (who haven't logged into an account on your site) or authenticated users (who have).
- Administrator: Someone with privileges to perform the action being discussed.

I use the word *people* when referring to that text on Drupal's interface: Clicking People in the Toolbar leads to a page that says "People" at the top of it, so it's the "People administration page." But I can't bring myself to use it in descriptions, such as "the People-creation process." (I'm somewhat familiar with *that* process, and this ain't it.)

For insight, see **drupal.org/node/538526**.

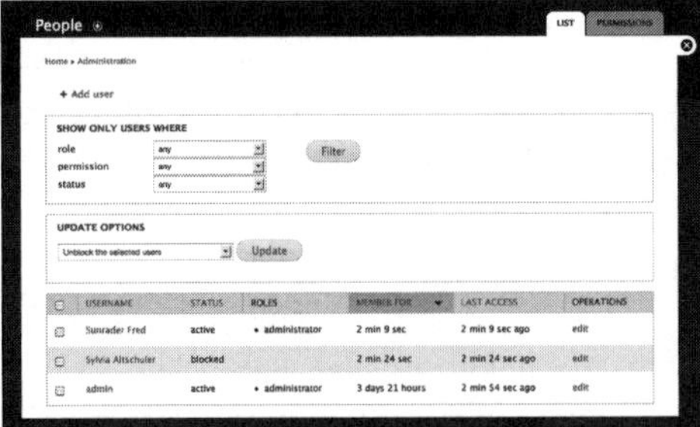

D The list of people on a Drupal site

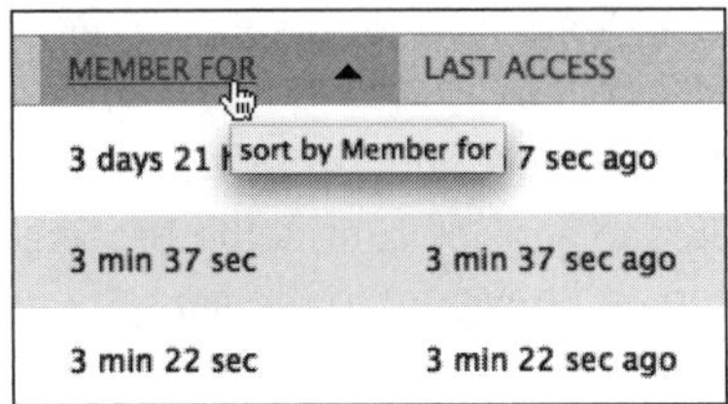

E Sorting the user list, with help text displayed when you hover your pointer over a sorting option

F The list of users, already filtered to show only administrators, with the imminent application of another filter

To view a list of user accounts:

1. Click People in the Toolbar to reach the People administration page **D**.
2. The People screen lists the 50 users who joined most recently, sorted from newest to oldest. If your site has more than 50 users, links at the bottom of the screen lead to other screens of up to 50 users each.

   To reverse the sort order so the oldest registrations float to the top of the list, click the "Member for" header. To sort by Last Access, Status, or Username, click the corresponding header **E**.
3. In the "Show only users where" section, you can filter the user list by any combination of three criteria, so you see only a subset of the complete list.
   - Role filter: Lets you show only users who have been granted a certain collection of site-access permissions. (For details about user roles, see the section "Defining User Roles and Permissions" in this chapter.)
   - Permission filter: Lets you show users who have permission to perform a specific action.
   - Status filter: Shows users who are either Active (permitted to log into their accounts) or Blocked.

   To specify criteria, select options from the pop-up menus and then click Filter.

   After you've filtered by at least one criterion, three buttons take the place of the Filter button **F**. To change or add criteria, indicate them as before and then click Refine. Filters are additive, so you'll see only users who meet *all* the specified criteria. To remove the most recent criterion, click Undo; to remove all criteria and return to showing the entire list of users, click Reset.

To modify an individual user's account:

1. Click People in the Toolbar to reach the People administration page.
2. To modify a single user's account, *either*:
   - Click the "edit" link at the end of that user's row.

   or

   - Click the user's name to view that person's profile and then click the Edit tab.

   The resulting page is very similar to the one you saw in the section "To create a user account." (It's also very much like what logged-in users see when they edit their accounts by going to **`http://`*`domain-name`*`/user`** and clicking the Edit tab.)
3. Here you can control the same aspects of the user's account as when you created it, with a few additional options at the bottom of the screen **G**:
   - Picture section: Lets you associate this user with a graphical representation, commonly known as an *avatar*. This field is only available if you've selected the "Enable user pictures" option. It's enabled by default, but if for some reason it becomes disabled you can learn how to enable it again in the section "To allow (or forbid) user signatures and avatars."

     To upload a graphic, click the Browse button and navigate to the file through your computer's file-selection dialog box. Drupal will upload the graphic when you click Save at the bottom of the screen.

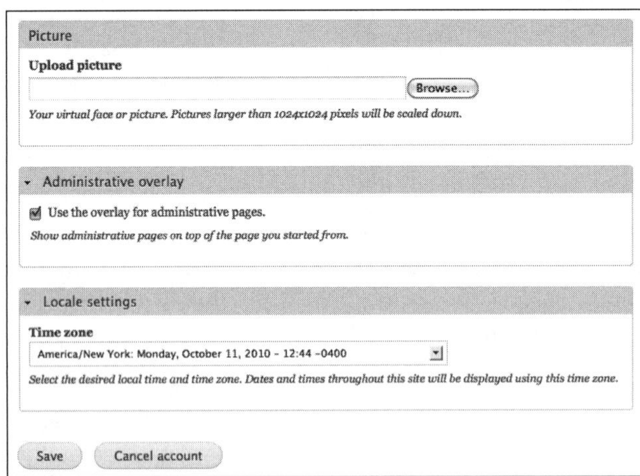

G Account-editing options that weren't available when you created the account

- Administrative overlay section: Lets you decide whether the overlay will appear when the user performs administrative tasks. (This option is available only for users with administrative privileges.) For more about the overlay, see the section “Using the New Administrative Interfaces in Drupal 7” in Chapter 2, “Establishing Your Drupal Site.”
- Locale settings section: Lets you change the user’s apparent time zone, which affects the display of time-related information, such as timestamps for posts and comments.

Other sections on this page may appear as you configure your site and add new modules.

4. When you’ve finished making changes to the account, click Save.

To cancel an individual user's account:

1. Go to the form to edit the user's page, as the section "To modify an individual user's account" described.
2. Click "Cancel account" at the bottom of the form.
3. The "When cancelling the account" confirmation page appears, providing a way to determine what to do with content that the user created, such as nodes, comments, and blog and forum posts **H**. Note that these options embed a subtle difference between whether to disable or delete a canceled account. The four options are:
   - Disable the account and keep all content: The user's account status changes to Blocked, and all content remains as before.
   - Disable the account and unpublish all content: The user's account status changes to Blocked. All content is hidden from view, but it is still accessible to administrators on the Content administration page. (For more information see Chapter 3, "Creating and Managing Content.")
   - Delete the account and make all content belong to the *Anonymous* user: The user's account is permanently removed from the system and no longer shows up on the People administration page. All nodes that the user created are now attributed to "Anonymous"—that is, a person who didn't log in to your Drupal site before creating the content. Comments by that person keep the same author name, but with the annotation "(not verified)" as if the commenter provided the user's name without logging in.
   - Delete the account and all content: Both the user's account and all content attributed to it disappear.

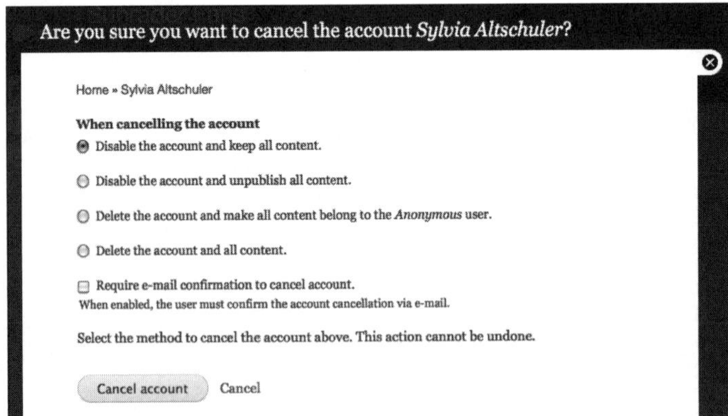

Are you sure you want to cancel the account Sylvia Altschuler?
Home » Sylvia Altschuler
When cancelling the account
Disable the account and keep all content.
Disable the account and unpublish all content.
Delete the account and make all content belong to the Anonymous user.
Delete the account and all content.
Require e-mail confirmation to cancel account.
When enabled, the user must confirm the account cancellation via e-mail.
Select the method to cancel the account above. This action cannot be undone.
Cancel account
Cancel

H The account-deletion page with options regarding user status, notification, and content

You can change which radio button is selected by default on the Account settings page. For more information, see the section "To change Drupal's behavior for account creation and cancelation."

4. The "Require e-mail confirmation to cancel account" check box lets you give the user the final choice on whether to cancel the account. When you select this option and then click "Cancel account," Drupal sends an email message to the address associated with the account. That message contains a secure link: If the user clicks it within 24 hours, Drupal completes the action of disabling or deleting the account. Otherwise, the account remains as it was.

   When you've made your choices, click "Cancel account." To leave the account as it was, click Cancel.

Deleting an Account: How Hard Could It Be?

This one account-deletion page looks simple: just a few radio buttons and a check box. But it's made more complicated when you allow users to cancel their own accounts, as Drupal 7 does for the first time. Figuring out what should happen to such accounts—and the content created in their names—has the distinction of being Drupal's longest-running puzzle. Discussion about it started in 2001 as the eighth node (**drupal.org/node/8**) created on the Drupal project's official web site, which now contains nearly a million nodes. (Drupal 7 *maintainer* Angie Byron tells the story of the hero who took charge and worked it all out at **webchick.net/contributor-spotlight/daniel-kudwien**.)

Node 8 is a good example of the saying "easy is hard"—and a sign of just how much goes on behind the scenes to make Drupal work well. Both Drupal and its thousands of contributed modules have "issue queues" full of difficult problems like Node 8, and thousands of developers (and others) volunteer countless hours every year to fix them. So whenever you come across something in Drupal that doesn't work right, remember the many things that *do*—and show Drupal's maintainers some love.

Controlling How Users Interact with Their Accounts

With Drupal's account settings at their most liberal, anyone who can find your site can create an account on it, thereby gaining permission to post comments, create a user profile, and do anything else you allow authenticated users to do. That's good in terms of accessibility: Your site's user population can grow large without your intervention. But on the down side, spammers and other online vandals have developed tools that automatically sign up for accounts on Drupal sites to place advertisements, contact users, and otherwise wreak havoc.

Fortunately, it's easy to change Drupal's default user-registration behavior to let you decide on a case-by-case basis whether to allow users to join your site. Your control of signup behavior goes well beyond that, though. You can also allow (or forbid) signatures and user graphics, choose whether users need to confirm their email addresses before being allowed in, and change the messages they get when they join.

To change Drupal's behavior for account creation and cancelation:

1. Click Configuration in the Toolbar and then click "Account settings."
2. Scroll down to the "Registration and cancellation" section. Select your preferred option in the "Who can register accounts?" field, which contains three radio buttons **A**:
   - Administrators only: Means that users can neither register themselves nor request a user account through Drupal. The "Create new account" link disappears from the User login block that appears in the left column in most themes (including Drupal's default theme, Bartik). Visitors who try to reach the "Create new account" page directly at **`http://`*`domain-name`*`/user/register`** get an "Access denied" message.
   - Visitors: Means that anybody can get an account without any intervention by an administrator.

     With this option set, and assuming you've left the "Require e-mail verification" check box (described below) selected, a user who clicks

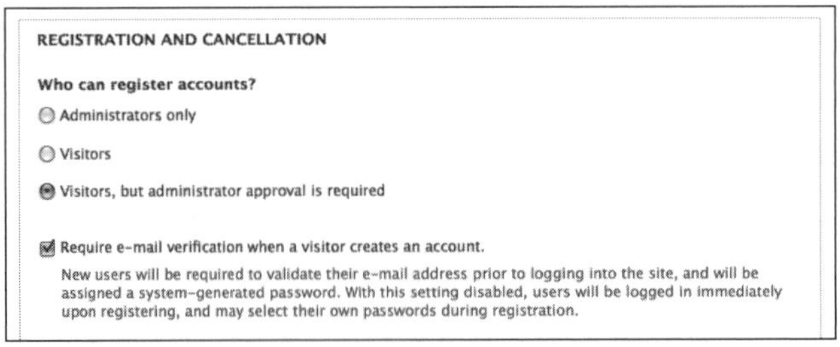

REGISTRATION AND CANCELLATION

Who can register accounts?

- ( ) Administrators only
- ( ) Visitors
- (•) Visitors, but administrator approval is required

[x] Require e-mail verification when a visitor creates an account.

New users will be required to validate their e-mail address prior to logging into the site, and will be assigned a system-generated password. With this setting disabled, users will be logged in immediately upon registering, and may select their own passwords during registration.

A Options to decide how much control you have over the creation of new accounts

the “Create new account” link and submits the form sees a message on the resulting screen that reads, “Your password and further instructions have been sent to your e-mail address.”

- Visitors, but administrator approval is required: Means that visitors can set up an account, but its status will remain as Blocked until someone with “Administer users” permission approves it. (To understand how to grant that permission, see the section “Defining User Roles and Permissions.”) This is Drupal’s default setting.

  With this option set, a user who clicks the “Create new account” link and submits the form sees a message on the resulting screen that reads, “Thank you for applying for an account. Your account is currently pending approval by the site administrator. In the meantime, a welcome message with further instructions has been sent to your e-mail address.”

Drupal also sends an email message to the superuser that reads, “***username*** has applied for an account,” along with a link to the page where that administrator can approve the application.

3. To require users to confirm their email addresses before their accounts become active, leave the “Require e-mail verification when a visitor creates an account” check box selected.

   In this case, the user does not have the opportunity to set a password when joining the site; instead, Drupal sends a temporary password to the email address the user provided. (To learn how to change the text of that email, see the section “To modify automated administration emails and determine when to send them.”)

   If the address was a fake (as is common in accounts created for abusive purposes), the user will never receive the password and will therefore never be able to log in to your site.

   If you decide to deselect the check box, Drupal will require the user to choose a password when creating the account, and no email confirmation will occur.

continues on next page

4. The next section on the page, "When cancelling a user account," provides four options **B**.

   The selection you make here becomes the default, but you can change it when you actually delete an account. For details on the differences among the four settings, see the section "To cancel an individual user's account."

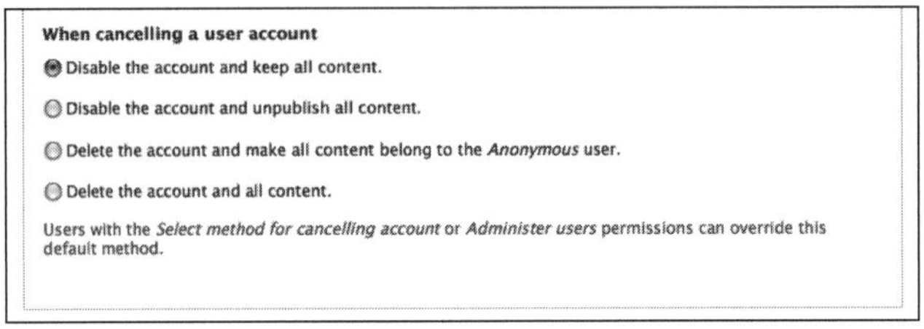

When cancelling a user account

- (•) Disable the account and keep all content.
- ( ) Disable the account and unpublish all content.
- ( ) Delete the account and make all content belong to the *Anonymous* user.
- ( ) Delete the account and all content.

Users with the *Select method for cancelling account* or *Administer users* permissions can override this default method.

B Setting Drupal's default option when canceling an account

Should I Require Email Verification?

The history of email verification is a long and contentious one. On one hand, you protect yourself from spam accusations and get a better quality of user when you require it; on the other, some users will misunderstand the confirmation message and therefore fail to confirm their memberships. (Online marketers claim the confirmation failure rate to be as high as 70 percent.)

So should you require email verification? In a word: *absolutely*. Drupal's popularity means that there are already online robots that know Drupal's sign-up procedure well enough to take advantage of any site that doesn't use email confirmation. (One obscure site I ran got a dozen such attempts per week.) In addition, people could sign up others without their consent: If you don't require email confirmation, and you later send email to your site's members, you could expose yourself to legal liability by spamming unwilling recipients.

Fortunately, there's one simple thing you can do to improve the email confirmation rate: Customize the confirmation email, following instructions in the section "To modify automated administration emails and determine when to send them." Include some information about the site that will tickle their memories more than just the site's name does. Shorten the message, and highlight the need for confirmation. (The default messages are somewhat weak on these points.)

Finally, go through your list of users at **`http://`*`domain-name`*`/admin/user`** once in a while to make sure that none slipped through the cracks. You might even consider sending a message to those who joined a while ago but are still listed as Blocked, to find out whether they did, indeed, mean to become members of your site.

To allow (or forbid) user signatures and avatars:

1. Click Configuration in the Toolbar and then click "Account settings."
2. Scroll down to the Personalization section **C**. The first check box, which is deselected by default, lets you permit users to create text *signatures* that Drupal appends to every comment that user posts.
3. To allow users to upload pictures to represent themselves (avatars) in comments and user posts, ensure that the "Enable user pictures" check box is selected (as it is by default).

   However, these avatars appear on your site only if you've selected the "User pictures in posts" or "User pictures in comments" check boxes on your theme's settings page. For more information about changing theme settings, see Chapter 2.

continues on next page

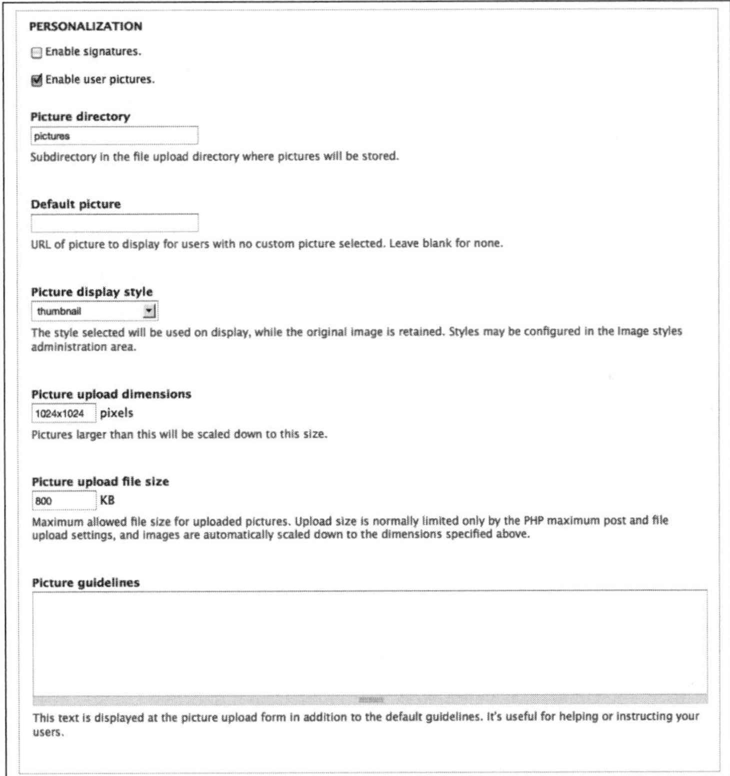

C The Personalization section of the Account settings screen

4. The remainder of the settings in the Personalization section are for determining how user graphics are managed.

   - Picture directory: Specifies what subfolder inside **`/sites/default/files`** will store avatar graphics. Drupal is quite fault-tolerant about this: If you name a directory that doesn't already exist on your server, Drupal attempts to automatically create it, and if you later change the directory, Drupal tries to figure out where to find the files. The path here should *not* have a leading slash, so **`pictures/users`** is correct while **`/pictures/users`** is not.
   - Default picture: Lets you specify an avatar for all users who don't choose their own. As with the "Picture directory" field, the path should not have a leading slash.
   - Picture display style: Tells Drupal which image style to apply to user avatars. The pop-up menu lists all image styles in your Drupal installation: The default one automatically scales avatars to 100 pixels square.

     To learn how to change these settings, see the section "To create or edit image styles" in Chapter 5, "Making Content Interactive."
   - Picture upload dimensions and Picture upload file size fields: Let you set the maximum allowable avatar size in pixels (in the format ***`widthxheight`***) and kilobytes, respectively. Users see these restrictions next to the file-upload field when they upload their avatars, and Drupal rejects any attempts to upload graphics larger than the allowable sizes.
   - Picture guidelines: Lets you can give instructions to users who are about to upload their avatars, in text that appears next to the file-size warnings **D**.

5. The rest of this screen lets you change the text of email messages sent to users, as is described in the next section, "To modify automated administration emails and determine when to send them." When you've made the desired changes, scroll to the bottom of the screen and click "Save configuration."

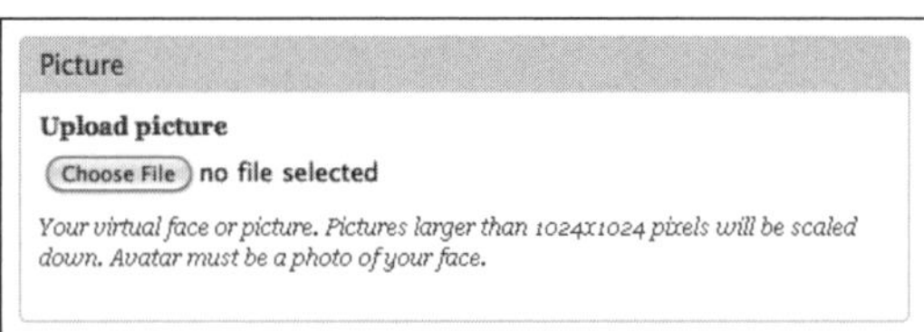

D Guidance that users see when they upload avatars, including the custom text "Avatar must be a photo of your face."

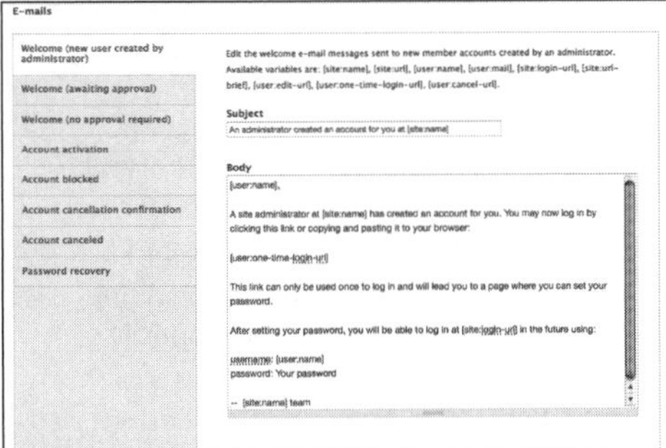

E The section of the Account settings page where you can change email messages sent to users

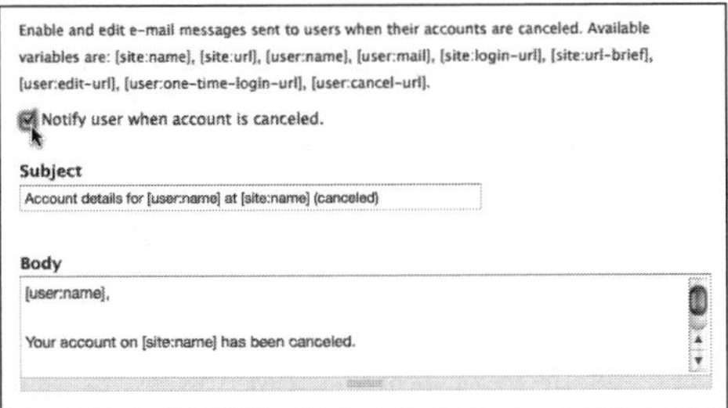

F Settings for some administrative messages include a check box to determine whether Drupal will send the message at all

To modify automated administration emails and determine when to send them:

1. Click Configuration in the Toolbar and then click "Account settings."
2. Scroll down to the E-mails section **E**.
3. Clicking any of the eight links on the left shows you the text of an email message that's sent to users under a specific circumstance, such as when you create accounts for them.

   Three of these message types—for account activation, account blocking, and account cancelation—offer you a check box to determine whether to send email when the action occurs **F**. Drupal *always* sends a message for the other five actions described.
4. To change the text of any of these email messages, simply click its tab and start typing in the Subject or Body fields.

   In addition to static text, you can enter dynamic "variables" that Drupal replaces with items specific to that user. In **F**, when Drupal sends one of these emails to the user **jimbo**, it replaces the text ***[user:name]*** with **jimbo**. The meanings of most of the variables that you can use are obvious, but here are clarifications for those that aren't:

   - ***[site:name]*** is the site's name—in our example that's **Sunrader Fans**.
   - ***[site:url]*** is the site's main page, which we've referred to in this book as **http://*domain-name***.
   - ***[site:url_brief]*** removes the **http://** part, delivering just ***domain-name***.

continues on next page

- *[site:login_url]* is always **http://*domain-name*/user** unless you explicitly change it.
- *[user:edit_url]* goes to the user's page for editing the account, generally **http://*domain-name*/user/*user-ID*/edit**, where ***user-ID*** is the serial number Drupal associated with the user's account. (The superuser's account has a user ID of 1, the second account created has a user ID of 2, and so on.)
- *[user:one-time-login-url]* and *[user:cancel-url]* are addresses on your site for the user to log in to or cancel the account. The ***login_url*** is generally in the form of **http://*domain-name*/user/reset/*user-ID*/*timestamp*/*random-hexadecimal-number***. The URL is only valid for 24 hours.

5. When you've made the desired changes, scroll to the bottom of the screen and click "Save configuration."

What About International Users?

There's one large area of Drupal we haven't talked about: internationalization. Possibly because it's been so successful outside its birth country of Belgium, Drupal has extensive controls for presenting your site in ways that are friendly to people in many countries, using many languages, and with varying standards for time and measurement.

Mastery of internationalization (commonly known as *i18n* to denote the many letters between the first and last) and localization (*l10n*) are crucial to anyone planning to launch an international site. But they're also complex subjects with many questions that need addressing. For example: Which parts of the site will you translate? If some languages read from right to left, how does that affect your layout? Are there local legal or cultural issues that could affect i18n?

We won't go into these details here, except to direct you to turn on the Locale module that provide controls for many of them. You can do so by clicking Modules in the Toolbar, clicking the Locale check box, and then clicking "Save configuration" at the bottom of the screen. You then see new options in the "Regional and Language" section when you click Configuration in the Toolbar. If you have further questions, the best place to find answers is in the Internationalization discussion group at **http://groups.drupal.org/i18n**.

Defining User Roles and Permissions

Drupal's security structure rests on two pillars:

- Categorizing users into roles
- Granting appropriate permissions to all users in a role

At first, this approach seems unwieldy. Let's say, for example, that you've just hired two people: one who needs to create, edit, and delete nodes, and another who'll be managing site users. It would be convenient to just edit the user accounts of those two people to grant those permissions. But Drupal doesn't work that way. Instead, you:

1. Create two new roles, such as "content manager" and "community manager."
2. Define permissions for those roles.
3. Apply those roles to the users who should have them.

The benefit of such a system is that it scales quite well. If your site becomes a huge success and you need to hire other people to manage it, you'll be able to give them the same permissions as their colleagues simply by selecting a check box in their user profiles. This role-based system encourages easy-to-maintain security practices: It's a lot easier to keep track of permission settings on a handful of roles than on thousands of users.

To add and delete user roles:

1. Click People in the Toolbar, then click the Permissions tab, followed by the Roles button **A**. This will bring you to the Roles administration page **B**.
2. Enter the name of the role you want to add in the blank field on the last line, then click "Add role."

   You can enter pretty much any text as the role name, including punctuation and eight-bit characters such as å and •.
3. Drupal adds the role to the list. To delete the role or change its name, click the "edit role" link to go to the Edit role page. Then click the Delete role button **C**.
4. You can change permissions associated with this role by clicking the "edit permissions" link on the Roles administration page seen in **B**. If you do, however, you'll see permissions for *only* that role, and you won't be able to compare them to those of other roles. For a better way to edit permissions, see the section "To change user access permissions."

TIP You can't delete or change the names of the "anonymous user" or "authenticated user" roles: They're essential parts of the Drupal software itself.

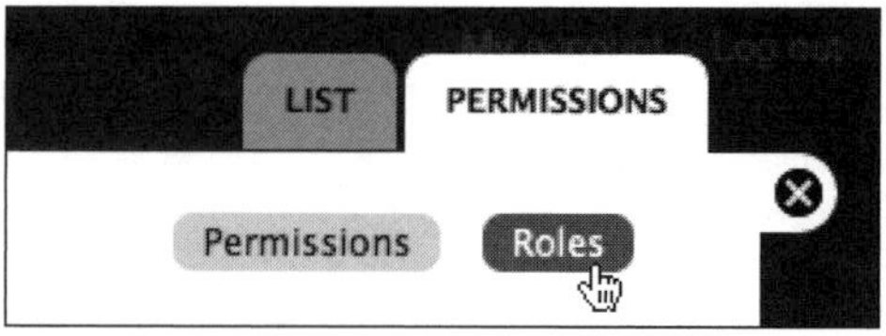

A The Roles button appearing after you click the Permissions tab

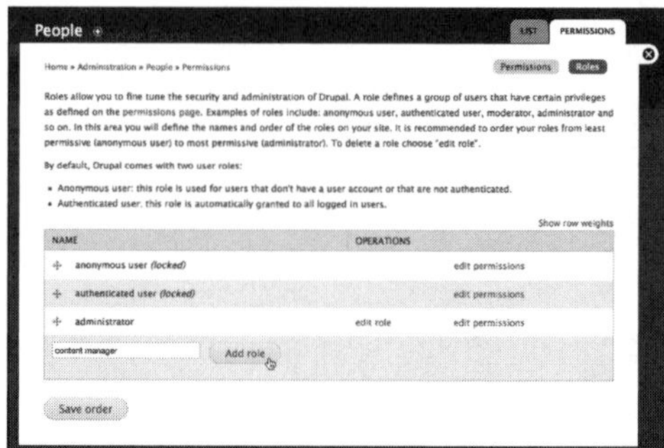

B The Roles administration page, shown during the addition of a "content manager" role

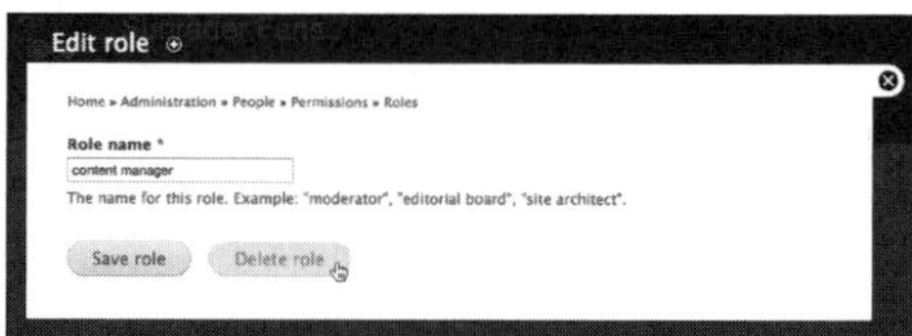

C Deleting the "content manager" role

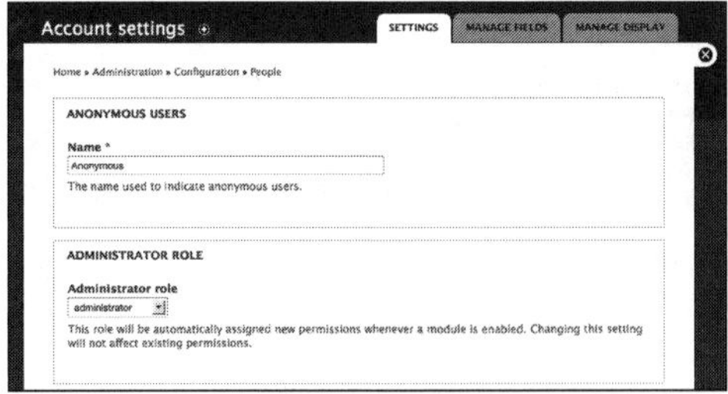

D Controls on the Account settings page that affect the anonymous user and administrator roles

To better define the administrator and anonymous user roles:

1. Click Configuration in the Toolbar and then click "Account settings." We'll examine only the first two sections of this page, labeled "Anonymous users" and "Administrator role" **D**.

2. The first section on this screen lets you change the way that Drupal refers to anonymous users—that is, those who haven't logged in to an account on your site. This mostly comes into play when you allow them to post content on your site, as the name you specify here typically appears near the content's title.

   Some sites use this setting as a way to encourage site registrations. For example, the popular technology site **`slashdot.org`** has called unregistered users "Anonymous Cowards" for years.

continues on next page

What's So Special About the Administrator Role?

Drupal's developers created the administrator role for Drupal 7 because many Drupal sites have multiple administrators. To manage this arrangement in previous versions of Drupal, you needed to either share the superuser account among several people—a terrible practice in terms of security—or create a role with all the permissions turned on. Since the latter is the better option, it became part of Drupal 7.

However, a user with the administrator role does not have exactly the same power as the superuser. For one thing, the superuser's powers are irrevocable, while you can turn off permissions for administrator users.

But there's one thing about the administrator role that's particularly handy: Whenever you install and enable a new module, users with the administrator role automatically gain power to administer it. However, administrators don't automatically gain permission to create nodes of newly made content types.

To learn how to grant and revoke specific administrator powers, see the section "To change user access permissions."

3. The "Administrator role" section has a pop-up menu that includes Drupal's special administrator role, all the roles you've created, and a "disabled" option **E**. Select the role that you'd like to have administrator privileges: Whenever you install and enable a new module, members of that role will have permission to use all its features.
4. When you've made the changes you want, scroll to the bottom of the screen and click "Save configuration."

To change an individual user's roles:

1. You can change the roles held by an individual user by editing that user's profile page. There are many ways to reach that page, among them:
   - Click People in the Toolbar and look through the list of users, filtering as necessary until you find the user; then click the "edit" link in that user's row. For more information about using controls on this page, see the section "To view a list of user accounts."
   - Click the user's name that shows up next to content that the user created, and then click the Edit tab.
   - Enter the user's name in the search box on the front page, click Users on the resulting page, click the user's name, and then click the Edit tab.
2. Scroll down to the Roles section of the user edit page. Click the check boxes as desired to select and deselect the roles this user should have **F**.
3. When you've made all the changes you want, scroll to the bottom of the screen and click Save.

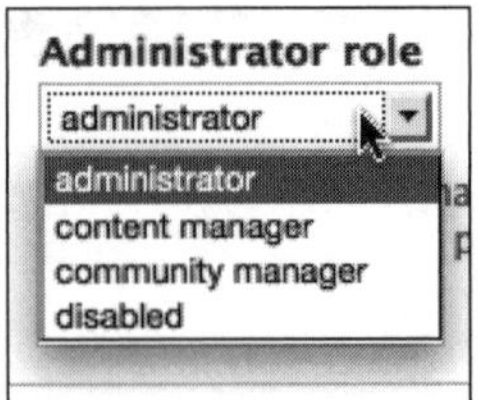

E Options for assigning a role to receive all permissions, including two custom roles

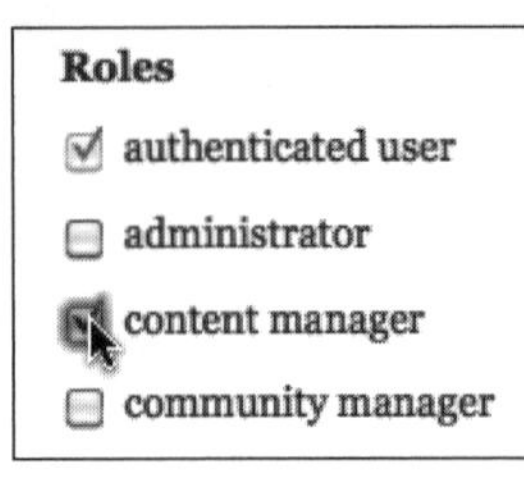

F Adding the "content manager" role via the user edit page

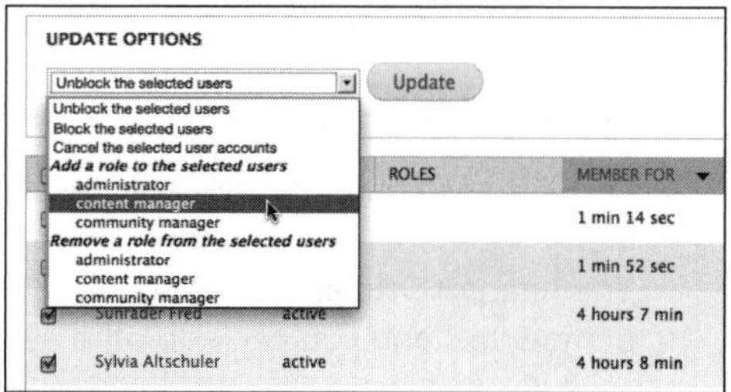

G Adding the "content manager" role to all indicated users

To change the roles of multiple users:

1. Go to the People administration page by clicking People in the Toolbar.
2. Sort and filter the list, as you learned in the section "To view a list of user accounts."
3. Choose the accounts you want to affect by selecting the check boxes next to their names.
4. In the Update Options section, select the role you want to add to those users under the "Add a role to the selected users" option G. To remove roles from those users, select the role under the "Remove a role from the selected users" option.
5. Click the Update button. The People administration page reloads, with the appropriate roles applied to the users you selected.

To change user access permissions:

1. Click People in the Toolbar and then click Permissions to go to the Permissions screen **H**.
2. To grant a permission, select the check box for the permission you want to grant and the role to which you want to grant it.

   This screen can seem overwhelming at first, with over 100 check boxes. But it's a lot easier to deal with when you understand its basic structure:

   - Each column is a role. When you select a check box in that column, you are giving permissions to all users who have that role. (For details, see the sections on roles earlier in this chapter.)
   - Each row is a permission: Such as "Access user profiles" or "Create new Article content." By selecting a check box in this row, you're granting that specific permission to a role.
   - Permissions appear grouped according to the module that controls them. The heart of Drupal is a collection of modules, and you can add other modules to extend Drupal's functionality. (For details, see Chapter 9, "Extending Drupal with Modules.")
3. When you've adjusted permissions as you like, click "Save permissions."

TIP Except for the anonymous user role, you can give a role only to someone who has a user name and password on your system—that is, to an authenticated user. Conversely, every person with a (non-anonymous) role is also an authenticated user. When you grant a permission to authenticated users, Drupal automatically grants it also to all non-anonymous roles.

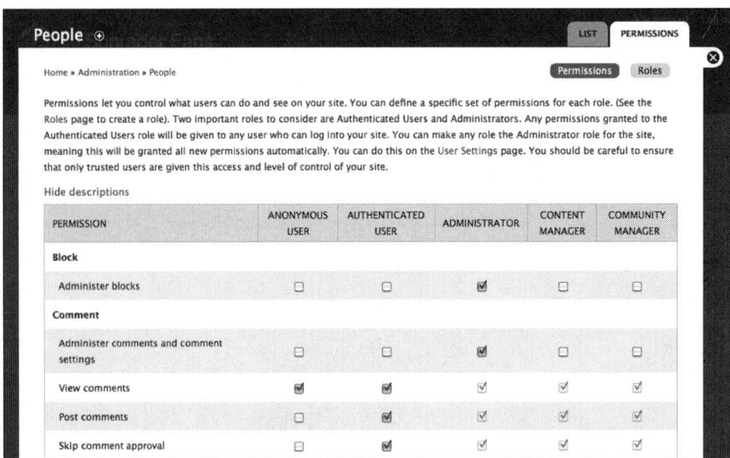

H A portion of the Permissions screen, showing Drupal's three default roles and the two additional roles we created

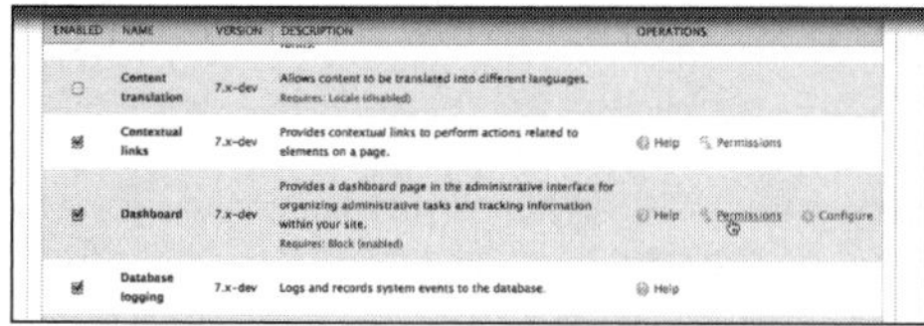

I Links to Help, Permissions, and Configuration pages for specific modules

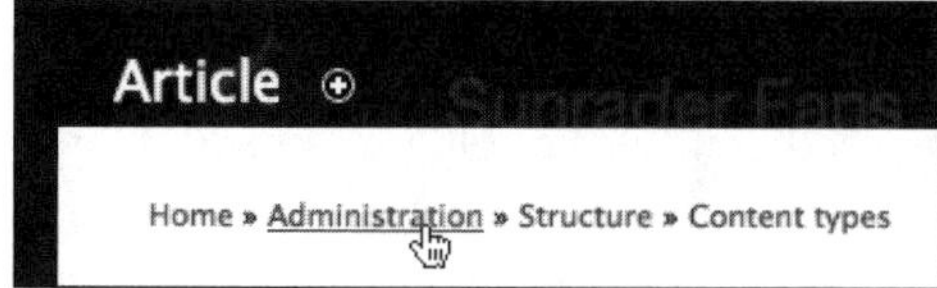

J The Administration link that's available on every administrative page

To find permission settings for a specific module:

1. There are two places in Drupal with links to permissions for specific modules. The first is on the Modules page: To go there, click Modules in the Toolbar. Next to some modules are Help, Permissions, and Configure links that take you directly to those controls **I**.
2. The second place where you can reach specific permissions settings is on the Administration page, which has no direct link through the Toolbar. To get there, go to any administrative page and click the Administration link in the upper-left corner **J**. (This is part of a string of links known as "breadcrumbs" that shows you where you are in relation to other administrative pages.)

   On the Administration page, click the Index tab to see controls categorized by module **K**, then click the permissions link under the relevant module.

Whichever method you use, Drupal takes you directly to the relevant section on the Permissions page.

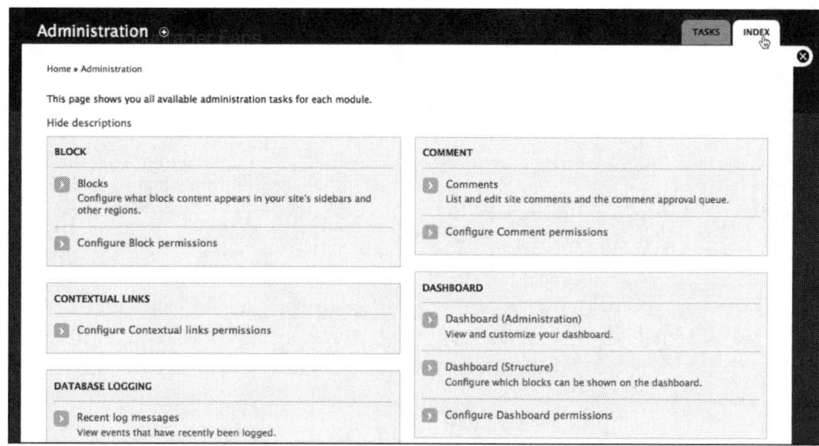

K A portion of the Administration page, with the Index tab selected

So Many Permission Settings... Which Are Important?

Version 7 is the first release of Drupal to undergo a thorough user-interface audit. Noted designer Mark Boulton led the charge, thanks to major funding from Drupal consultancy Acquia and contributions of time by hundreds of volunteers.

But the Permissions screen remains a bit of a bear. It's burdened with irreducible complexity, and the sea of check boxes so far appears to be the best way to address it.

After you've been using Drupal for a while, the complexity fades away because you'll find that you keep coming back to the same few permissions settings again and again, but you almost never touch others. While each administrator works differently, and each site has different needs, here are the permissions I most often need to tweak:

- Grant "Post comments" permission to anonymous users. These comments don't appear on the site immediately. Instead, they go into the Approval queue, which you'll learn about in the section "To moderate comment spam." Only grant this permission if you have the time to browse and act on the approval queue frequently—at least once a day is usually fine for sites with moderate traffic.
- Grant permissions to create, edit, and delete nodes of various content types to the appropriate roles. Administrators often forget to grant such permissions in the Node module to allow content growth.
- Grant "Use search" and "Use advanced search" permissions to anonymous and authenticated users.
- Grant "View user profiles," "Change own username," and "Cancel own user account" permissions to authenticated users—assuming that you run a fairly open site, and feel you can trust your users enough.

Building and Protecting Your User Community

Many online businesses fail for lack of an audience. If your site relies on user-contributed content and interaction, it won't live long unless it attracts people and keeps them coming back for more.

Early web sites did so through a variety of gimmicks, such as prize drawings and outright cash bribes. Then entrepreneurs realized that the promise of human contact was just as compelling—and a lot cheaper. And so the boom in online social networking began.

You've already learned how to use some of the tools that encourage social networking, such as forums, blogs, and polls. Some methods to create community are more subtle. Allowing users to apply tags to stories, for example, gives them a small-but-satisfying sense of power, while distributing the hard work of categorizing content among many people through a technique known as *crowdsourcing*. (Read about tagging in the section "Categorizing Content with Taxonomies" in Chapter 5.)

This section gives you three other ways to build community. You'll learn how to:

- Let users know each other through profiles they create.
- Enable contact forms so they can contact each other directly.
- Prevent comment spam, an extremely common problem that pollutes the river of human interaction.

To add fields to user profiles:

1. Drupal gives every user a profile with just enough information to maintain the account: user name, password, and so on. But you can add fields to those profiles through a process much like the one you learned in Chapter 4, "Customizing Content," to add fields to content types.

   We'll demonstrate by adding a field that lets users tell the world what vehicles they own. This information shows up on each user's profile, which is visible on the page at **`http://`*`domain-name`*`/user/`*`user-ID`*** to everyone with the "View user profiles" permission. (By default, only administrators have this permission. To learn how to make it more widely available, see the section "To change user access permissions" earlier in this chapter.)

   Controls to add fields are on the Account settings page. To get there, click Configuration in the Toolbar and then click "Account settings."

2. Click the "Manage fields" tab to see what fields are already part of user profiles **A**. Two fields are there by default: "User name and password" and "Timezone." You can move them, but you can't turn them off.

3. Now you add fields in the same manner as you learned in the section "To add fields to a custom content type" in Chapter 4. By way of demonstration, we'll add a field titled "Sunraders I own."

   In the "Add new field" area, enter a human-readable name and a machine-readable name. Then select which type of information the field will contain and the "widget" that determines how that information is collected. (I've chosen the Text field type and the "Text field" widget for our example.) Click Save.

4. You'll now need to decide on various criteria, such as field length, whether it's a required field, and so forth. These options will vary depending on the field type you selected.

   When you've finished filling out the field settings pages, click "Save settings."

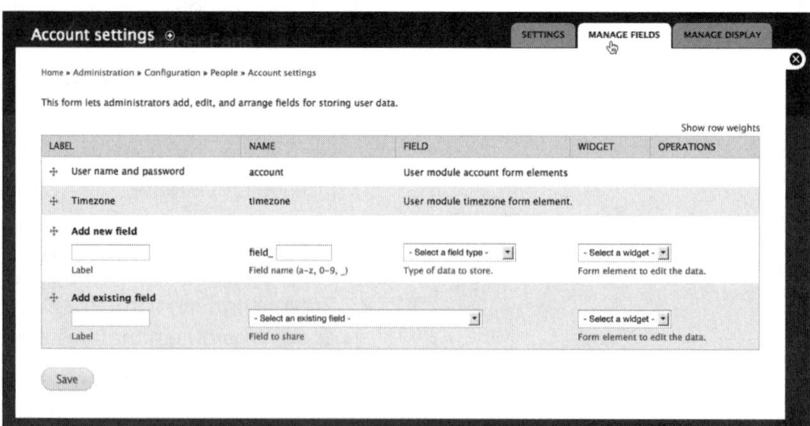

A The screen where you can change what fields are part of user profiles

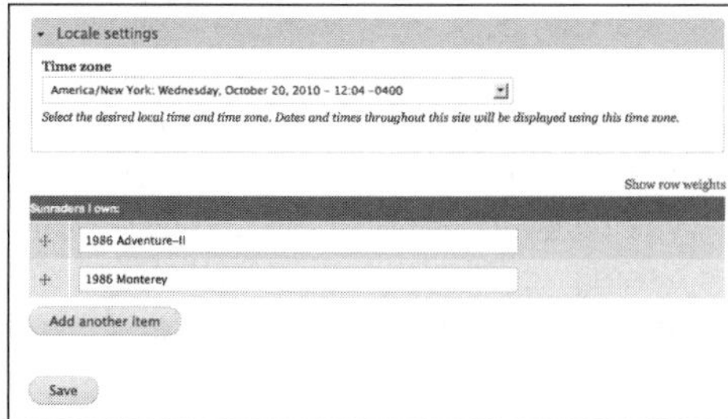

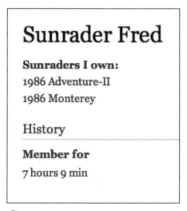

B The "Sunraders I own" multiple-value field in the user edit form, with the built-in "Locale settings" field above it

Sunrader Fred

Sunraders I own:

1986 Adventure-II

1986 Monterey

History

Member for

7 hours 9 min

C Viewing a profile that contains our newly added field

5. Drupal returns you to the Manage fields page, with your new field in place. You can change the order of fields as they'll appear in profiles by dragging them by their handles ✥ and clicking Save. Likewise, you can change their appearance by clicking the "Manage display" tab and altering their default settings. For help, see the "To change a field's display and input options" section in Chapter 4.

   Now when users edit their profiles, they'll see a field where they can fill in the information you requested **B**. When others view a profile, they'll see what the user put in that field **C**.

What About the Profile Module?

If you manage a Drupal 6 site, you might have noticed that the Profile module lets you add fields to user profiles in a manner very similar to what you saw here. You might also have noticed that the Profile module is still there in Drupal 7, although it's disabled by default. So why not use it?

The fact is, you could, and your users would never know the difference. However, the method you learned here is much more in line with Drupal's future architecture. Before, profiles and nodes were based on completely different field systems; now, both are "entities," equally able to enjoy Drupal 7's advances in field handling. (Comments and taxonomy terms are also entities.) How important is that? Well, Drupal creator Dries Buytaert called the introduction of entities "the biggest architecture change in the history of Drupal" in July of 2010.

The Profile module, by comparison, is only there to allow sites to keep profiles intact when migrated from Drupal 6 to Drupal 7. But Drupal 8 won't support those old-format profiles. So if you're building a new site, the choice is clear: Create profiles using the modern field system and avoid the Profile module.

To provide a form for users to contact you (and each other):

1. Click Modules in the Toolbar to go to the Modules page.
2. Enable the Contact module by selecting its check box. Scroll to the bottom of the screen and click "Save configuration."
3. Your contact form is now enabled and will send emails to the site address you entered when you created the site. By default, only users with the administrator role can use it. We'll make it available to everybody by changing its permissions.

   To do so, click People in the Toolbar and then click Permissions. Scroll down and grant the "Use the site-wide contact form" permission to those roles you'd like to have it. (You can also allow users to contact each other through individual contact forms by selecting the "Use users' personal contact forms" permission.) When finished, scroll to the bottom and click "Save permissions."
4. To change the contact form's features, click Structure in the Toolbar and then click "Contact form." On the resulting page is a list of contact categories that contains one entry, labeled "Website feedback." Click Edit in that row to go to that category's configuration page **D**.

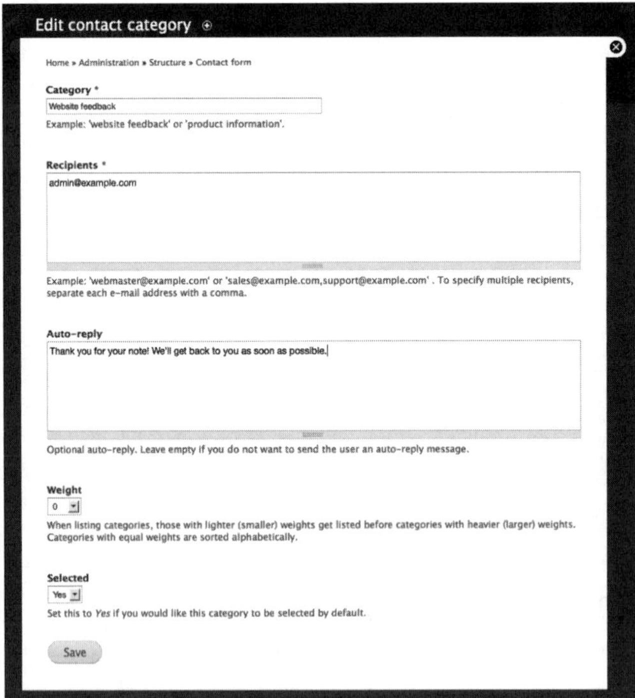

D Editing the "Website feedback" contact category

5. Fill out the resulting form. Its fields are:
   - Category: What users see in a pop-up menu on the contact form. Typical categories are "Business inquiries," "Technical problems," and so forth.
   - Recipients: Determines where these messages will go. If you want them to go to multiple recipients, separate the email addresses with commas.
   - Auto-reply: Tells Drupal to send an email message to people who fill out the form. Such a message is a nicety, letting them know that you'll respond to the message as soon as possible. Enter the text of the message you'd like Drupal to send.

     If the person trying to reach you using the contact form is an authenticated user, Drupal uses the email address from the user's profile. Drupal prompts anonymous users to provide an email address in the contact form. However, it doesn't authenticate those addresses in any way, so there's no guarantee that your auto-reply message will reach the correspondent.
   - Weight: As elsewhere in Drupal, lets you put this category before or after others in the contact form's pop-up menu.
   - Selected: Determines whether the contact form will use this category if the user doesn't select any other. Whenever you set this field to Yes on a category, Drupal automatically changes it to No on all other categories so that only one category is ever pre-selected. If you don't set the Selected field to Yes on any categories, then Drupal will prompt people using the contact form to select a category.

   When you've filled out this form, click Save.
6. You can set up additional contact categories by clicking the "Add category" link on the Contact form administration page, filling out the form, and clicking Save.
7. Your contact form is now ready! Users with sufficient permission who go to **http://*domain-name*/contact** see it **E**.

continues on next page

Contact

Your name *

Jimbo Jones

Your e-mail address *

jimbo@example.com

Subject *

Found a broken link

Category *

Website feedback

Message *

Thanks for the great site! I just wanted to let you know that the link to your personal site from the seems to be broken from the "About" page.

Keep up the good work!

Send message

E A typical contact form, as an anonymous user sees it before typing and sending a message

8. You (or individual users) can also turn on *personal* contact forms that allow users to contact each other.

   First, go to the profile page of the user you'd like to be able to receive contact email. As the administrator, you'd do this by clicking People in the Toolbar and then clicking "edit" next to the user's name; the user would do this by clicking "My account" and then clicking the Edit tab.

   Then, scroll down and select the "Personal contact form" check box and click Save **F**.

   Now users with both the "View user profiles" and "Use users' personal contact forms" permissions can contact that user by going to the appropriate user page and clicking the Contact tab.

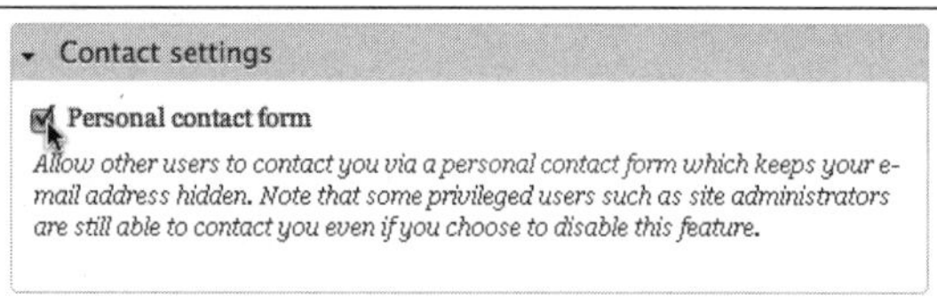

F Enabling a personal contact form on the user's profile edit page

To moderate comment spam:

1. Go to the Permissions page by clicking People in the Toolbar and then clicking the Permissions tab. Ensure that the "Skip comment approval" permission is not selected for the roles whose comments you want to moderate.
2. Users who have the "Post comments" permission but not the "Skip comment approval" permission see a message at the top of the resulting page after attempting to post a comment on your site. ("Your comment has been queued for review by site administrators and will be published after approval.") In addition, Drupal sends the administrative email address a message that says a comment is waiting for your approval. That email message includes a URL that takes you to the Approval queue, at `http://`***`domain-name`***`/admin/content/comment/approval`.
3. When you go to that page, you see a list of comments awaiting approval. (You can also go to that page by clicking Content, clicking the Comments tab, and then clicking the "Unapproved comments" button.)

   Select the check boxes of those comments you want to either approve ("publish") or delete. Then select the appropriate option from the "Update options" pop-up menu and click Update **G**.

TIP Think hard before granting the "Skip comment approval" permission to anonymous users if your site is visible to the entire Internet. Any area where a comment can be posted will fill to the brim with spam. If you have the time, I recommend you moderate comments from authenticated users as well, as some spammers now use scripts that automatically join Drupal sites just to become "authenticated" enough to spam your site.

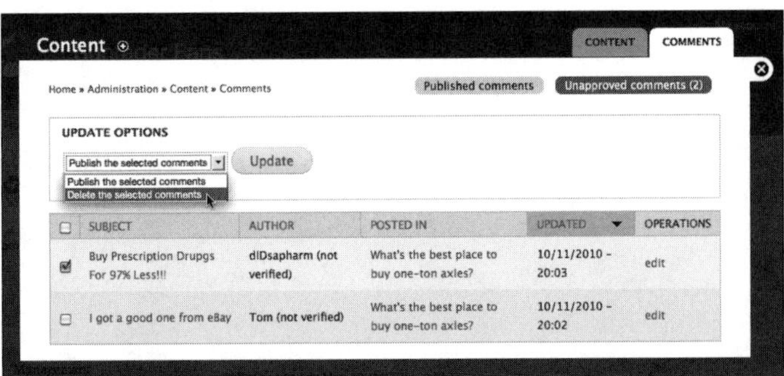

G The comment approval queue, as seen during the process of deleting a spam message

Customizing Drupal's Look and Feel

Drupal is first and foremost a *functional* tool. You feed it data in the form of text and graphics, and it spits them back at you in controlled and useful ways. But it's not a completely colorless tool. Members of the Drupal community have made unprecedented efforts to improve the software's appearance and interactivity—its "look and feel."

And yet designing for Drupal remains somewhat difficult, relying on text-based tools to change Cascading Style Sheets (CSS) and PHP code. Very little in Drupal's layout system has a drag-and-drop interface, and there are few handles to resize objects. Further, you control how design files interact with each other by configuring a **`.info`** file that's entirely unique to Drupal.

But as is typical in Drupal, you're rewarded for your efforts with an extremely high level of flexibility. With a rudimentary knowledge of HTML and CSS, coupled with the tips you'll learn here, you'll know enough to make substantial and effective changes to your site's appearance. For much, much more about Drupal theming, see **`drupal.org/theme-guide`**.

In This Chapter

Creating a New Theme

A new Drupal themer's temptation is to try to write a first theme from scratch. That's a valuable way to learn theming from the ground up, but unnecessary. With dozens of well-constructed themes available for free download at **drupal.org/project/themes**, it's much easier to simply modify an existing theme. That can also be a better way to learn, since many existing themes incorporate standards and tricks that aren't obvious from a cold reading of the theming guide on **Drupal.org**.

We're going to start by basing our new theme on one that's very simple, but I want to reiterate that you can build your own theme on the shoulders of *any* Drupal theme—assuming, of course, that its copyright permits that use. (All Drupal core themes and those found on **drupal.org/project/themes** are licensed under the GNU Public License, which explicitly allows such use as long as the derived work also permits such modification. For details, see **gnu.org/copyleft/gpl.html**.)

It's amazing what a difference small changes can make. Often, you can satisfy your design needs by simply replacing a few graphics, colors, or CSS classes. On that note, this is a good time to review the section "Selecting a Visual Theme" in Chapter 2, "Establishing Your Drupal Site," for a reminder on how to change basic theme settings—for example, to replace the theme's default logo with your own.

To duplicate and rename an existing theme:

1. In your computer's file system, find the theme you want to copy. This could be either a core theme (which you'll find in the **/themes** folder of your Drupal installation) or a theme you downloaded earlier from **drupal.org/project/themes**. (For more information about downloading themes, see the section "To find, download, install, and enable an alternative theme" in Chapter 2.)

   New in Drupal 7 is a bare-bones theme named Stark that we'll use as a basis for our changes. In practice, you'll often start with a more complete theme, but the less-complex and less-distracting Stark is better for our purposes.

2. Copy the theme's entire folder (in this case, **/themes/stark**) to inside either **/sites/all/themes**, **/sites/default/themes**, or another appropriate folder if you're running a multisite installation. (For further direction, see the sidebar "Understanding the sites Folder" in Chapter 2.)

3. Inside this new folder, you'll find one file that ends in **.info**—in our case, that's **stark.info**. Rename the file to what you want for the theme's *machine-readable name*. (You'll give it the *human-readable name* in another step.) In our example, I've renamed it **peachpit.info**.

   Rename the theme's enclosing folder with the same name so that it's clear both to you and to Drupal itself **A**.

continues on next page

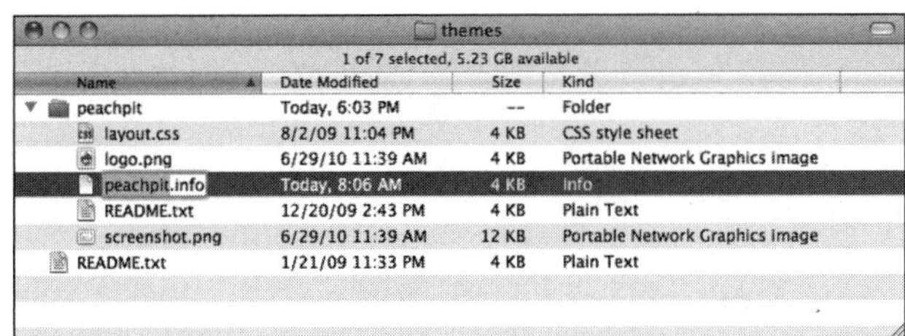

A Renaming the theme's **.info** file and enclosing folder

4. Now you're going to edit the newly renamed **.info** file to add the human-readable name and several other important pieces of information. Open it with a text editor, such as Mac OS X TextEdit, Windows Notepad, or *nix nano **B**.

5. The **.info** file has several parts, which the theming guide at **drupal.org/node/925532** will explain in great detail. (Parts of this guide are incomplete as I write this. You may be able to fill in some of the gaps by looking at the Drupal 6 theming guide at **drupal.org/theme-guide/6**. In particular, see "Structure of the .info file" at **drupal.org/node/171205**.)

   The only part you need to change is the "name" line, shown as Line 2 in **B**. Whatever you put here becomes the human-readable name of the theme, which appears on the Appearance page. Any changes that you make to the "description" (Line 3) also show up there.

   Both the first line and Lines 10-14 are added automatically to themes that are distributed through the Drupal project's web site at **drupal.org** and don't directly affect your installation of Drupal. There's no need to change them unless you plan to redistribute your theme through the **drupal.org** web site.

6. In a web browser, go to the Appearance page by clicking Appearance in the Toolbar. You now see your theme alongside any core and contributed themes you've installed **C**. You can enable it in the same way you learned in the section "Selecting a Visual Theme" in Chapter 2.

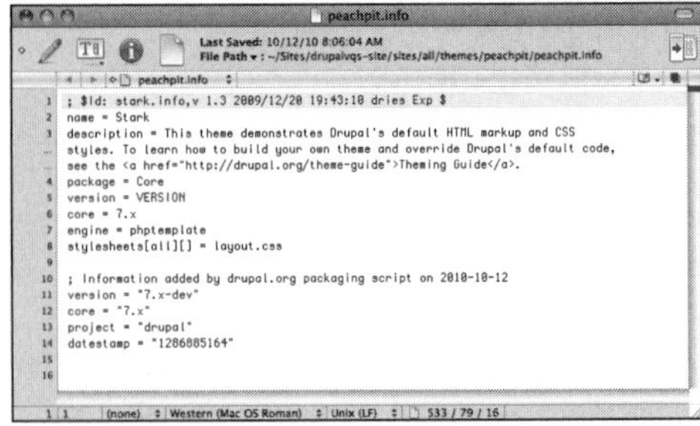

B The **peachpit.info** file opened in the Mac program TextWrangler, before applying any changes to it

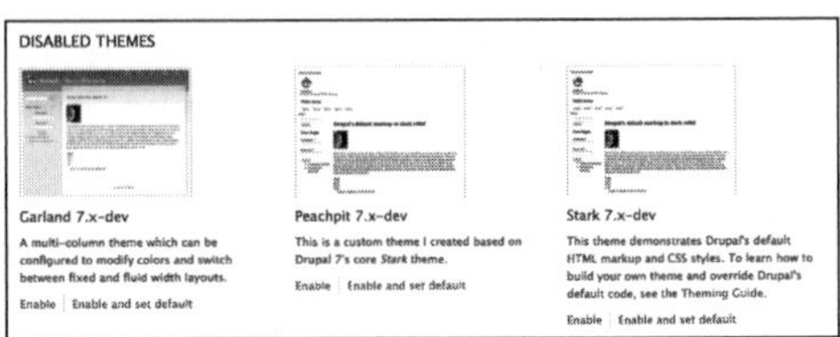

C The Appearance page, showing the newly created Peachpit theme next to the Stark theme on which it was based

Why Not Just Change the Existing Theme?

You may wonder why we bothered to copy the Stark theme. Couldn't we have just renamed it and changed it where it was?

The short answer is: Yes, we could have. But doing so would violate the central rule of Drupal development: Never touch anything outside the **/sites** folder. Or, as experienced Drupal developers frequently warn: Don't hack core.

There are several reasons why:

- Any changes you make in the **/themes** directory (instead of **/sites/all/themes** or similar) will simply be wiped out when you update Drupal, as you'll probably do about every month or two. (See the section "To update Drupal" in Chapter 2 for details.)
- Your changes will be hard to track, because anybody else who's tasked with administering your Drupal site will look for theme changes inside the **/sites** folder.
- Making changes directly to Stark prevents you from easily "rolling back" to its original, core version should problems arise.

Fortunately, Drupal's design makes modifying anything outside the **/sites** directory unnecessary. Its architecture specifically allows you to make any changes you could possibly want within that directory—you only need to learn to do things "The Drupal Way." That way is not always obvious, but one dictum is clear: Don't hack core.

TIP You can add HTML styling to the "description" field in the `.info` file. In C, you can see that I've added the `<em>` tag to the word *Stark*.

TIP As with any other Drupal development, you should work on a backup of the site, not its live version. Theming errors could make the site difficult to navigate or even inaccessible.

TIP Although we're using Stark to build our new theme, a note in its `layout.css` file warns that it "shouldn't be used on a production site because it can break." Its weaknesses are fixable with good CSS, however. If you prefer to start with something a little more robust, you can reuse any Drupal 7 theme you find at `drupal.org/project/themes`.

TIP You might also want to create your new theme using a different technique on top of themes designed as "base themes," such as Basic (`drupal.org/project/basic`), Genesis (`drupal.org/project/genesis`), Zen (`drupal.org/project/zen`), or NineSixty (`drupal.org/project/ninesixty`). Several of these come with excellent documentation.

TIP When you have developed your theme to a point where its basic appearance won't change much, replace the 150-by-90-pixel screen shot file (as was shown in C) that gives administrators a preview of the theme on the theme administration page. You can specify the screen shot's name in the `.info` file by adding the line `screenshot = *path/filename.ext*`. If you don't specify a location, the theme looks for a file named `screenshot.png` at the top level of the theme's directory.

Changing Theme Graphics and Typography with CSS

If you've studied CSS, you know that there are three ways to include styles in a web page:

- Inline styles: Temporary instructions defined immediately before the content they affect.
- Internal styles: Defined at the top of an HTML page and affect only that page.
- External styles: Contained in a separate text document that's referenced from within HTML pages.

Drupal uses all three methods to some extent. For example, you can style individual snippets of text within a node by using inline styles and applying the "Full HTML" text format. And by adding internal styles to a theme's template files—that is, the ones ending in **`tpl.php`**—you can apply changes to specific content types or pages.

We'll concern ourselves with changes in external styles, as they pervade your entire Drupal site. Implementing them is a two-stage process. First, edit your theme's **`.info`** file to tell Drupal which external CSS files to use; second, create (or edit) those files to add the styles you want.

We're now entering a somewhat advanced area of Drupal administration, and this chapter is only intended to help you get your feet wet. The Drupal.org theming guide at **`drupal.org/theme-guide`** will take you the rest of the way.

```
package = Core
version = VERSION
core = 7.x
engine = phptemplate
stylesheets[all][] = layout.css
stylesheets[all][] = local.css
```

A Adding a style sheet named **local.css** as the last-loaded CSS document in the **peachpit.info** file

To indicate a theme's CSS files:

1. Open the **.info** file for the theme you want to change. We'll continue using the Peachpit theme we created in the section "To duplicate and rename an existing theme."
2. In the middle of the **.info** file is at least one line that starts with **stylesheets**. This is the section where you define which CSS documents your Drupal theme uses to build pages.

   Add the names of any style sheets you want Drupal to use, in the following format: **stylesheets[*media-type*][] = *stylesheet-name.css***. Drupal loads these style sheets in the order this file

continues on next page

Anatomy of a Drupal Theme

For simplicity's sake, we've worked with the Stark theme throughout this chapter. That simplicity has provided clarity, but at the expense of exposing you to the many parts found in a more complex theme. Look in the Garland theme's folder (at **/themes/garland**) to see the difference: There are simply a lot more files.

Here's a description of those files you didn't see in the **Stark** folder. Keep in mind that Garland is far from the most complex theme out there. Some themes have additional parts, such as files containing JavaScript code that spices up the theme's user interface.

- Other CSS files. Garland includes several, most notably **fix-ie.css** (to correct bugs in Microsoft Internet Explorer) and files ending in **-rtl.css** (for languages that read right to left, such as Arabic).
- A color folder contains graphics, a CSS file, and a PHP support file to make Garland a recolorable theme (as was demonstrated in Chapter 2).
- An **images** folder keeps theme images from being littered throughout the theme's top-level directory.
- Several files ending in **.tpl.php**. These are the theme's *template* files, written in PHP to define where (and whether) information will appear on the screen. Template files can contain complex logic, and you can create different ones for individual content types or nodes. As always, the Drupal theming guide at **drupal.org/theme-guide** is a great source to learn how to do this. There is further information in the book *Front End Drupal*, co-authored by this book's technical editor, Emma Jane Hogbin.

lists when it renders a page: If there are style conflicts, the last-listed style sheet wins. One very common practice is to put all custom styles into a file named **`local.css`** and list that filename last in the **`.info`** file **A**.

The ***`media-type`*** value denotes the contexts in which the style appears. The most common values are **`all`**, **`screen`**, and **`print`**, although several others are possible. See **`w3.org/TR/CSS21/media.html`** for a complete list.

3. Save the **`.info`** file.
4. Click Configuration in the Toolbar and then click Performance. Clear the theme cache by clicking the "Clear all caches" button. Drupal normally caches the contents of the **`.info`** file to improve speed, so changes to that file won't be visible until you clear the cache. (A visit to the Appearance page also clears the cache.)
5. Create and edit the style sheet document (or documents) you named in the **`.info`** file, as shown in the next section, "To add styles in a CSS file."

TIP In practice, you could skip this step and just edit a theme's existing style sheets. Resist the temptation! Creating a new external style sheet that contains your custom styles makes upgrading (and rolling back to earlier versions) a lot easier.

TIP If you clear the cache as step 4 describes but still don't see the changes you expect, force your web browser to reload the page. For most browsers, the key command is Shift-Command-R on Mac and Shift-Control-R on *nix or Windows.

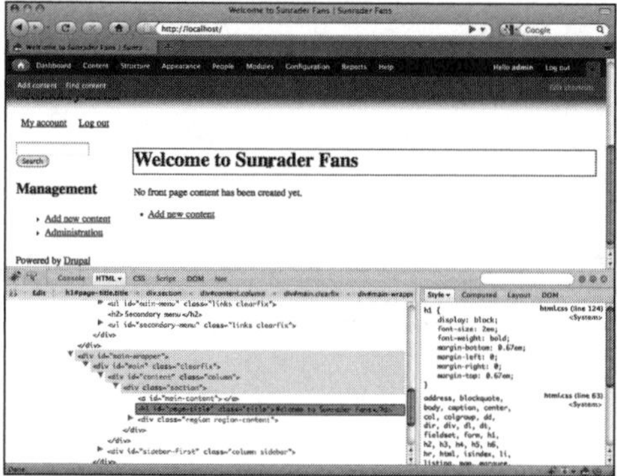

Ⓑ Using the Firebug plug-in to determine which styles affect a specific text block on a Drupal page

To add styles in a CSS file:

1. Before making a change, you first have to discover *what* to change. Drupal conveniently adds style tags to most page elements in a logical fashion, so there are plenty of opportunities for styling pages. But figuring out the names of specific styles takes some detective work.

   Most Drupal themers find the task easier with a tool called Firebug (**getfirebug.com**) that works together with the Firefox browser (**mozilla.com**). With this combination, you learn what styles affect an object on your Drupal page by clicking the "Inspect element" icon and then the object Ⓑ. (Alternatively, you can simply right-click an

continues on next page

Do I Really Need to Know CSS?

Yes. Yes. A million times yes.

There's just no way around it: CSS is the 21st-century way of designing for the web, and with good reason. Most obviously, CSS provides an ocean of layout and styling options. But just as importantly, CSS helps ensure that pages will look good on any browser, including portable devices, printers, and machines used by vision-impaired people. Drupal recognized its value early on, and its layout is now designed around CSS.

But CSS can seem overwhelming at first, especially if you try to learn it by dissecting existing themes. Five or ten styles affect a typical bit of text on a Drupal page, and changing the wrong one can have far-reaching effects you might not see right away. On the other hand, it's valuable to get practice with CSS *as it's used in Drupal*, since many naming conventions appear again and again. So here's what I suggest:

- Set up a test Drupal site where you can play around with theming as much as you want without worrying about the consequences. (For help, see Chapter 1, "Getting Drupal Up and Running.")
- Get a good tutorial/reference book (or six!) about CSS. I recommend *CSS3: Visual QuickStart Guide* by Jason Cranford Teague.
- Use online resources to quickly look up CSS syntax when needed. I always find myself going back to the one at **w3schools.com/css**, which also has "sandbox" areas where you can try out unfamiliar CSS code.

element on a Windows or *nix computer, or Control-click on a Mac, and choose the “Inspect element” option from the pop-up menu.) You can then decide how specific (or general) you want your style changes to be by adding the appropriate styles to your custom CSS file.

2. Add CSS styles to your custom style sheet. We’ll use the Peachpit theme we created in the section “To duplicate and rename an existing theme” **C**.

   The following CSS code is an example that changes the font and several layout elements when added to the **local.css** file **D**.

```
body
{
  font-family: sans-serif;
}

#site-name {
  font-size: 2em;
}

#header {
  border-style: dotted;
  border-width: 5px;
}
```

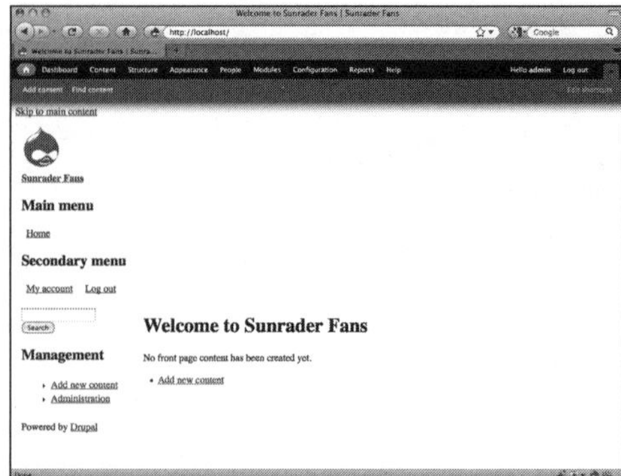

C The Peachpit theme before applying any style changes

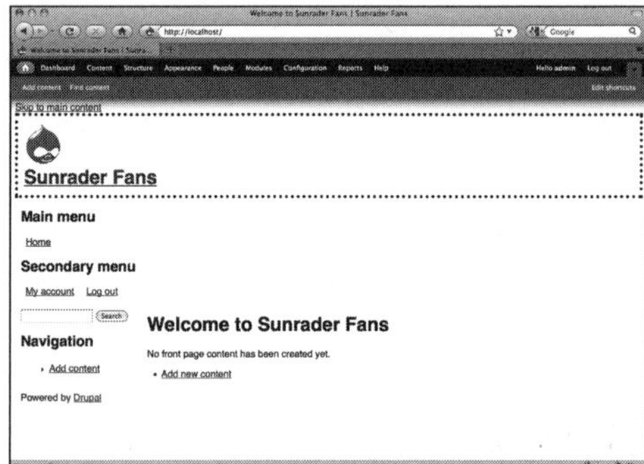

D The Peachpit theme with its new styles applied

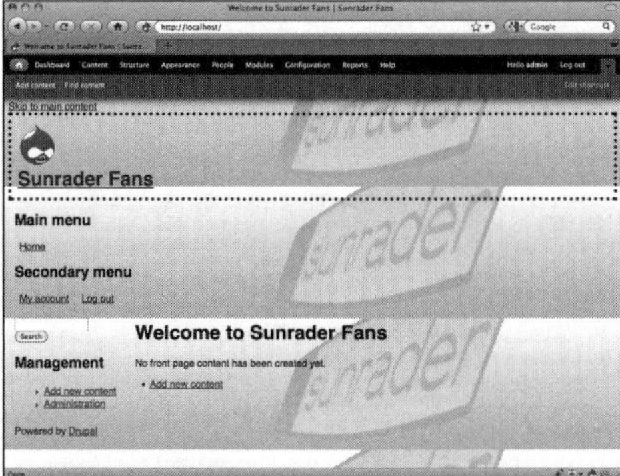

E The repeating effect of a **background-image** tag that's not modified by any other tags

To add a background graphic:

1. Use an image-processing program such as the GNU Image Manipulation Program (GIMP) or Photoshop to create the GIF, JGEP, or PNG graphic you want to use as the background. You could use an image intended to cover the entire screen, or just part of the screen.
2. Move this new image into the theme's folder, at either the top level or in a subfolder. In our example, a typical location is **/sites/all/themes/peachpit**.
3. Open one of the custom CSS files you designated in the **.info** file. If you haven't created this one yet, do so by following the instructions in the section "Changing Theme Graphics and Typography with CSS."
4. Add CSS to reference the background graphic. The properties you'll use are:
   - **background-image**
   - **background-repeat**
   - **background-attachment**
   - **background-position**

   If you're not familiar with CSS, the tutorial at **w3schools.com/css/css_background.asp** will quickly get you up to speed. Here's a quick-and-dirty way to change the graphic behind the entire page (assuming your graphic is named **background.jpg**):

   ```
   body {
     background-image:url(
     → 'background.jpg');
   }
   ```

   This is the simplest form of background image. However, there's one problem: If the viewer's screen is bigger than the graphic, it will repeat, possibly in unattractive ways E.

continues on next page

By adding the **background-repeat: no-repeat;** directive, the graphic appears only once **F**. Here's the code:

```
body {
  background-image:url(
  → 'background.jpg');
  background-repeat:no-repeat;
}
```

(**E** and the graphics following it mix in a few of the styles we applied earlier for clarity. Of course all **body** tags need to be mixed into a single **body** declaration.)

CSS has several other background properties to determine where the background image appears, whether it moves when the viewer scrolls down, and so forth. For more information about them, see **w3.org/TR/CSS2/colors.html**.

5. Add other CSS styles to complement your background. Here, for example, the background has a gradient down to a light gray (**#CCCCCC**), but then abruptly cuts off. By adding a **#CCCCCC** background color behind it, the graphic blends in with the rest of the screen **G**. The complete style is:

```
body
{
background-image: url(
→ 'background.jpg');
background-repeat:no-repeat;
background-color: #CCCCCC;
}
```

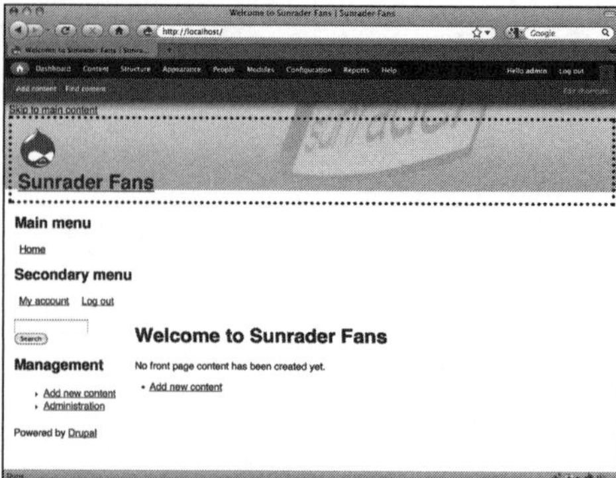

F A background image with additional CSS styling to make it appear only once

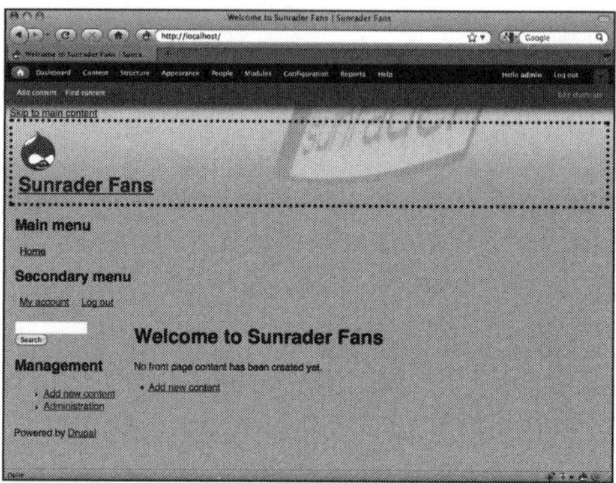

G A background image blended seamlessly with a background color

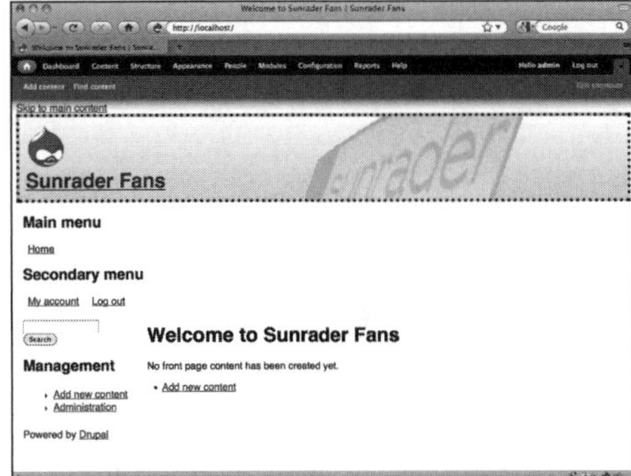

H A background image placed in the **#header** section so it stays within the dotted lines

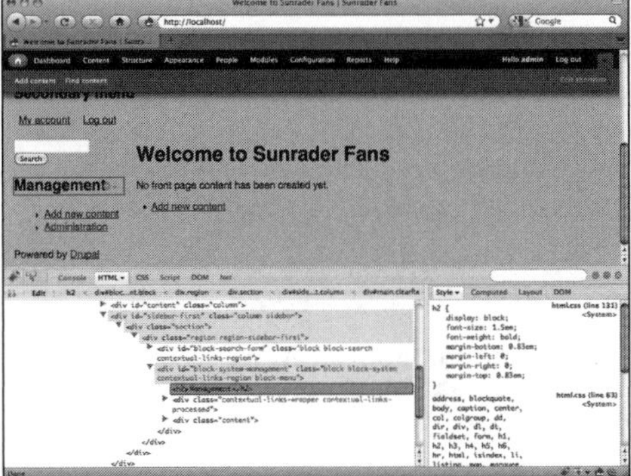

I Using Firebug to figure out what CSS styles affect block titles

TIP The style in the example affects the entire page because it's in the `body` tag, but you can associate a background with any tag. This technique is common for adding backgrounds to `div` regions that the theme defines, such as `#content`, `#header`, `#footer`, `#sidebar-first`, and so on H.

TIP Since they cover such a big area, background graphics can cause slow page loads. Try to cut down on their sizes as much as possible, for example by lowering image quality in an image-manipulation program. (Remember, background images function best when they convey a *feeling* rather than specific information.) Alternatively, use background images in clever ways so they don't have to be so big. In G, we put the background on only a part of the page and let the `background-color` style cover the rest.

TIP When creating background graphics, make sure they won't interfere with the text that will be placed on top of them. First, avoid images with sharp changes in color or texture; second, make the overall color contrast with the site's text color. For black text, lighten up the background; for light text, use a black or nearly-black background.

To add incidental graphics

1. One way to dress up a theme is to add icons or other small graphics to accentuate titles, headings, or section changes. First, you need to decide what part you want to accentuate. We'll add a small icon next to the title of all blocks, for example the block titles in the sidebar.

   Once again, Firebug (**getfirebug.com**) is an effective theme detective's tool. (For more about Firebug, see the section "To add styles in a CSS file.") With Firebug and a solid knowledge of CSS, you see that block titles have the **<h2>** tag and the **block** class. Put together in the unique syntax of CSS, the style we'll affect is **.block h2** I.

continues on next page

2. Create the graphic and move it into your theme's folder, either at the top level or in a subfolder. The icon we'll use in this demonstration is the **info.png** file in Lullacons Pack 1, a free set of graphics created by Nate Haug and licensed under the GNU General Public License. (You can download it at **lullabot.com/articles/free-gpl-icons-lullacons-pack-1**.) We've renamed the icon **bullet.png**.
3. Open one of the custom CSS files you designated in the **.info** file. In the section "Changing Theme Graphics and Typography with CSS," we used the **local.css** file.
4. Add the appropriate style. Once again, there's no substitute for a strong understanding of CSS. In our case, we're going to add the graphic as a background image and then shift the text to the right of the image by adding padding to the text's left. Since padding doesn't affect background images, only the text will move, while the graphic will remain where we put it.

   This CSS style has three directives:

   - Specifying the graphic itself: **background-image: url(→'bullet.png');**
   - Making the graphic appear only once: **background-repeat: no-repeat;**
   - Moving the text to the right so it doesn't appear on top of the graphic: **padding: 0px 0px 0px 25px;**

   The final style looks like this:

```
.block h2 {
  background-image: url(
  →'bullet.png');
  background-repeat: no-repeat;
  padding: 0px 0px 0px 25px;
}
```

5. Save the custom CSS file and reload the page in your browser to see the change **J**.

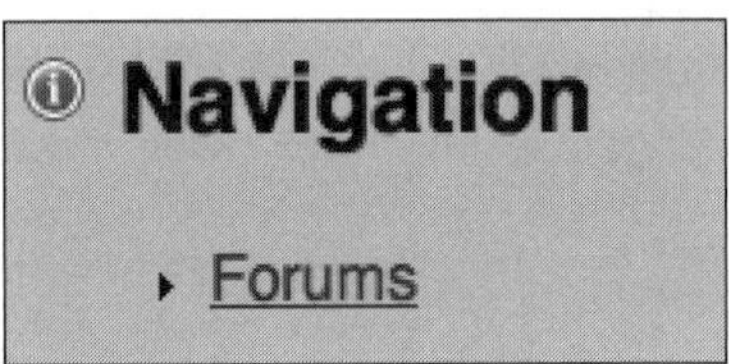

J The result of using CSS to add a small icon next to block titles

Extending Drupal with Modules

Modules are truly at the heart of Drupal. Besides those that come with its core package, a wealth of additional ones is free for the taking on **drupal.org**.

But choosing the right modules for your site is a daunting task. The list at **drupal.org/project/modules** is enormous, running into thousands of projects. How do you know which are right for you? How can you judge whether developers will still maintain a module in the years to come?

You have an advantage: The **drupal.org** site hosts virtually all open-source Drupal modules in existence, providing a single source to evaluate and compare modules. But like many oracles, it can be cryptic, and you sometimes have to poke around for the truth. This chapter gives you ways to determine the rightness, value, and stability of modules for your site. It also walks you through the process of installing and enabling modules, tells you how to keep them up to date, and helps you get the most from them.

In This Chapter

Using Modules

When you want to add functionality that's not part of core Drupal, your first stop is the module list at **`drupal.org/project/modules`**.

We'll talk about how to decide which module is right for your site in the section "Resources for Evaluating Modules." But for now we'll assume that you've found the module you want and just need to install and configure it.

Your job doesn't end once the module is up and running: Modules, like Drupal itself, need updates to improve security and stability. And when you encounter a bug in a module—which happens more often than people like to admit—you need to know where to get support.

To install, enable, and configure modules:

1. For our example, we'll use the Wysiwyg module discussed in Chapter 4, "Customizing Content." We start by going to the Wysiwyg project page at **`drupal.org/project/wysiwyg`**.
2. Find the Download link for the latest Drupal 7 version of the module. At the time this book was written, the final version hadn't been released. Therefore, you'll need to download the development version **A**. (When it's available, download the Drupal 7 version from the "Recommended releases" list instead.)
3. If you have a two-button mouse, right-click the Download link; on a Mac with a one-button mouse, press Control while clicking. Then select Copy Link Location from the pop-up menu.

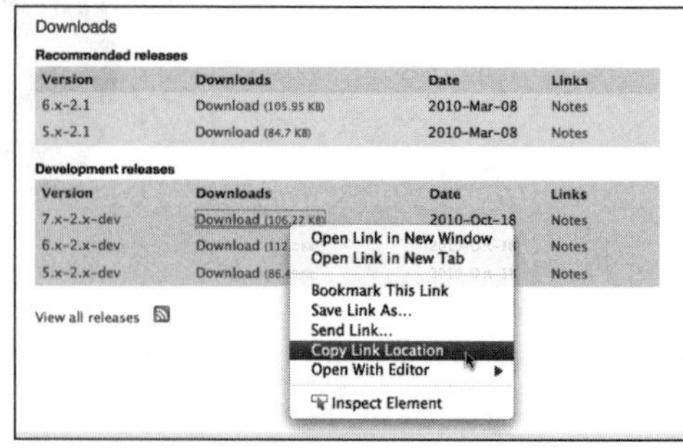

A Copying the URL for the current Drupal 7 version of a module

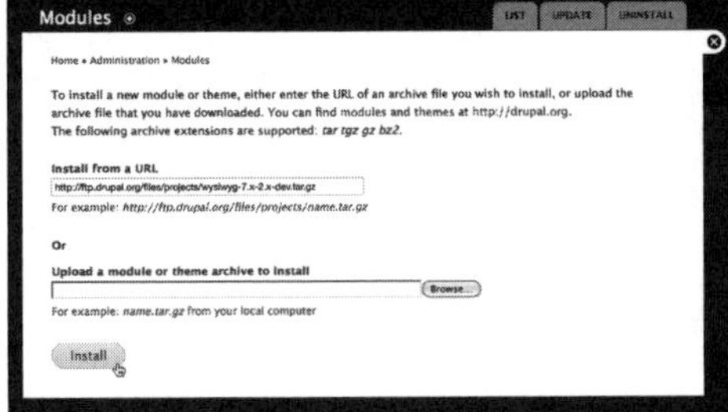

B Installing a module via its URL

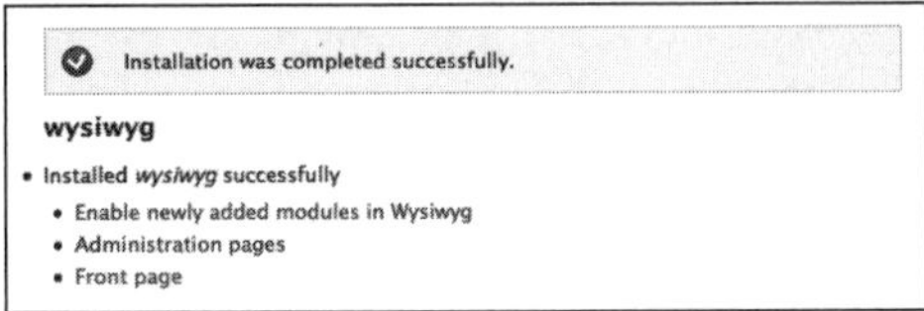

C Drupal's post-installation message

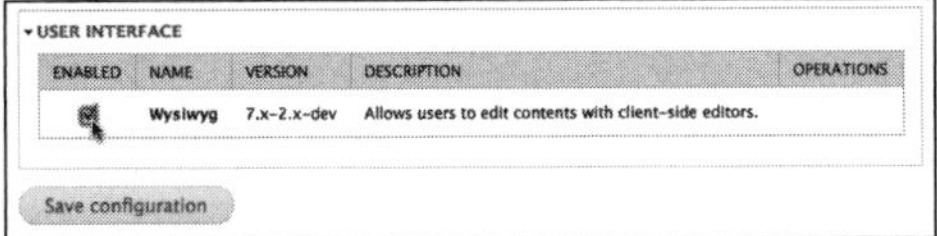

D Enabling the Wysiwig module

4. On your site, click Modules in the Toolbar and then click "Install new module."

5. In the "Install from a URL" field, paste the URL you just copied and then click Install **B**.

6. When Drupal has finished installing the module, you'll come to a page that tells you "Installation was completed successfully" **C**. From here, you can click to go to the front page or the Administration page; some modules (including this one) provide other links.

7. Just-installed modules remain disabled until you explicitly enable them. To do so, click Modules in the Toolbar and then scroll to the bottom of the page. Select the module's check box and click "Save configuration" **D**.

   Some modules depend on others to work; such dependencies are shown on the module management page with the words "Requires" and "Required by" under a module's description, along with lists of which modules are required or dependent.

   If you turn on a module that requires another, disabled module, Drupal will present a screen for you to confirm that you want to enable both modules. If you don't have the module that's required, Drupal won't allow you to enable the one that requires it.

   If one module requires another, you won't be able to disable it until you've also disabled the one that depends on it. As a result, you might need to go through the module management page two or more times to disable certain modules, because you'll have to untangle layers of dependencies first.

continues on next page

8. Depending on the module, you might need to take additional steps to make it work. Unfortunately, Drupal isn't completely consistent about how it warns you that such steps are needed, or where to find the controls. A few places to check are:
   - The Modules page, which you reach by clicking Modules in the Toolbar. Look next to the module for a Configure link. (Not every module has one.)
   - The Administration page, which you reach by clicking Administration in the upper-left corner of most administrative pages and then clicking the Index tab. (See the section "To find permission settings for a specific module" in Chapter 7, "Wrangling Users.")
   - The Status report page, which you reach by clicking Reports in the Toolbar and then clicking "Status report." Some modules alert you to installation problems this way, and include links to solve them.
   - The Configuration page, which you reach by clicking Configuration in the Toolbar.

TIP Remember: If you're using Drupal 7, you can use only modules designed to work with Drupal 7. (Believe me, I know how frustrating it is to find a module that's perfect, but not available for the version of Drupal you're using. Them's the breaks.)

TIP You can also install a module by downloading it to your computer and then re-uploading it to your Drupal site. Simply use the field labeled "Upload a module or theme archive to install" instead of the one labeled "Install from a URL." The Drupal 6 method of manually placing the module's files in your Drupal installation still works as well.

TIP If you click to go from the post-installation page C directly to any administrative page—that is, any except the front page—it will appear without the administrative overlay. To make the overlay appear, go first to the front page.

TIP Some modules don't have direct configuration pages and instead affect other parts of Drupal in subtle ways. One example is the Token module (`drupal.org/project/token`): It has no configuration page itself, but instead adds controls to various administrative pages.

Modules' Lives Outside the drupal.org Web Site

The **`drupal.org`** web site is the official source for modules and is where you can file public bug reports in the module's "issues queue." (For more about this queue, see the "To evaluate a module's past" section in this chapter.)

But because those modules are free software, there's nothing to stop people from republishing Drupal modules on their own sites. One enterprising person named John Forsythe does something like that by providing an alternative module directory at **`drupalmodules.com`**, where he invites users to rate and discuss modules in an environment quite unlike that on the **`drupal.org`** site.

Along the same lines, there's nothing to stop developers from withholding their modules from the **`drupal.org`** repository. In fact, that site lists only modules that have been released under the GNU Public License (GPL), so you won't find any modules there with proprietary (non-free) code.

In truth, I've never heard of anyone attempting to sell Drupal modules to the general public. However, custom module development is a profitable business, and I'd guess that there are thousands of client-specific Drupal modules that never find their way onto **`drupal.org`**.

To update installed modules:

1. To determine whether it's necessary to update any installed modules, go to the Available updates page by clicking Reports in the Toolbar and then clicking "Available updates." This process checks only enabled modules; you don't need to worry about disabled modules, since any out-of-date code they contain can't affect your site.

2. Near the top of the page is a note that says when your installation of Drupal last checked **`drupal.org`** for new versions of installed modules. Visiting this page automatically performs that check, but if you want to force Drupal to check again, click "Check manually" **E**.

3. If you see an icon that says you need to update a module—like the one next to the Token module in **E**—click the Update tab. If not, no further action is necessary.

4. Select the check boxes next to the modules you want to update. You can select them all by selecting the check box at the top of the column **F** and then clicking "Download these updates."

5. You'll see a progress bar as the modules download, followed by a confirmation screen **G**.

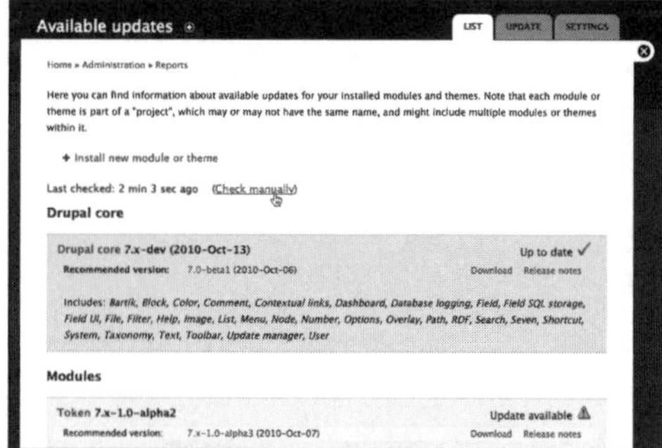

E Forcing Drupal to check for new versions of Drupal software and contributed modules

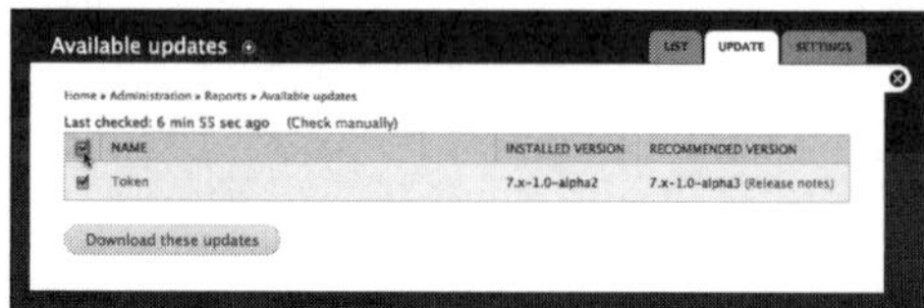

F Selecting the check box that updates all out-of-date modules

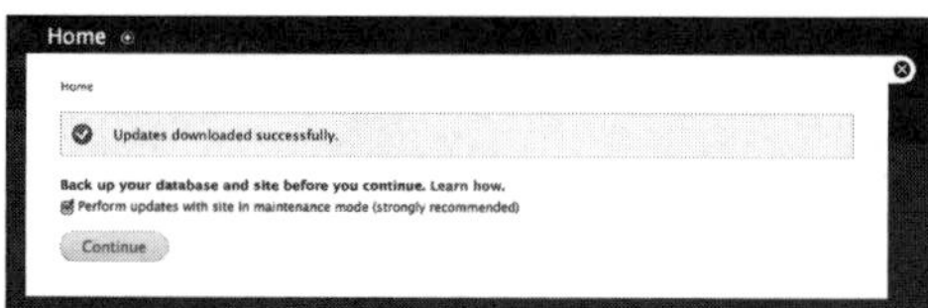

G Confirmation that Drupal downloaded new module versions successfully

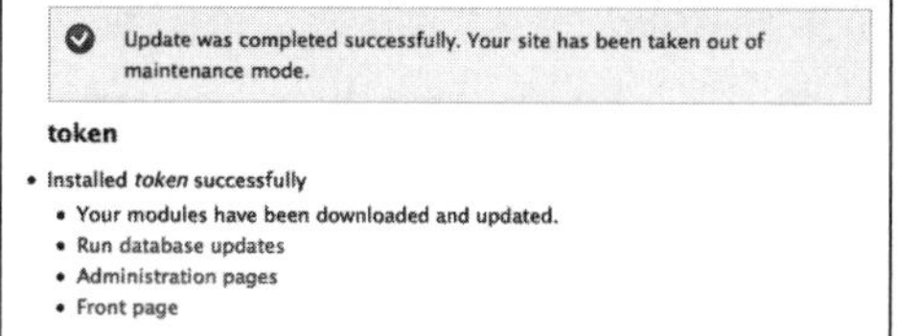

H Confirmation that Drupal updated a module successfully

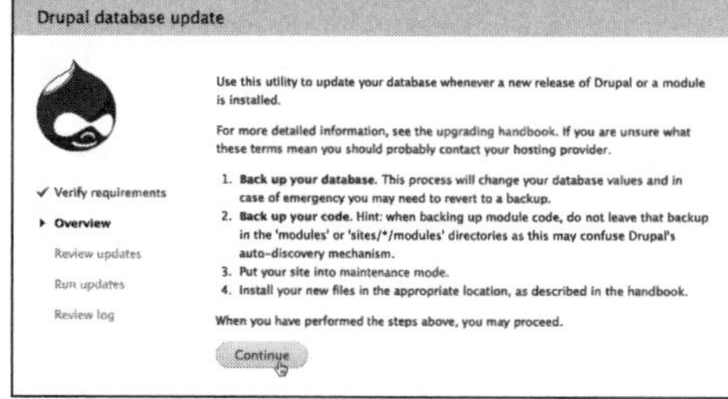

I Preparing to update your site's database

6. Back up your site's files and database, following the instructions in the "Packaging your Drupal Site" section of Chapter 2, "Establishing Your Drupal Site." This step is optional, but I highly recommend it: Module updates occasionally go horribly wrong and can take your site down with them.

7. The check box offering to put your site in maintenance mode effectively takes it offline during the update process, then turns it on again when the update is finished. If you deselect that check box, there's a chance that user activity could interfere with the update, or that data will disappear as a result. That's highly unlikely, but better safe than sorry: Unless an unusual circumstance dictates otherwise, leave this check box selected.

   Click Continue when ready.

8. Drupal performs the update, then takes your site out of maintenance mode. When finished, you see a confirmation screen **H**.

9. If you were to visit the "Available updates" screen at this point, the warning icon should have changed to an all-clear "Up to date" icon. However, you've updated only the module's files: Your job isn't finished until you also update the database. To do so, click "Run database updates."

10. The resulting screen warns you again to perform a backup and put the site in maintenance mode **I**. (There's no need to do a backup, as we just backed up the site a moment ago.) Click Continue.

continues on next page

11. The resulting screen tells you whether the updated modules will cause changes in your site's database; clicking the "Pending updates" link provides details on the changes, if any **J**.

    Click the "Apply pending updates" button.

12. You'll see a progress bar, followed by a confirmation screen **K**. Your site is now up to date.

    If you turned on your site's maintenance mode in step 10, turn it off now.

TIP We only updated a single module—and then only because the page shown in E told us there was an "update available," not that there was a security issue. In practice, you might find yourself putting off non-critical updates until you can do several in one go. That process is more complex only in that there are more check boxes to select and more information to review on the page shown in J. But generally it's the same business whether you're updating one module or ten.

TIP What can you do if there's an error when you update the database? In truth, not much. Sometimes the error message provides advice, but usually you have only two options: Restore the site from backup and try again, possibly waiting for the module's next version; or, if you're a MySQL expert and deeply understand the module's code, try to hack the database manually. In any case, you should go to the module's issue queue at `drupal.org/project/issues/`*`module-name`* to see whether anyone's reported the problem, and if there's a solution. If not, report it! Doing so will help the module's developers fix it faster.

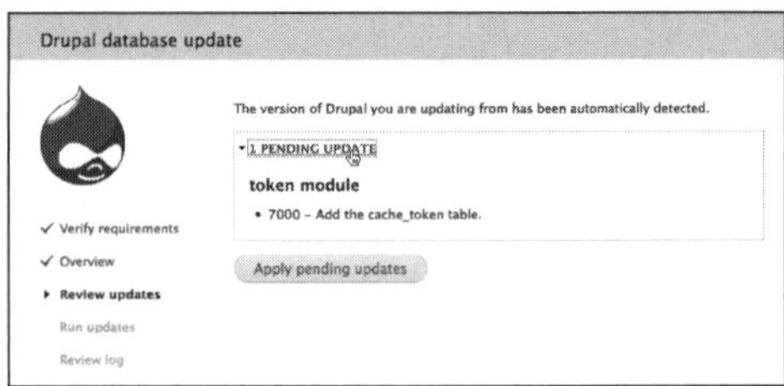

J Examining details of pending database changes

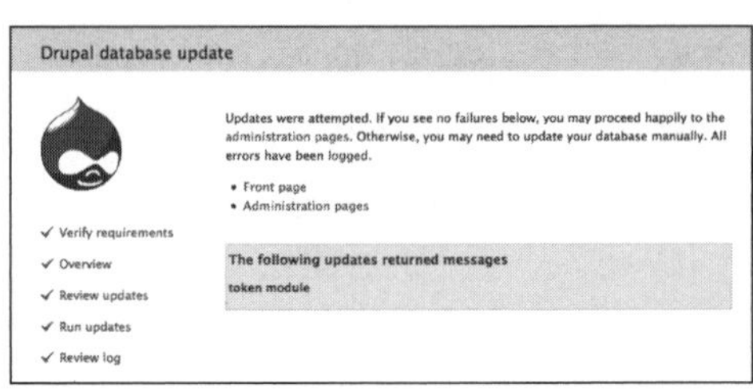

K Success! Your site's database updated without error.

All About Module Updates

Module updates fall into a few categories:

- Security fixes: Stop abuse of your site through a module's vulnerability
- Bug fixes: Make the module work as expected and without errors
- Feature improvements and additions: Often made in response to feedback from site administrators
- Minor updates: Enhance existing features, clarify points, or affect the module's internal structure

Security and bug fixes are obviously the most urgent of these, so the reasons to update are clear: You want to keep your site running well and in your control. On the Available updates page, modules with these sorts of updates due are generally indicated with a red "urgent" icon.

The other two sorts of updates are only recommended, but still worth installing. Sometimes those minor changes address issues you didn't even notice had been bothering you. (Most developers keep a close eye on user suggestions in the project's issue queue, found at **drupal.org/project/issues/*module-name***, and implement at least some suggestions.)

But remember: A vast majority of the modules available from the **drupal.org** web site were created by volunteer programmers in their spare time. As a result, they vary widely in their upkeep. One module may receive a substantial update monthly; another languishes for years without even a single *patch* (bug fix). Further, developers differ in what they consider urgent, so when you pick and choose which updates you'll apply, you'll never know for sure whether you're missing anything important.

So my advice is to check the Available updates page frequently and install updates as they come along. But be careful: Not all module versions on the **drupal.org** web site are ready for prime time, so to speak. Those that the developer believes are stable and safe appear in the Releases list with a light green background; those that are questionably safe have a pink background; and those that are considered unsafe have a red background Ⓛ. Don't replace a module with a less-safe version unless you have a special reason to do so and are prepared to return to a safe version if you have problems.

Downloads

Recommended releases

Version	Downloads	Date	Links
7.x-1.0-alpha3	Download (22.92 KB)	2010-Oct-07	Notes
6.x-1.15	Download (63.63 KB)	2010-Oct-07	Notes
5.x-1.15	Download (31.13 KB)	2010-Aug-11	Notes

Development releases

Version	Downloads	Date	Links
7.x-1.x-dev	Download (22.92 KB)	2010-Oct-07	Notes
6.x-1.x-dev	Download (67.89 KB)	2010-Oct-11	Notes
5.x-1.x-dev	Download (31.38 KB)	2010-Sep-24	Notes

View all releases

Ⓛ A module's release list, with versions in varying states of readiness. (All "Development releases" here have a red background, while "Recommended releases" have a green background.)

Modules: The Drupal 7 Challenge

Drupal's cheerleaders sometimes point to the "thousands" of modules available for it. But that number is false. While **drupal.org/project/modules** ostensibly lists over 6000 modules, each one's compatibility is limited to specific versions of Drupal. More precisely, integer versions aren't compatible, so a module written for Drupal 5 won't run on Drupal 6, although it usually runs equally well on both Drupal 5.6 and 5.12. (As I write this in November 2010, about 650 have some kind of Drupal 7 version.)

This incompatibility among versions is the result of a fundamental Drupal philosophy, usually phrased as "the drop is always moving," meaning Drupal's developers are forward-looking and don't put much emphasis on backward compatibility.

So the first thing to check when you're considering a module is whether it's compatible with your version of Drupal. But here's the predicament: Developers can't update their modules for new integer versions of Drupal until Drupal itself is stable. That was a big problem for Drupal 6, which most people couldn't use for months after its release because the modules they needed simply weren't ready.

Remembering that issue, long-time Drupal *contributor* Moshe Weitzman proposed (on his blog at **cyrve.com/d7cx**) that developers pledge to have their Drupal 7 modules available on the day of Drupal 7's release, and that they add the text "#D7CX" to their module's description on the **drupal.org** web site to make such modules easier to find. The results have been remarkable: At the time of this writing, several weeks before Drupal 7's expected official release, over 200 modules have signed on. Among them are some of Drupal's most popular modules, so Drupal 7 is well positioned to enjoy a faster adoption rate than any previous version.

Table 9.1 lists the 20 most popular modules for Drupal 6 as of mid-October 2010, according to the statistics at **drupal.org/project/usage**. In each case, I've said whether the module has taken the D7CX pledge, is in active development (but not taken the pledge), or has become part of core Drupal itself.

Of course, the **drupal.org** web site remains your primary source of up-to-date information on module availability.

TABLE 9.1 Drupal's Top 20 Modules

Module Name and URL (drupal.org/project...)	Drupal 7 Status	Description
Views (`/views`)	In active development, but has not taken the D7CX pledge.	A flexibly "query builder" that lets you extract information from Drupal's data store and present it in interesting and useful ways.
Content Construction Kit (CCK) (`/cck`)	Most of CCK is in core Drupal 7. The few parts that aren't are in active development, but have not taken the D7CX pledge.	Allows you to add fields to content types. See Chapter 4, "Customizing Content."
Token (`/token`)	Most of Token is part of core Drupal 7. The parts that aren't have taken the D7CX pledge.	Exposes certain Drupal variables for entry in nodes and the like. For example, Token replaces **`[user]`** with the user's actual name.
Pathauto (`/pathauto`)	Has taken the D7CX pledge.	Creates URL paths based on patterns that the administrator defines. For example, Pathauto could assign a node titled "Hello, world!" the URL **`http://`*`domain-name`*`/hello-world`**.
FileField (`/filefield`)	Part of core Drupal 7.	An extension to CCK to provide fields that hold (generic) uploaded files.
Administration Menu (`/admin_menu`)	Has taken the D7CX pledge.	Exposes administrative links in a CSS/JavaScript-powered toolbar at the top of the screen. It's similar to Drupal 7's Toolbar, but with additional functionality.
ImageField (`/imagefield`)	Part of core Drupal 7.	An extension to CCK to provide fields that hold uploaded images, with some controls to display those images.
ImageAPI (`/imageapi`)	Part of core Drupal 7 but has also taken the D7CX pledge. According to its developer, the non-core component of the ImageAPI module "provides an ImageMagick toolkit and extends core's toolkits to add an unsharpen mask action."	Behind-the-scenes support for other image-related modules (such as ImageCache).
ImageCache (`/imagecache`)	Part of core Drupal 7.	Automatically resizes, crops, and adds effects to uploaded images.
Date (`/date`)	Took the D7CX pledge but later rescinded it because of "significant [Drupal] API changes... long after [the stated] code freeze that forced me to rewrite significant portions of the code several times."	Adds a behind-the-scenes "Date API" that gives other modules access to time- and date-related functions, and includes an extension to CCK that lets you add date fields to content types.

table continues on next page

TABLE 9.1 *continued*

Module Name and URL (drupal.org/project...)	Drupal 7 Status	Description
IMCE (`/imce`)	In active development, but has not taken the D7CX pledge.	Extends WYSIWYG editors to improve users' ability to upload and place images in content.
Google Analytics (`/google_analytics`)	In active development but has not taken the D7CX pledge.	Integrates Drupal with Google Analytics (`google.com/analytics`) to provide site usage and tracking statistics.
Webform (`/webform`)	Has taken the D7CX pledge.	Lets you easily set up fill-in forms, the results of which can be mailed to a specified address.
Wysiwyg (`/wysiwyg`)	Has taken the D7CX pledge.	Simplifies the installation of rich-text editors for Drupal content.
Poormanscron (`/poormanscron`)	Part of core Drupal 7.	Takes the place of *nix `cron` program; forces periodic functions to run.
Advanced Help (`/advanced_help`)	In active development but has not taken the D7CX pledge.	Improves Drupal's built-in help system by making it more context-sensitive, providing help links where they're most needed.
Image (`/image`)	Part of core Drupal 7.	Provides support to manage and display image files.
CAPTCHA (`/captcha`)	In active development but has not taken the D7CX pledge.	Anti-spam tool that forces visitors to successfully answer a challenge before they can post content. The challenge is designed to be easy for people but hard for machines to solve, preventing automated posts.
jQuery UI (`/jquery_ui`)	Part of core Drupal 7.	Connects Drupal to a library of functions that provide user-interface effects.

Resources for Evaluating Modules

Confronted with hundreds of available modules, how can you know which to trust? Without good information, you might pick one that is nearing the end of its life and soon to be replaced, or is known to be buggy, or is inferior to another that satisfies your need better.

While you can never be sure that what you're getting is right for you, what follows are a few tips to help you find, sort through, and evaluate modules. In short, you should consider:

- The module's track record
- Its developer's reputation
- Statements about it from its developer and its user base
- Which tool is best for the job, particularly when several similar modules perform the same function

Expert opinion is also invaluable for judging module quality: Who would know a module better than the people who use it? Drupal blogs such as those listed at Planet Drupal (**drupal.org/planet**) often feature module comparisons. One good example is Michael Anello's presentation "45 Modules in 45 Minutes: The Best Modules You're Not Using" at **drupaleasy.com/45**; another is NodeOne's series "49 Modules You Should Know" at **nodeone.se/blogg/49-modules-you-should-know**.

Finally, the page about contributed modules at **drupal.org/node/340271** provides additional resources for finding and selecting modules for your site, while **drupalmodules.com** hosts module ratings and reviews.

To evaluate a module's past:

1. The best way to understand a module's history is to look at its issue queue. To get there, *either*:

   ▸ Go to the module's project page at **drupal.org/project/*module-name*** and then click one of the links in the Issues block in the right column **A**.

   or

   ▸ Go to **drupal.org/project/issues/*module-name***.

2. At the top of a module's issues page are several controls that let you search the entire issue queue based on such criteria as whether a reported issue has been corrected (Status), how important the issue is (Priority), and which version of the module the issue affects **B**. You can also search for any string of text, which is extremely helpful in figuring out whether an issue you've encountered has already been reported. Clicking "Advanced search" provides more search options **C**.

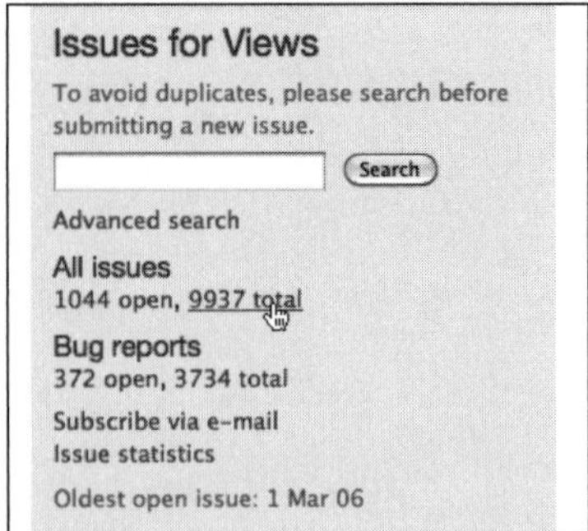

A An Issues block on the **drupal.org** web site, with links to examine a project's bug reports and feature requests

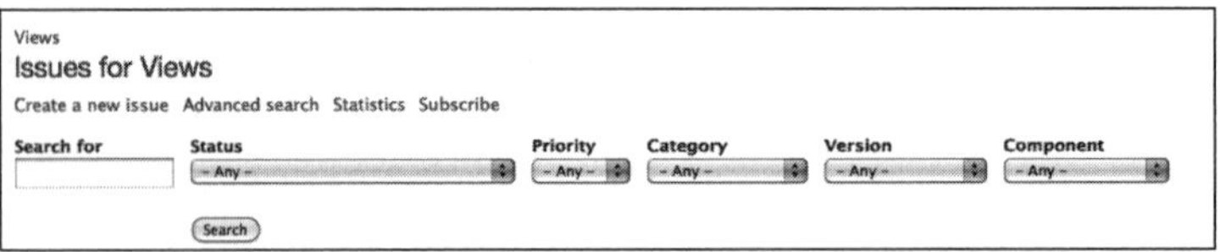

B Search controls for a module's issue queue

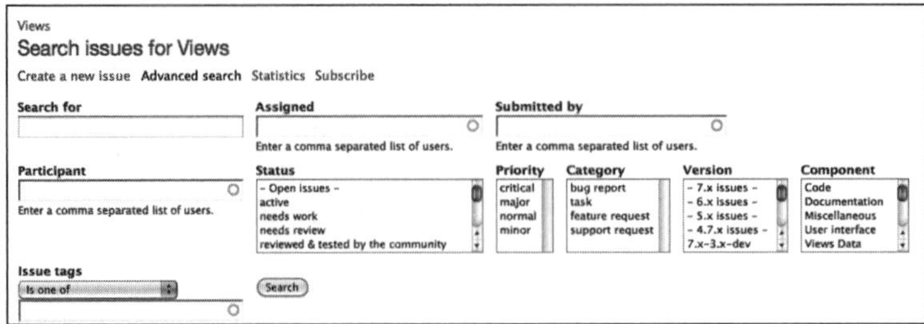

C An issue queue's advanced search options

Statistics

Create a new issue Advanced search **Statistics** Subscribe

Average lifetime

Category	Overall	Last month
bug reports	18 weeks 5 days	4 days 13 hours
feature requests	31 weeks 5 days	4 days 21 hours
support requests	15 weeks 5 days	1 week 1 hour
tasks	24 weeks 5 days	1 day 23 hours

Issue activity

Status	Overall	%	Last month
active	574	6%	162
fixed	93	1%	93
closed (duplicate)	1053	11%	48
postponed	87	1%	7
closed (won't fix)	1605	16%	23
closed (works as designed)	374	4%	15
closed (fixed)	5823	59%	145
needs review	132	1%	58
needs work	90	1%	54
reviewed & tested by the community	1	0%	1
patch (to be ported)	27	0%	17
postponed (maintainer needs more info)	40	0%	35
closed (cannot reproduce)	38	0%	15

D A module's statistics page

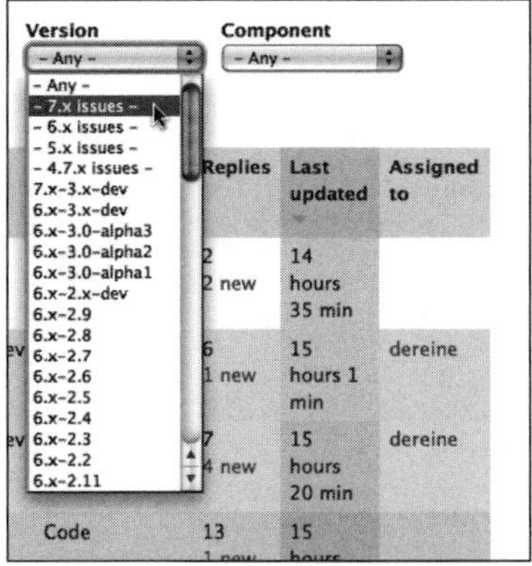

E Finding all issues related to the 7.x version of a module

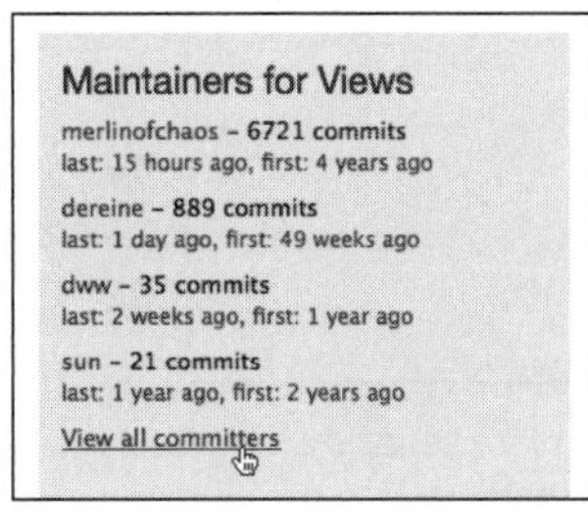

Maintainers for Views
merlinofchaos - 6721 commits
last: 15 hours ago, first: 4 years ago
dereine - 889 commits
last: 1 day ago, first: 49 weeks ago
dww - 35 commits
last: 2 weeks ago, first: 1 year ago
sun - 21 commits
last: 1 year ago, first: 2 years ago
View all committers

F The link to see a list of everyone who committed code to a module

Some things to look for in the issue queue to get a sense of a module's quality:

- How many outstanding bugs are in the version you're using, as compared to those that have been fixed? The **drupal.org** web site conveniently hosts a page of statistics, which you can reach by clicking the Statistics link on the issue queue page, or by going to **drupal.org/project/issues/statistics/*module-name*** **D**.

  You can look at the bugs themselves by going to the issue queue page and then setting up a search with the Status pop-up menu set to "- Open issues -" or "active," the Category pop-up menu set to "bug report," and the Version pop-up menu set to either "- 7.x issues -" or the specific version you're using **E**.

- How active is the issues queue? By default, the queue appears sorted by how recently there's been discussion of issues in the queue. Look down the "Last updated" column to get a sense of community activity.

- How often do the module's maintainers take part in issue queue discussions? Sometimes a developer creates a module but then can't afford the time to support it after it becomes popular. The result is an active issue queue, but nobody's taking the lead in getting problems fixed.

To see who the module's maintainers are, go back to the module's home page at **drupal.org/project/*module-name*** and click "View all committers" **F**. (*Committers* are highly trusted project

continues on next page

contributors who are allowed to incorporate changes into the project's code.) This may be a long list: By clicking "Last commit" and "Commits" at the top of the table, you can sort according to the most-recent committers and more-prolific committers, respectively. Then, go back to the issue queue at **drupal.org/project/issues/*module-name***, search for the committers' names, and see how engaged they are with the community that's using their module.

3. Another criterion for judging module quality—especially new modules—is the reputation of its developers. Click the user names of the project's maintainers and its most active contributors to go to their **drupal.org** user profiles **G**. A few fields are particularly informative:

   - Member for: Tells you how long a user has had an account on the **drupal.org** web site. This site is essential both for community interaction and learning how to program Drupal correctly, so a long-standing membership implies (but doesn't guarantee) substantial Drupal experience.

   - Projects: Lists other modules and themes to which the user has contributed. The **drupal.org** site maintains this list automatically: It can't be faked. Obviously, an experienced developer is likely to have worked on more than one project and to have committed a substantial number of changes to them.

   The profile may also include information the user entered by hand, such as professional affiliations, interests, DrupalCons attended, web sites, and availability for custom development work.

KarenS
Profile
Posts
View
Contact
Drupal
I contributed Drupal modules
I contributed Drupal documentation
I provide Drupal-related services
I attended OSCMS 2007, Sunnyvale
I attended DrupalCon Barcelona 2007
I attended DrupalCon Boston 2008
I attended DrupalCon DC 2009
I attended DrupalCon Paris 2009
I attended DrupalCon San Francisco 2010
Work
Companies worked for
Lullabot
Personal information
Full name
Karen Stevenson
My Drupal site
http://www.elderweb.com
Country
United States
History
Member for
4 years 39 weeks
Projects
Date (5181 commits)
Calendar (2435 commits)
Content Construction Kit (CCK) (1619 commits)
OG Galleries (142 commits)
Views Calc (103 commits)
Views Gallery (72 commits)
Event (52 commits)
Pollfield (43 commits)
Sandbox (37 commits)
Location (33 commits)
DruBB (30 commits)
Switchtheme (28 commits)
HTML2Book (11 commits)
Comment Manager (10 commits)
Custom Contact (10 commits)
Variable Dump (6 commits)
Profile Migrate (6 commits)
Views Bonus Pack (6 commits)
Flickr (3 commits)
Embed filter (3 commits)
Upcoming.org (3 commits)
Admin (2 commits)
Views (1 commit)
Administration theme (1 commit)
Total: 9837 commits

G The user profile of an especially active Drupal developer

Click the Posts tab to see what discussions the user has participated in, from most to least recent. The Contact tab lets you send the user a note. (You'll see that tab only if you're logged in to the **drupal.org** web site and the user has enabled it.) However, resist the impulse to contact the developer for support questions and trivial concerns. Chances are you'll find an answer to your questions in the issue queue. Leave the developer more time to work on modules.

Drupal's "Hall of Shame" for Duplicated Projects

Because they're part of such a wide-ranging and active community, it's inevitable that Drupal module developers will sometimes find themselves duplicating efforts. On one hand, that's good because modules that are similar aren't exactly the same. Each typically has features and advantages that the other lacks. On the other hand, modules that compete for the same audience run the risk of diluting the efforts of both projects.

That's the *raison d'être* for the Similar Module Review group at **http://groups.drupal.org/similar-module-review**. As the name implies, it's intended to identify modules that do essentially the same thing and to help their developers join efforts where possible. Along the same lines is the "Comparisons of contributed modules" page at **drupal.org/node/266179**, which archives and organizes many of the discussions from that group and provides tables that clarify how similar modules differ from each other.

Getting (and Giving) Help

They say an organization reflects the personality of its founder. Bill Gates tends toward "big system" thinking, so Microsoft's employees follow suit, leading to system-minded software; meanwhile, Steve Jobs's emphasis on appearance leads Apple products to be fashionable. Successful founders are wise to ally themselves with partners of complementary strengths, as Jobs did with technical genius Steve Wozniak. Without some ability to escape the founder's personality, an organization's audience will always be limited to those who are like its founder.

Drupal founder Dries Buytaert is unquestionably a technology-focused person, and the Drupal project reflected his personality through its first six years or so. Since 2007, he's seemed to recognize Drupal's yearning to grow beyond its gearheaded roots and has aggressively courted businesspeople, designers, and others whose expertise is outside the field of software development. But it's a big ship and turns very slowly, so much of Drupal's existing documentation is still developer-centric.

That's most obvious on Drupal's official home, the web site **drupal.org**. Most of the discussions are highly technical, and simple questions often garner overly technical responses. Simply put, there's a big communication gap between those who are just learning Drupal and the Drupal pro community that wants to encourage them.

Fortunately, that gap is closing. A major redesign of the **drupal.org** web site launched in October 2010, and the Documentation Team Lead, Addison Berry (**drupal.org** user name: **add1sun**), has taken pains to encourage more beginner-level materials on the site.

This appendix is a snapshot of **drupal.org** and other supporting resources at a given moment in time—by the time you read it, both the quantity and quality of Drupal help will have improved from when I wrote it. But some things never change, and you'll always benefit from a constellation of group, individual, and packaged help. Here's an overview of all three.

The Messy Feast on drupal.org

No matter what your Drupal question, the response is the same: "You'll find the answer on **drupal.org**." That's true, but the site is wildly wide-ranging and pretty disorganized. The problem is that it's a community of writers with few editors. Irrelevant ramblings have the same weight as concise how-tos, and obsolete information can remain prominent for years.

But once you know your way around, it's not all that bad. In particular, four methods of navigating the **drupal.org** site yield especially rich results:

- Read handbooks.
- Search.
- Delve into help forums of specific projects.
- Follow discussion groups for Drupal-related interests.

But before you can take part in discussions on the **drupal.org** site, you must become a member of the community by registering for an account. (You can read any part of the site without an account, though.)

To create a user account on the drupal.org site:

1. In a web browser, go to **drupal.org**.
2. If you're not already signed in, click the Login / Register tab near the top of the page **A**.
3. Complete the form on the resulting page.
4. You'll receive a message at the email address you provided, typically within a few minutes. If it doesn't arrive within a few hours, try again or use a different

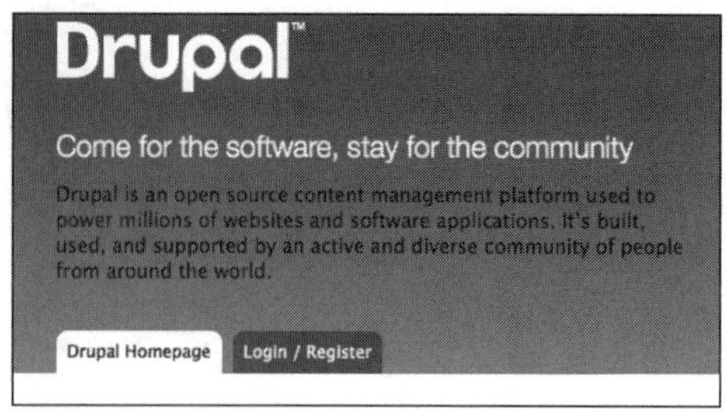

A The top of the **drupal.org** site, showing the Login / Register tab

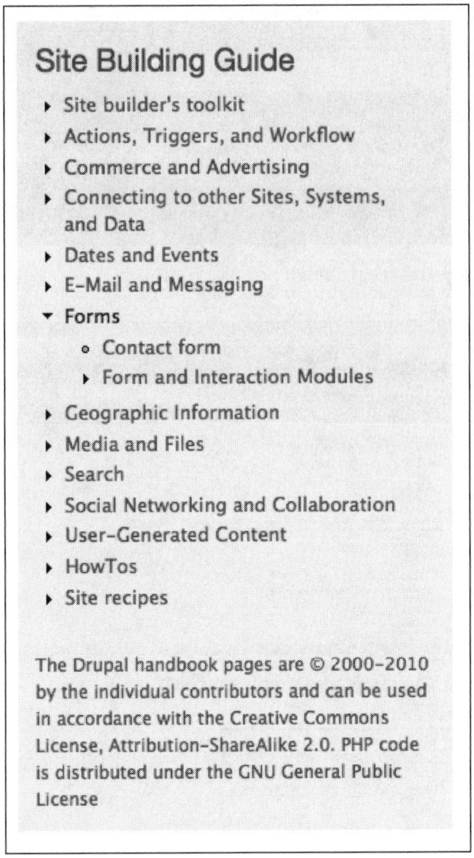
Site Building Guide
Site builder's toolkit
Actions, Triggers, and Workflow
Commerce and Advertising
Connecting to other Sites, Systems, and Data
Dates and Events
E-Mail and Messaging
Forms
Contact form
Form and Interaction Modules
Geographic Information
Media and Files
Search
Social Networking and Collaboration
User-Generated Content
HowTos
Site recipes
The Drupal handbook pages are © 2000–2010 by the individual contributors and can be used in accordance with the Creative Commons License, Attribution-ShareAlike 2.0. PHP code is distributed under the GNU General Public License

B A block for the Site Building Guide, as it appears while viewing the Forms page

email address, as it's possible that your mail-service provider blocked it.

Follow instructions in that message to change your password from the temporary one that **`drupal.org`** provided to one you'll remember.

You now have an account on the **`drupal.org`** web site. Be sure to log in to it whenever you want to take part in discussions there.

To get basic help via handbooks:

Site administrators for **`drupal.org`** use the term *handbook* somewhat loosely to mean "a collection of content packaged together using Drupal's Book module." As you might remember from the "Creating Other Types of Content" section of Chapter 3, the Book module links related nodes of information in a (somewhat) easy-to-navigate structure. It's an advantage over haphazardly linked nodes, especially on the **`drupal.org`** site where handbooks can run into dozens or even hundreds of pages.

To reach the main portal for Drupal handbooks, click the Documentation link at the top of any page on the **`drupal.org`** site (when logged in) or go directly to **`drupal.org/handbook`**. When you start reading a handbook, a block appears in the right column of the page that shows all pages within that handbook **B**. Links with small arrows next to them indicate pages that contain child pages with further, related instructions. (The bottom of each handbook page also lists its child pages.)

One final note: If you're having a problem, read the Troubleshooting FAQ at **`drupal.org/Troubleshooting-FAQ`** before going further. It's full of tips that will help you either solve the problem yourself or diagnose it well enough to talk about it clearly.

To search drupal.org:

The simple appearance of the search box in **drupal.org**'s upper-right corner belies some remarkable powers **C**. Specifically, **drupal.org** has what's called a *faceted search*, allowing you to narrow the results list in a convenient way.

The first step is obvious: Enter text into the search box and click the Search button. The resulting page resembles **google.com**. Having searched through a million or so nodes, it returns with titles, brief excerpts, and other information from search hits **D**.

If you don't immediately see what you want, don't give up! **drupal.org**'s search lets you go further in two ways:

1. The links labeled IRC Nicks, Users, and Advanced Issues in the right column immediately perform your search in those spaces **E**. (The first page of hits lists only nodes.)

   So let's say you get help from someone in IRC who goes by the nickname "tha_sun." Perform a search for that, then click the IRC Nicks link. You quickly learn that you were gifted with the wisdom of none other than the **drupal.org** user **sun**, or (as one further click on the name tells you) Daniel F. Kudwien.

2. The other links on the right side of the page let you limit your search results by several criteria. The numbers next to each link indicate how many hits will be left after you click. Click any of the links in the "or filter by..." block to narrow your selection. To remove a facet and return to the previously found set, click the All link at the top of the block.

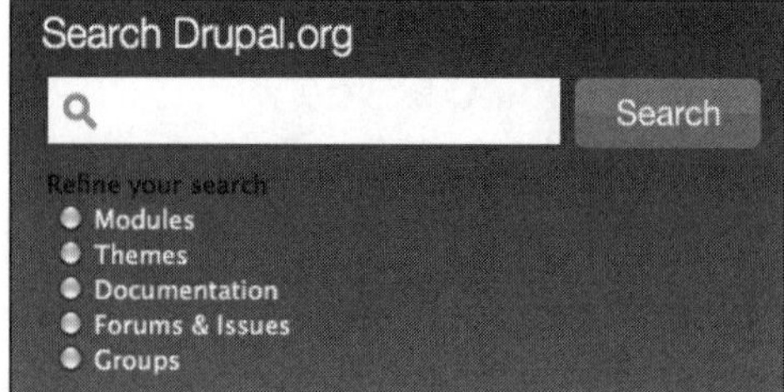

C The main search box on drupal.org

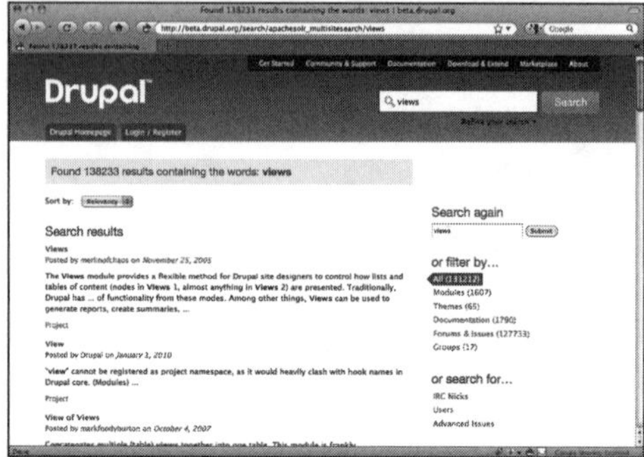

D The result of a simple search

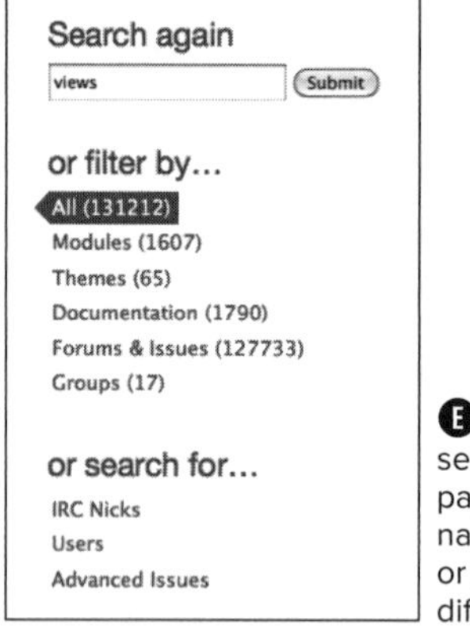

E Blocks on the search results page that let you narrow your search or perform it in a different data space

Download & Extend

Download & Extend Home | Drupal Core | Modules

Rules » Issues

Node Reference from the URL

Posted by Parkes Design on *September 8, 2009 at 11:23pm*

F Clicking the last item in the breadcrumb trail takes you to the node's parent area

TIP To search for a phrase, enclose it in quotation marks. If you don't include them, a search for `node reference` will, for example, find nodes that contains the words "node" and "reference," even when separated by several sentences, rather than the term "node reference."

TIP The site `groups.drupal.org` is intended for subject-related discussions, for example to help people build real-estate sites with Drupal or to integrate mapping software. It's an incredibly useful resource but is unfortunately separate from `drupal.org`, so a search on one doesn't see items on the other. I definitely recommend searching on both, particularly if your issue is subject-specific. (At the time I write this, there are plans to better integrate the two sites.)

TIP Many people find it simpler to search the `drupal.org` site through the search engine they usually use. On `google.com`, for example, you'd search for "node reference" by entering `site:drupal.org "node reference"` in Google's search box. You could further search within a specific project by changing the `site:` parameter. For example, the same search within the CCK module project's pages would be `site:drupal.org/project/CCK "node reference"`.

TIP Sometimes you'll click a search result and find yourself deep in the bowels of a project about which you want more general information. Links in the breadcrumb trail above the node's title give you a broader view. **F**

To ask questions:

So you've searched the **drupal.org** web site and not found a satisfactory answer. You've looked through the Troubleshooting FAQ at **drupal.org/Troubleshooting-FAQ** and feel confident that you haven't overlooked something obvious. Now it's time to ask your question directly in the appropriate forum. The bad news is that it's sometimes hard to determine which forum is most appropriate; the good news is that a well-placed question on **drupal.org** is part of the site's permanent record, with the potential to help everyone who follows you. So don't hesitate to ask.

But be prepared to wait for a response—and for some of the answers to be less useful than you'd like. Remember that everyone on **drupal.org** is there as a volunteer, on their own free time: Every response, even the ones that are snotty or wrong, represents some effort. With that in mind, here are some tips for asking questions:

- If it's a basic, general question, consider posting in the main forum area at **drupal.org/forum**. However, don't post in the forums labeled "deprecated." They're no longer actively used. They remain visible on the site only as an archive.
- Search for a similar question that has gotten good responses, and post in that discussion area.
- Post in a way that fits in with the rest of the **drupal.org** site, as is outlined in the sidebar "Discussion Etiquette."

To get help for specific modules and themes:

Most of the advice in the "To ask questions" section is true for finding help for specific modules and themes. But rather than starting with the search box, I'd recommend first going to the project's home page at **drupal.org/project/*module-name*** and clicking the relevant links (such as "Read documentation") in the right column of that page, or searching that project's issue queue. To learn how to navigate the issue queue better, see the section "To evaluate a module's past" in Chapter 9, "Extending Drupal with Modules."

Discussion Etiquette

Every society has its standards, and the one that's grown up around Drupal is no different. Many of its social expectations are common to the society at large (be polite), some are common to technical groups (be concise), and some are Drupal-specific (know who the major developers are). Here's a list of some of the most important points.

- Include the meat of the question in the title. Writing good headlines is a difficult but profitable art: "Can't edit newly created book page" will get more (and better) help than "Please help me."
- Post in only one place at a time. Posting in multiple forums, also known as *cross posting*, might result in a faster response. But it's considered spam and is such an antisocial practice that knowledgeable Drupal experts may ignore your questions out of spite once they discover your bad behavior.

  But what if you posted in an inappropriate place, and therefore didn't get any responses? If you posted an issue, anyone (including you) can change where it's posted by changing the information in the "Edit issue settings" section. Otherwise, it's reasonable to post a second time in a more appropriate forum after a fair amount of time has gone by—say, a few days. When you do, include a link back to the original issue, and then put a note in your first post directing people to the second one.
- Resist the temptation to contact developers directly. It's the most natural belief in the world: A project's creator is the person most knowledgeable about how it works, right? So they should be able to quickly answer your question! But the reality is quite different: Knowing how something works isn't the same as knowing how it's used. More importantly, a project's developer is often overwhelmed with requests and can focus only on those that help the most people—for example, fixing bugs or adding features. So chances are you'll get silence rather than the quick help you need.
- Provide details. Include the version of Drupal you're using; the version of relevant modules and themes; details of changes you made to your site before encountering problems; and, most importantly, how to reproduce the issue. (I try to include numbered steps in every issue I post.)
- Report back. If you discover something that affects the issue, post a comment to that effect. And if you end up solving the problem yourself, write to tell everyone how you did it. Chances are good that others will be waiting for that information—or that someone will find the discussion months later and be glad that you gave it closure.
- Give back. Look through the discussions at **drupal.org/forum** once in a while. When you see a question you can answer, do so! Another place you'll find people in need is in the issue queues of specific projects. Just go to **drupal.org/project/issues/*project-name***, choose "Open issues" from the Status pop-up menu and "Support request" from the Category pop-up menu, and click Search.

Getting One-on-One Help on IRC

The Drupal community has a secret back room for getting immediate help: channels on the real-time Internet Relay Chat system hosted at **irc.freenode.net**. In truth, it's not a *secret* chat system, and in fact there's a page of step-by-step instructions for using it at **drupal.org/irc**, advertised prominently on drupal.org's support page at **drupal.org/support**.

But IRC (usually) requires you to use an unfamiliar program and learn some obscure commands, so few people who aren't hard-core technologists use it. On one hand that's unfortunate, because IRC's technical complexity freezes some people out; on the other, it means that IRC channels are generally populated by dedicated people with a high level of technical knowledge.

The fastest way to get into Drupal IRC chats is to log on via a web-based interface, such as the one at **http://webchat.freenode.net** Ⓐ. Enter a user name and the channels you want to join, and solve the CAPTCHA challenge. In the Channels field, type channel names separated with a comma and no space; many are listed at **drupal.org/irc**. Click Connect, and you're in!

Upon connecting, you see a window with a main chat area and a few other features Ⓑ:

- In the page's upper-left corner is an icon that looks like [IRC▾]. Clicking it gives you a pop-up menu with options that let you change certain settings (such as the background color) and lead to further information about the IRC program.

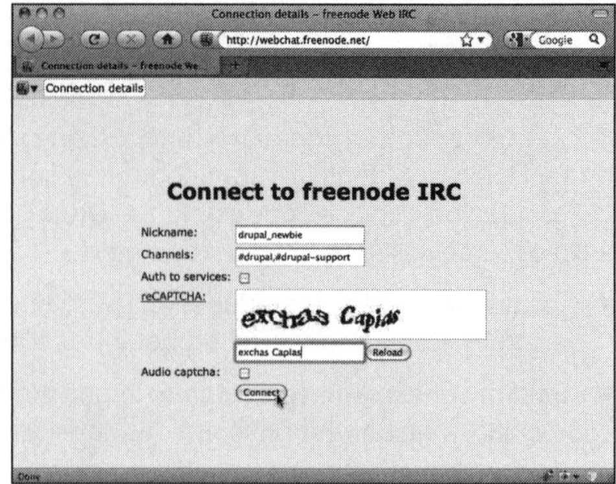

Ⓐ Connecting to two Drupal IRC channels via a web-based interface at **http://webchat.freenode.net**

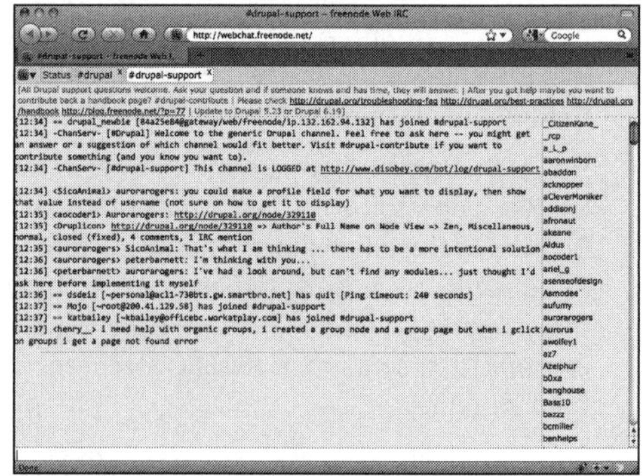

Ⓑ An IRC session on the **#drupal-support** channel.

- Immediately to the right of the icon are tabs that show which channels you've joined—in Ⓑ, that's **#drupal** and **#drupal-support**—along with a tab for the Status window that shows connection messages as people enter and leave the chat channel. The tab for the currently visible channel appears in white, while the others have the background color. To switch to another channel, click its tab; to leave a channel, click the x on its tab.
- In a non-scrolling area above the main chat are messages about the currently visible channel. Pay attention: This area often contains valuable information for newcomers.
- The area to the right shows a list of everybody currently in the channel. Clicking a name gives you the option to find out more about that person ("whois") or to talk directly to that person ("query"). When you query someone, a new tab appears to show that you've opened a private channel with that user. Use this feature sparingly.

For better control over IRC sessions, download and use a dedicated IRC client. Some popular free clients are:

- Mac: Colloquy at **colloquy.info**
- Windows: Miranda at **miranda-im.org**
- Any computer running the Firefox browser: ChatZilla at **http://chatzilla.hacksrus.com**

TIP Definitely read the tips at drupal.org/irc before venturing on. That page contains some extremely useful aspects of IRC that wouldn't fit here, such as registering your nickname and getting automatic help from the IRC robot.

TIP Despite its name, the #drupal channel is *not* for general support chat. Rather, it's for developers of core Drupal, modules, and themes, and for business related to maintaining Drupal projects. Some support questions are tolerated, particularly if related to using the Drupal API, but Drupal administration questions usually get ignored.

TIP The #drupal-support channel is the best place to ask general questions, unless a more specific forum exists (for example, #drupal-views or #drupal-themes). A list of many other channels is at drupal.org/irc.

TIP New channels often appear during Drupal conferences and can provide an important "back channel" venue for chatter during the sessions. Even if you can't attend a DrupalCon, you can still listen in on #drupalcon during the event. Read the event's promotional materials for other conference channel names.

TIP As in drupal.org forum discussions, everybody taking part is a volunteer. They're not getting paid to answer your questions and are under no obligation to do so. Often, questions simply don't get an answer. That's the way it is. One way to get more help is to offer it yourself. Helpful people recognize and honor one of their own.

Hiring Drupal Experts

They say that "volunteer work is worth every penny you paid." While that's overly cynical—the Drupal project itself is the result of expert, painstaking, nearly all-volunteer labor—it is true that being on the payroll increases motivation. When you pay, you can direct efforts, specify (and enforce) deadlines, and ensure that the less-fun parts of the job get done. As a parody version of the Golden Rule says, "Thems with the gold makes the rules."

But how do you know whom to hire? Drupal is still young and obscure enough as a technology that there are no widely accepted certifications, no competency tests, and very few standards. You shouldn't expect any to appear soon, either, as ongoing discussions show that Drupal consultants take a dim view of standardized competency testing. At the same time, there *are* criteria that will tell you whether a Drupal consultant has what it takes.

Projects

Pathauto (701 commits)

Comment Notify (220 commits)

Token (124 commits)

S5 presentation player (80 commits)

Hyperlocal News (55 commits)

Prediction Markets (41 commits)

A The bottom part of a profile on the **drupal.org** web site, showing how many times the user committed code to various projects

To find clues from looking at a user's drupal.org account:

Drupal's history is intimately connected to its community on the **drupal.org** web site, which has been in active use since 2002. It tracks and makes public its users' activities, creating a record that helps you determine whether someone's experience is sufficient and relevant for your job. Here are some particularly informative nuggets of data from that record.

- Length of time with a **drupal.org** account. The **drupal.org** web site is by far the most central source for information, education, and community for Drupal. While someone without an account could read texts and download software from the site, that person would be unable to take part in discussions or contribute code—two central facets of learning.

  To find out how long someone's had a **drupal.org** account, search for the user name with the techniques you learned in the "To search drupal.org" section, or go directly to **drupal.org/search/user_search/*user-name***. Click the user name, then scroll to the History section at the bottom.

- Other information on the **drupal.org** profile, which includes a list of involvement with the Drupal community (through conferences, code contributions, and so forth) and companies worked for.

  The **drupal.org** site automatically keeps track of how many times that user "committed" code to a project on the site—that is, made it an official part of the project **A**.

continues on next page

Keep in mind that people sometimes contribute substantially to a project without ever committing code, for example by testing, writing documentation, working through issues in forum discussions, offering assistance via email or IRC, or contributing money. Also, someone can contribute code without having the ability to commit it. (I personally don't have any commits to my name, although I've contributed minor patches.) Having said all that, a high commit count usually indicates impressive levels of open-source programming activity *and* trust among project maintainers.

- Drupal-based sites that the user has created. Profiles on **`drupal.org`** have only one space for "My Drupal site," and most people typically put the address of their blog there. However, other parts of the profile might contain clues leading to Drupal-based sites the user created.
- Activity on the **`drupal.org`** site itself. When viewing someone's profile, click the Posts link to see details on discussions the user has taken part in **B**. Clicking any of the items leads you to the content itself, where you'll see how the user interacts with colleagues on the site. (A "Commits" tab also appears on the profiles of users who have committed code to a Drupal project.)

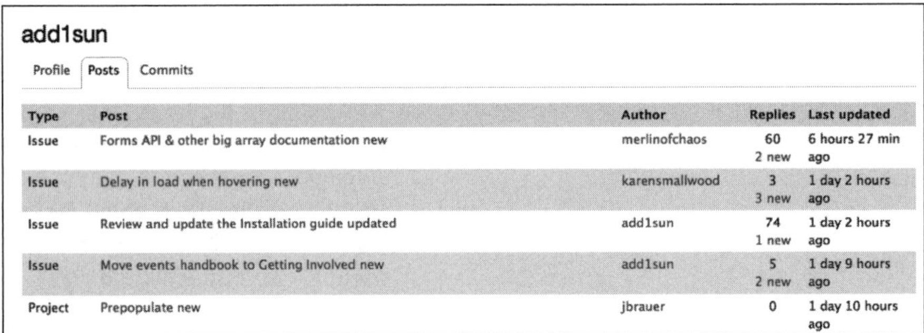

add1sun

Profile | Posts | Commits

Type	Post	Author	Replies	Last updated
Issue	Forms API & other big array documentation new	merlinofchaos	60 2 new	6 hours 27 min ago
Issue	Delay in load when hovering new	karensmallwood	3 3 new	1 day 2 hours ago
Issue	Review and update the Installation guide updated	add1sun	74 1 new	1 day 2 hours ago
Issue	Move events handbook to Getting Involved new	add1sun	5 2 new	1 day 9 hours ago
Project	Prepopulate new	jbrauer	0	1 day 10 hours ago

B The Posts page for a particularly active **`drupal.org`** user's account, showing discussions she's participated in

To find clues from other sources:

Let's say your detective work on the **drupal.org** site narrowed the search down to a few likely candidates, and you've contacted them by clicking the Contact tab on their profiles. (Not all users have a Contact tab, as they can turn it off if they prefer.) How else can you judge their abilities before you hire them? Consider both technical and non-technical criteria, including:

- Availability. A perfect consultant with no time for your project is the same as no consultant at all.
- Appropriateness. Module development, site building, site maintenance, documentation, and theme design all require different skills, which don't always overlap. (People who are good at both programming and design are particularly rare.) There are subspecialties even within these specialties, so someone who's created a great e-commerce module probably doesn't know much about modules for graphic manipulation. Hire right.
- Reputation. So your "perfect" candidates worked on some beautiful sites. But did they meet deadlines? Were they easy to work with? Did they leave important tasks for others to do? The only way to uncover these hidden competences (or incompetences) is to talk with those who worked with them. Request contact information and follow up. Keep in mind that consultants will only refer you to contacts they think will give them a good recommendation. If you can reach any *other* people who worked with them, all the better.

continues on next page

- Ability to communicate. "The whole is greater than the sum of its parts"—but only when those parts work together. If consultants seem to have trouble understanding your project or their part in it, don't hire them. You might find that they excellently perform the wrong tasks.

Finally, consider the tips in the article "Hiring a Drupal site developer" (**drupal.org/node/51169**).

It Goes Both Ways: Finding Drupal-Related Work

As I write this, unemployment in the United States is around 10 percent—nearly double the average during the 1990s. But Drupal is a growth industry, with more contracts than people to fill them. So how can you get a piece of this action?

First, realize that most Drupal jobs require advanced knowledge far beyond what's taught in this book. Judging from the want ads, Drupal-capable PHP programmers seem to have their pick of work, followed by themers and site builders. But there *is* work for those with only fundamental skills.

The first place to look is in the jobs board at **http://groups.drupal.org/jobs**. This page aggregates jobs posted in the many regional and topic-specific discussion groups on **http://groups.drupal.org**. Pop-up menus let you narrow your search by various criteria; clicking a link in the Groups column takes you to that group's home page, which includes posts both related and unrelated to jobs.

Beyond the **drupal.org** and **groups.drupal.org** sphere, many employers list their Drupal-related jobs in job-bank sites such as **monster.com** and **careerbuilder.com**. A search for **Drupal** on those sites quickly finds them. (As I write this, that search returns about 120 jobs on each site. The same search a year ago—in late 2009—netted 65.)

But if you're serious about making Drupal your career, your best bet is to first demonstrate your value, then let it shine. Take part in discussions on the **drupal.org** sites; provide support on IRC; most importantly, go to face-to-face Drupal meetings. In the Drupalsphere, as in the world at large, most hires happen among existing friends and colleagues. Prove your worth and the work will come.

Giving Back

Drupal's commercial outlook is bright, partly because Drupal is the right software at the right time. But Drupal business stands on the shoulders of the non-commercial, volunteer support provided by thousands of people. The need for community support is ongoing and ensures the future of Drupal in every context. Without it, your Drupal skills (and mine) could become irrelevant as other, better-supported technologies overtake it.

That reason alone compels us all to provide support to Drupal community projects, but there are two far more selfish reasons. First, in figuring out the solutions to others' problems you learn at least as much as the person you're helping; second, by supporting Drupal you become better known among those who will eventually support your own efforts.

The page at **`drupal.org/contribute`** gives details on how to help in the areas of:

- User support
- Documentation and translation
- Usability, graphic design, and theming
- Development of modules and core Drupal
- Marketing

I've organized ways for giving back to Drupal into two larger groups: technical and non-technical support.

To provide non-technical support:

- Respond to questions in the Support forums at **drupal.org/forum**.
- Respond to questions on the Support email list, after first joining at **http://lists.drupal.org/listinfo/support**.
- Respond to real-time questions on the **#drupal-support** IRC channel. (See the section "Getting One-on-One Help on IRC" to learn how to use this chat venue.)
- Help solve problems in the issue database at **drupal.org/project/issues**. (For tips on navigating this database, see the section "To evaluate a module's past" in Chapter 9.)
- Create or (better yet) improve documentation, using links found at **drupal.org/contribute/documentation**. In my opinion, Drupal's core documentation needs editing and organization more than it needs new materials: If you have a librarian's mind, go for it. Modules and themes, on the other hand, often have no documentation other than the brief notes provided by their developers, and benefit from the input of creative educational writers.
- Translate modules and core Drupal. If you speak a language other than English, the Drupal project needs you! Core Drupal 6 was available in over 50 languages (including my own obscure second language, Esperanto), and each one was the result of the efforts of polyglots like yourself. See **drupal.org/contribute/translations** to learn how you can help.
- Identify issues in modules, themes, and core Drupal. Even if you can't develop solutions, uncovering and documenting issues you come across is the first step to fixes. When you find something wrong, create an issue that clearly states the problem, documenting all the steps necessary to reproduce it. To do so, navigate through the appropriate issue database as you learned in the section "To evaluate a module's past" in Chapter 9, search to ensure that the issue hasn't been reported already, click "Create a new issue," and complete the resulting form. There are further details on the "Helping with Testing" page at **drupal.org/contribute/testing**.
- Spread the word. If you have an evangelical bent, encourage Drupal's growth with help from the resources at **drupal.org/contribute/marketing**.
- Donate money to the Drupal Foundation, a not-for-profit organization created to pay for such matters as event management and computers to host the **drupal.org** web site. The group's home page is at **http://association.drupal.org**.
- Sponsor module development. Is there a module you wish were better? Contact its maintainers (using techniques you learned in Chapter 9) and offer to pay for their time to work on it. Often module weaknesses are the result of simple economics: Their developers need to make a living, and module development doesn't pay anything. By paying for their time to work on the module, you create improvements that directly benefit every Drupal administrator that uses it.

To provide technical support:

Although the Drupal community is heavy with programmers, there's always room for more—especially if you're willing to do some of the hard, under-recognized work that makes existing code stronger. Here are some ways to do that.

- Familiarize yourself with Drupal's development resources at **drupal.org/contribute/development**.
- Learn how Drupal's API and central code repository works. Drupal has some unique programming patterns, and the multi-user system for contributing code presents its own challenges. Doing things "the Drupal way" ensures that any code you create will meld well with that of its thousands of other contributors. Besides the **drupal.org/contribute/development** resource, **http://api.drupal.org** will serve you well.
- Fix bugs in the issue database. As always, you can search through the entire database by pointing a web browser at **drupal.org/project/issues**, or focus only on specific projects at **drupal.org/project/issues/*project-name***.
- Help test others' fixes. Every code fix (known as a *patch*) goes through several steps, from attempted fix to committed code. An automated testing system ensures that the patch *works*—that is, that it doesn't cause problems. But human interaction is needed to make sure the patch does what's expected. Learn how to help with this important step by reading **drupal.org/contribute/testing**.

Face-to-Face with the Drupal Community

It's easy to feel lonely in your Drupal pursuits, especially if you aren't already comfortable in the disembodied world in which software geeks live. Fortunately, the Drupal community is now large enough to host hundreds of face-to-face meetings a year.

All such events appear on the calendar at **http://groups.drupal.org/events**. Some of them are linked to groups on the **http://groups.drupal.org** site. If that's true of an event you're interested in, click to go to the group that's sponsoring (or at least discussing) the event.

There are essentially four types of face-to-face meeting:

- *Drupal User Groups (DUGs)* often have regular meetings that feature speakers, discussions, and hands-on help. They tend to attract a core group of experienced Drupal enthusiasts but are extremely welcoming to new and inexperienced users.
- *DrupalCamps* are special events, usually sponsored by a local DUG or Drupal-focused business. Typically, they're one day long, free (or low cost), and have sessions geared toward both new and experienced Drupal users.
- *DrupalCons* occur twice a year: in the spring in the U.S., and elsewhere (traditionally Europe) in the autumn. Sponsored by the Drupal Association, these are must-attend events for Drupal professionals and developers. They feature talks, special-interest group meetings, exhibits, and social get-togethers over a four-day period. Information about the next DrupalCon is at **drupalcon.org**.
- *Drupal classes* are held by various Drupal experts and training companies. They tend to be highly focused events of a day or more, held in a classroom-style setting, for "corporate" (that is, comparatively high) prices.

Drupal Terms and Culture

Drupal isn't only a software package. It's also a community of computer professionals, hobbyists, students, and just plain folks who have shepherded it since its origin in 2001.

Like any community, it has its jargon and peculiar way of doing things. Some terms and practices are opaque to all but professional-level programmers and administrators—Drupal's family of origin.

As the project continues to grow, it attracts more and more people who don't have a background in computer science, a fact that's caused some conflict within the community itself. One sign of disorder is evident from browsing the official documentation on **drupal.org**. What words does it explain? What Drupal standards are non-obvious? Who, exactly, constitutes Drupal's audience?

Overall, the Drupal community is a welcoming and helpful one, as is evident from the thousands of person-hours its members contribute every day to make Drupal clearer and easier to use. But definitions of its jargon and culture are scattered among **drupal.org**'s half a million pages. The following terms are defined in a Drupal context to give you the foundation you need in order to follow—and participate in—community conversations.

Acquia Drupal: A version of Drupal comprising *core Drupal* with several additional *modules* and *themes*. Commercial support for it is available from Acquia, Inc. (**acquia.com**), a company co-founded by Drupal's original creator, *Dries Buytaert*.

administrator: This word has two meanings:

1. A person who manages a Drupal site.
2. One of the user *roles* that come built in to Drupal in its default installation. (The other two are *anonymous user* and *authenticated user*.) The administrator role automatically gains permission to use and manage features of new modules that you install.

anonymous user: The *role* given to site visitors who have not logged in to a user account. Such visitors have no *profiles*, user names, or signatures. As an *administrator*, you control how much access anonymous users have by setting controls on the *permissions* screen. (To reach it, click People in the Toolbar and then click the Permissions tab.)

authenticated user: The *role* automatically given to site visitors who have logged in to a user account. Such people have individual identities (in the form of *profiles*), and they're identified as the source for any content they create. An authenticated user may have other roles, including the *administrator* role.

block: Content that can be placed in any of a theme's *block regions*. A block can contain many kinds of content: static or dynamic; created by a *module*, an *administrator*, or Drupal itself; resulting from a script; or fed from another web site. You add, modify, and delete blocks on the Blocks administration page; to go there, click Structure in the Toolbar and then click Blocks.

block region: A part of the screen where you can place *blocks*. Drupal requires that themes have one block region, the "content" region, where node content appears by default. However, most themes have at least a header, a footer, and two sidebars, while some themes have many more block regions. (The default Bartik theme has 15.) You can see a map of a theme's block regions by going to its settings page and clicking "Demonstrate block regions."

code: Instructions in a language that computers understand. Most Drupal code is written in PHP, although JavaScript is also common and other languages are possible. While instructions in descriptive languages such as CSS and HTML are technically code, the term is usually reserved for languages that define steps to a goal.

comment: Content that's attached to a *node*, usually created in response to it.

committer: Someone with permission to put project changes into Drupal's official code repository on **drupal.org**.

content type: A pattern for making *nodes*. Content types differ in their settings and the *fields* they contain. Drupal comes with two content types enabled by default: article and basic page. You can create additional content types by clicking Structure in the Toolbar and then clicking "Content types."

contributor: Someone who works on a Drupal *project*, whether as a *developer* or in another capacity—for example, by providing documentation.

contrib: Short for "contributed." Refers to Drupal-compatible *projects*—particularly *themes* and *modules*—that are freely available, but not part of *core Drupal*.

core Drupal: The main, "official" form of Drupal available for download at **drupal.org**. Because Drupal is open-source software, anybody could legally put together a *distribution* that mixes pieces of Drupal with other software. By comparison, every piece in core Drupal goes through a unified development and review system overseen by *Dries Buytaert* and his volunteer deputies.

dashboard: An administrative page showing recent site activity and useful controls. The dashboard is highly customizable. See "To customize the Dashboard" in Chapter 2 for details.

developer: Someone who creates Drupal-compatible *code*, whether as a *contributor* to a *project* or *core Drupal*, or in service of an individual Drupal site.

distribution: A version of *core Drupal* that excludes some of its pieces, includes additional pieces, or has installation or configuration features that differ from core Drupal. One example is CiviCRM (**civicrm.org**), which is designed for online management of organizations such as non-profit and advocacy groups.

Dries Buytaert: Drupal's original creator and the trademark holder for its name Ⓐ. He started writing Drupal in 2000 while a student at the University of Antwerp (Belgium), releasing it as open-source software in 2001. He still maintains close ties to the Drupal community, contributing and managing its code, serving as a board member of *Drupal Association*, and delivering a "State of Drupal" address at each semi-annual *DrupalCon*.

Ⓐ Dries Buytaert

Drupal: A free and open-source software package that works with a web server (such as Apache), a database server (such as MySQL), and the PHP scripting language to develop and deliver web sites. Its name is the result of an error. *Dries Buytaert* originally intended to register the domain **dorp.org** to host the project, after the Flemish word for village. But he mistyped the application as **drop.org** and later named the software Drupal after "druppel," the word for "little drop." Drupal is pronounced DROO-pl or (less frequently) DROO-pahl.

Drupal Association: A Belgium-based not-for-profit organization founded in 2006 to "provide support to the Drupal project."

DrupalCon: A meeting of Drupal professionals and fans occurring twice a year, typically as a spring event in the United States and a smaller European gathering in autumn. The event has grown steadily, with the April 2010 event in San Francisco drawing over 3000 people. (The August 2010 European DrupalCon in Copenhagen drew over 1200.)

Druplicon: The Drupal project's mascot, which looks like a drop of water with a face Ⓑ. It plays on the project's original domain name, **drop.org**.

Ⓑ The Druplicon

entity: A kind of information container that can contain *fields*. *Nodes*, *profiles*, *taxonomy terms*, and *comments* are all examples of entities in Drupal 7.

field: A space for information stored in Drupal's database. You can add fields to *entities* such as *content types*, after which every *node* of that content type contains that field. For example, you might design a content type to organize the books in a public library, where each book is a node of the content type **`volume`**. That content type could have a field for each book's catalog number, another field that says whether the book is fiction or nonfiction, and so forth. An example of a field you might add to *profiles* is one for phone numbers.

maintainer: The chief decision-maker of a *project*. The maintainer is usually one of the project's most active *developers* and is always a noted *contributor*. The name of a project's maintainer is given at the upper-left corner of the project's home page **C**.

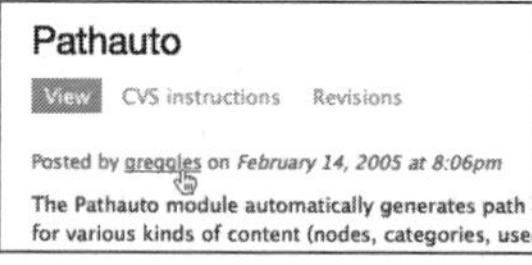

Pathauto
View
CVS instructions
Revisions
Posted by greggles on February 14, 2005 at 8:06pm
The Pathauto module automatically generates path
for various kinds of content (nodes, categories, user

C A link to the *profile* of a *project*'s *maintainer*.

module: A software package that adds functionality to Drupal. Hundreds of such packages are available for free at **`drupal.org/project/modules`**. For details on how to select and install modules, see Chapter 9, "Extending Drupal with Modules."

node: The basic unit of content in Drupal, such as an article, basic page, poll, or blog post. You create nodes by clicking "Add new content." In virtually all *themes*, node content appears in the center of the page, in the content *block region*.

permissions: Controls on a Drupal site that allow users to have different access levels to site features, based on their *roles*. You control permissions by clicking People in the Toolbar and then clicking the Permissions tab.

profile: A place for details about an *authenticated user* on a Drupal site. By default, profiles are hidden from everybody except the *superuser* and those users with the *administrator* role, and contain only such basic administrative matters as a user's user name, email address, and time zone. By enabling more-liberal *permissions* and adding profile *fields*, you can use profiles as a way for your site's users to better understand and interact with each other.

project: *Themes*, *modules*, translations, and other community-managed software found at **`drupal.org/project/`*`project-name`***—including Drupal itself.

role: A categorization for users. All visitors to your site who haven't logged in have the *anonymous user* role; those who have logged in have the *authenticated user* role, and may have additional roles as well. You assign *permissions* based on role, so all users with a specific role have the same *permissions*.

Shortcut bar: A collection of administrative links displayed in a gray strip just below the *Toolbar*. You can add and remove links to it: See the section "To change which items appear in the Shortcut bar" in Chapter 2.

superuser: The user that's created when you first install Drupal. This user has absolute access to all content and administrative functions on the site. The superuser is sometimes known as User ID 1, being the first user on the system. Because superuser is a commonly used term in other computer science contexts, some Drupal documentation *contributors* prefer the more-specific term "site maintenance account."

taxonomy: A system of categorization. Drupal lets you categorize content, where each type of categorization is known as a *vocabulary* and each label is a *term*. Collectively, this system is a site's taxonomy. For better understanding, see Chapter 5, "Making Content Interactive."

template: A PHP file that's part of a Drupal *theme,* which defines the kind of information that appears at different places throughout your site. (The theme's CSS files define the format of that information.) For further details about templates, see the "Core templates and suggestions" page at **drupal.org/node/190815**.

term: Part of Drupal's system of categorization, a term is a specific selection in a category. Terms belong to *vocabularies* that define the kind of category. For example, you might categorize cars by the kind of transmissions they have: The *vocabulary* would be "transmission type," which would contain the terms "automatic" and "manual."

theme: A package of PHP, CSS, image, and other files that defines your Drupal site's look and feel. Drupal 7 comes with four themes, and **drupal.org/project/themes** offers dozens more as free downloads. You can also create your own themes or buy them from commercial vendors. Drupal's default content theme is Bartik, while its default administration theme is Seven. To select and configure your site's theme, click Appearance in the Toolbar. A person who creates Drupal themes is called a "themer."

Toolbar: The black strip of administrative links you see at the top of your web browser's window when you're logged into a Drupal site as an *administrator*.

Views: The most popular contributed module for Drupal, Views gives your site substantial new ways to present data. You can download it from its project page at **drupal.org/project/views**.

vocabulary: A category in Drupal's system of *taxonomy*. If you wanted to categorize cars, for example, you could have a vocabulary for "transmission type," which would contain the *terms* "automatic" and "manual."

Index

A

B

C

D

E – F

G

H

I

J – L

M

N

O – Q

R

S

T

U

V – W

X – Z